FREE TO BE
RUTH BADER GINSBURG
THE STORY OF WOMEN AND LAW

FREE TO BE
RUTH BADER GINSBURG
THE STORY OF WOMEN AND LAW

TERI KANEFIELD

Armon
Books
San Francisco

Armon
Books
San Francisco

945 Taraval Street, #130
San Francisco, CA 94116
Cover design by Streetlight Graphics
Painting of Ruth Bader Ginsburg by Simmie Knox
Commissioned by the Supreme Court of the United States.

Images: From the Collection of the Supreme Court of the United
States: Frontpiece, 184, 209. Alamy: 46, 137, 215. Shutterstock:
196. All others are from the Library of Congress, the National
Archives, are in the public domain, or were made free to the public.

ISBN-978-0692723210

CONTENTS

Ruth Bader Ginsburg as a college senior in 1954.

Author's Note: While describing Ruth Bader Ginsburg's childhood and early life, I will refer to her by her first name. After she becomes a judge, I will refer to her as Judge Ginsburg, Justice Ginsburg, or—as is common when referring to Supreme Court justices—just plain Ginsburg.

1

ONE LAWYER'S
BEGINNINGS

Nathan Bader was born in 1896 in a shtetl near Odessa in the Russian Empire, the kind of village immortalized in the work of Yiddish writer Sholem Aleichem and the musical *Fiddler on the Roof*. It was a place where life had continued unchanged for generations, where Jews—while sharing a village with Gentiles—largely governed themselves and lived separate lives. Nathan was nine years old when a violent series of pogroms broke out in the region, leaving thousands of Jews dead and many more homeless. That same year, the Baders decided there was no future for them in Imperial Russia.

Nathan's father left first, journeying to the United States to earn passage for the rest of the family. Four years later, the rest of the family joined him, becoming part of the great migration that brought one and a half million Jews from Eastern Europe to America.

They settled in New York's Lower East Side, a crowded and gritty district packed with tenement buildings, synagogues, libraries, shops, department stores, and grocery stores. Known as a "notorious slum,"[1] the capital of Jewish America, almost everything was Jewish-owned and Jewish-run—banks, shops, grocery stores, even the garment factories and department stores. By the time the Baders arrived, the district was packed with more than seven hundred people per acre, making it one of the most crowded neighborhoods in the world.

The young man who would become father to one of the century's most brilliant legal minds had no formal education other than night school, where he learned English. Nathan, described as warm and likable, followed the time-honored path of Jewish immigrants and went into the garment business. He specialized as a furrier.

Unfortunately, Nathan didn't have a good head for business.

The original caption read: How the 'other half' lives in a crowded Hebrew district, Lower East Side, NY. 1907.

Fortunately, he married Celia Amster, who did. Celia's roots were also Eastern European. Her parents immigrated to the United States from somewhere in the Austrian Empire, arriving in New York just four months before her birth in 1902, making her the first member of her family to be born in the United States. The fourth of seven children, she was smart, driven, and a voracious reader, graduating at the age of fifteen with top grades from Washington Irving High School in Manhattan's Gramercy Park neighborhood. Because she was a girl, her grades meant little to her family, who pinned their hopes of higher education and social advancement on her oldest brother. All family members were expected to work to send the oldest boy to college, so when Celia went to work as a bookkeeper in the garment industry, part of her salary went toward her brother's college expenses.

Celia quit her job once she and Nathan were married. Nathan held the view, common at the time, that a working wife meant a man was unable to support his family. From inside the home, Celia was able to give Nathan the help he needed to keep his business profitable. She performed clerical and bookkeeping duties, helping to keep the business afloat even during the Great Depression, when very few people were buying furs.

Nathan and Celia Bader lived in a small, well-kept house on East Ninth in the Flatbush district of Brooklyn. Their first child, Marilyn, was born in 1927. Next, in 1933 when Marilyn was six, came Joan Ruth, nicknamed Kiki—pronounced Kicky—by her sister.

Kiki was a year old when Marilyn died of meningitis. Although Kiki was too young to remember Marilyn, her sister's death lent an ever-present air of sadness to their home. Marilyn's death left Kiki an only child, but her childhood was anything but lonely, surrounded as she was by a large, closely-knit extended family—lots of aunts, uncles, and cousins. Kiki particularly enjoyed the Passover Seder when she was still the youngest at the table and was thus the child who asked the traditional four questions.[2] Each summer, she attended the Jewish Camp Che-Na-Wah in the Adirondacks, a camp founded by her uncle Solomon—Celia's oldest brother, who she had helped send to college.

Among Kiki's early memories were weekly trips with her mother to the local library, which was housed over a Chinese restaurant. Kiki selected her books for the week. She enjoyed reading mysteries and Greek mythology. While at the time, Kiki didn't question the prescribed order for girls and boys, later she credited the Nancy Drew series with planting the idea that a girl could be an adventurer who thought for herself, a doer who didn't fit the usual gender stereotypes of the 1930s and 1940s. She wanted to be either Nancy Drew or Amelia Earhart when she grew up.

Celia changed the order of her daughter's names from Joan Ruth to Ruth Joan when enrolling her in school. Celia saw several other Joans already signed up, so she enrolled Kiki as Ruth Joan Bader. Kiki attended Public School 238, grades K–8, a tall brick building with hardwood parquet floors and high windows located a mere block and a half from the Baders' home. The school was crowded, with more than a thousand students, and often as many as thirty children per class. Kiki wrote an editorial for the school newspaper entitled "Landmarks of Constitutional Freedom," tracing the foundations of American law from the Magna Carta to the present day.

Easygoing Nathan was the soft touch, the parent who would have spoiled Kiki had Celia allowed it. Celia was the parent with demanding standards, who went over Kiki's homework and made sure she practiced piano. Once, when Kiki brought home a less-than-perfect report card, Celia made clear her displeasure. That was the end of less-than-perfect report cards from Kiki.

The Jews in the Baders' neighborhood mixed freely with immigrants from Ireland and Italy. Kiki's best friend, Marilyn DeLutio, was the daughter of Sicilian immigrants, and Kiki was often in their home. Beyond the safe confines of the Baders' circle of family and friends, however, lurked the specter of anti-Semitism. Brooklyn during Kiki's childhood was a place where boys on the street had fistfights over whether the Jews had killed Jesus, and where many still believed that Jews needed the blood of Christian boys to make their matzos. Once in the 1930s Kiki was driving with her parents through Pennsylvania when she saw a sign in front of a hotel that said, "No dogs or Jews allowed"— the same sort of sign that appeared in Germany, instilling in American Jews the fear that the violent wave of anti-Semitism taking hold in Germany might find a footing in America as well. Much later, during the hearings in which Kiki—then, of course, Judge Ginsburg—was confirmed to the U.S. Supreme Court, Senator Kennedy asked her about her sensitivity to racial issues. She explained that growing up Jewish during World War II sensitized her to the marginalization of groups.

Celia introduced both Kiki and her cousin Richard to art at the Brooklyn Academy of Music, buying subscriptions to the Saturday children's performances. When Kiki was eleven, one of her aunts took her to a condensed version of *La Gioconda*, a production designed to stimulate a child's appreciation of opera. The settings were bare, and sections were narrated so the entire opera could be performed in an hour, but the vocals were glorious, and Kiki fell in love with opera. Now she had a new fantasy—to be a great diva. She learned early, though, that she had no talent for singing. A grade school teacher told her she was a sparrow and not a robin, so when the others sang, she was to simply mouth the words. Later she said she sang in two places, her dreams and the shower.

Celia also brought Kiki to the Lower East Side to remind her of her roots, the neighborhood that remained as a step in time from the shtetls of Eastern Europe. By the time Kiki visited the Lower East Side as a child, the New York City Housing Authority had replaced the worst of the structures to relieve the slum conditions, but the district was noisy, crowded, and boisterous—and Kiki did not love it. Many years later, though, she teared up with nostalgia remembering the foods she ate at those delicatessens and shops, which she called the best in the Jewish tradition.

At the age of thirteen, Kiki graduated first in her class from Public School 238. She attended high school at James Madison High School, founded in 1925, a school with top academic standards, reflecting the ambitions of the community. The school was housed in an imposing red brick building on Bedford Avenue in the Madison section of Brooklyn. Most of Kiki's classmates, girls as well as boys, were college-bound. Today James Madison High boasts a large roster of distinguished graduates, including four Nobel Prize winners and three senators, one of whom was 2016 presidential candidate Bernie Sanders. Representative Charles E. Schumer, a James Madison alumnus, said the school did more for his education than college at Harvard.

During Kiki's first year of high school, just before her fourteenth birthday, tragedy struck: Celia was diagnosed with cervical cancer. Celia underwent her first surgery during Kiki's first year of high school, and was in and out of the hospital for the next four years. Kiki understood that not much could be done to save Celia's life. Despite the daily pain of living with "the smell of death," [3] Kiki never let on to her classmates that her mother was dying.

Kiki was a baton twirler, a member of the Go-Getters pep club, and a cello player in the school orchestra. She ran for student government, but was beaten by one of her best friends. She was confirmed with honors from the East Midwood Jewish Center. At home, she often did her homework at Celia's bedside because it pleased Celia to see her studying.

Kiki was petite—just over five feet tall and very slender—with bobbed hair and blue eyes. Classmates described her as pretty and popular. Reserved, she didn't speak unless she had something of substance to say. She had a slow, deliberate way of talking, liberally sprinkling pauses into her conversation. Self-controlled by nature, she took Celia's advice that she should always be a lady, by which Celia meant rising above destructive and petty emotions. A lady, according to Celia, remained calm and was always modest. Kiki's tranquil exterior masked the inner strength and determination that allowed her to flit through high school in her pep club jacket, hiding the secret that her mother was dying.

Celia's illness was not the only thing Kiki hid from her classmates. Behind a pretty face and shy smile, she hid a sharp intelligence. To the outward eye, there wasn't much to give her away as a future law professor and Supreme Court justice, as she was more likely to be found wearing the Go-Getters black satin jacket and selling tickets to games than holed up in the library. Girls in the 1940s were supposed to be fun and popular—party girls—not bookish and smart. Kiki, always the perfectionist, was for all the world to see the perfect high school girl. For those looking closely, though, there were hints of a lawyer in the making. Her grades were almost perfect. She was editor of the school newspaper. She was admitted into Arista, the elite honor society. Outwardly fun, inwardly serious, she was a girl who smiled often, but rarely laughed.

"She was very modest," a classmate said later, "and didn't appear to be super self-confident. She never thought she did well on tests, but of course, she always aced them."[4]

Celia expected Kiki to go to college. In particular, Celia had her sights set on Cornell—the school her oldest brother had attended. Cornell, located on the southern shore of Cayuga Lake in central New York, was considered one of the best schools for girls, not only because Cornell accepted a fair number of girls, but also because it was thought to be a good place to find a man: The ratio was four men for each woman admitted. With its high academic standards, Cornell was not the place to find just *any* man, but one who was smart and capable, with a good career ahead of him. Celia didn't just want Kiki to find a man—she also wanted Kiki to have a career and be independent. Of the jobs generally open to women—nursing, teaching, and secretarial work—it was evident to Celia that Kiki, with her love of history and civics, was best suited to being a high school history teacher.

Kiki was admitted to Cornell and awarded several scholarships, including Madison High's English Scholarship and a New York State Scholarship. She graduated from high school ranked sixth in her class and was scheduled to speak at the graduation ceremony as part of the Round Table Forum of Honor.

The day before Kiki's graduation ceremony, Celia died of cancer at the age of forty-seven—almost as if she'd held on until she knew her daughter was ready to venture forth into the world as a young adult. Kiki, in mourning, did not attend her high school graduation ceremony. Teachers brought her medals and awards to her home. Upon Celia's death, her family discovered that she had been secretly saving money to pay for

Kiki's college education. She had saved $8,000, a fantastic sum in 1950. Ever prudent, Celia never bought anything on credit. She had five separate bank accounts with no single account having more than $2000.

Because of her scholarships, Kiki was able to return the money to her father, which he soon needed. Not long after Celia's death, Nathan's business went quickly downhill, a testament to the help Celia had been able to give him.

Kiki insisted that growing up she never had any sense of herself as what we might today call a feminist. However, when asked about certain topics, like her attitudes toward Judaism, her answers indicated a heightened awareness of the limitations placed on girls. For example, she talked about how only men could participate in the *minyan*, the quorum required for public prayers of mourning. One of the mornings the family was sitting *shiva* for Celia there were not enough men present to make up the *minyan*.[5] So someone had to go searching for a man—despite the abundance of women in the house. Kiki felt particularly stung. She'd not only worked hard at her confirmation but also was one of the few to take it seriously. At camp, after being confirmed, she'd often been the "camp rabbi," leading the others in prayer. Yet, her Jewish education meant nothing during one of the most important moments of her life—because she was a girl.

2

A TOP STUDENT
AND A TOP GOLFER

In the fall of 1950, when Kiki was seventeen years old, she arrived at Cornell—a university known for top academics, demanding and knowledgeable professors, long, cold winters, and a strikingly beautiful natural landscape. Kiki was one of seven Jewish women in the freshman class. All seven were housed on the same floor in Clara Dixon Hall. They became friends and remained close all their lives. Later, Kiki suggested tongue in cheek that it could have been happenstance that the seven Jewish women in the class were housed together, or perhaps the Jewish women were grouped together in an effort to make them feel more comfortable. But she knew the real reason. They'd been segregated. Sororities and fraternities, too, were segregated. Some were for Jews. Most were for Christians, with no overlap permitted. She felt snubbed when non-Jewish friends she'd met during a summer waitressing job avoided her on campus and issued her no sorority invitations.

Kiki—still known to her friends by her childhood nickname—joined a Jewish sorority, AEPhi, and majored in government. She took part-time clerical jobs to supplement her scholarships, and joined the Women's Self-Governance Association.

Later, when asked to talk about her time at Cornell, she often mentioned the different rules that applied to men and women at the university. Women were required to live in dormitories, whereas men were allowed to find independent housing in town. Women had to sign in to the dormitory each night. They had to be back in the dormitory by 10:00 p.m. on weekdays, midnight on Fridays, and 1:00 a.m. on Saturday. If a woman wasn't back on time, she was locked out and had to find somewhere else to sleep that night. Kiki later admitted to having found herself locked out of the dormitory—but only once.

Even at Cornell, there was pressure on women to hide their intelligence, to make the men feel like they were smarter—even though, because of quotas and thus higher admission standards for women, the women were often stronger students. Kiki, still feeling that she needed to live up to the image of a fun sorority girl, found obscure libraries so others wouldn't know how much she studied.

Kiki met Martin David Ginsburg, known as Marty, during her first year at Cornell. Marty was eighteen, a year older than Kiki. He was a second-year student, and social chairman of the Jewish fraternity Tau Delta Phi. He came from a well-to-do Long Island family—his father was vice president of the Federated Department store chain, the corporation that now owns the Target stores, among others. One of the six other Jewish women on Kiki's floor, Irma Hilton, was dating a man who was friends with Marty. Irma and her boyfriend introduced Marty and Kiki, even though both were dating others. Kiki had a boyfriend from Camp Che-Na-Wah, who was then a law student at Columbia. Marty had a girlfriend at

Smith. But, as Irma explained, the weeks between visits with an out-of-town boyfriend were long, and the nights in Ithaca were cold. Besides, Marty was the owner of a gray Chevrolet. Irma had the idea that if Kiki and Marty would get together, the four of them could go places in Marty's car.

Kiki described their first meeting as a blind date, but Marty later revealed that the date was only blind on Kiki's side. "I cheated," he said.[6] The date was arranged after Marty told Irma's boyfriend that he thought Kiki was really cute.

Kiki and Marty were friends for a full year before their relationship turned romantic—enough time for them to get to know each other without the complications of courtship. "He would tell me everything on his mind," Kiki said. "Not a bad way to start a relationship."[7] Marty was the first to fall in love. He came to see who Kiki was underneath, and he wooed her with promises that he respected her intelligence and admired her quiet intensity. Marty was the first boy she'd met who cared that she had a brain. Most men, she felt, actually preferred that a woman *didn't* have much of a brain. She also came to realize that Marty was much smarter than her Columbia Law School boyfriend. She felt it was Marty's deep confidence in himself borne of his own superior intelligence that prevented him from feeling intimidated by her. One of Marty's friends said, "Ruth was a wonderful student and a beautiful young woman. Most of the men were in awe of her, but Marty was not."[8]

On the surface, the two were as different as could be. Whereas Kiki was reserved and careful, Marty was gregarious and irreverent. Many years later, after decades of marriage, and after Kiki became Justice Ginsburg of the U.S. Supreme Court, she and Marty were at a social gathering consisting mostly of her former clerks when Marty, unbeknownst to her, taped a sign on her back that said, "Her Highness."[9] With Marty as her partner, Kiki didn't have to live up to cultural expectations and be the fun-loving life of the party—Marty willingly took on that responsibility.

Once Kiki stopped hiding her intelligence it became evident to her peers that she was "scary smart."[10] She often sat cross-legged, reading, while the others played bridge or gossiped. She enjoyed Gilbert and Sullivan, sometimes playing selections on the piano. While later portraits showed her as serious and even dour, Irma Hilton said, "She was actually a lot of fun. It was just that she had her priorities straight: She never partied until her work was done."[11]

Marty, modest as well as irreverent, was always eager to shine the spotlight on Kiki. He joked that at Cornell, she was a top student while he was a top golfer. Indeed, he was a talented golfer and member of the college golf team. He started college as a pre-med student, but he dropped chemistry when he discovered that the labs interfered with his golfing schedule.

During Kiki's second year of college, in keeping with her goal of becoming a high school history teacher, she did some student teaching in a local high school. She discovered that high school teaching was just not her cup of tea. Meanwhile the nation was in the grip of Senator Joseph McCarthy's Red Scare. Cornell's Professor Marcus Singer was indicted before a grand jury in Washington, DC, when he refused to tell the House Un-American Activities Committee about his associates in a wartime communist study group. Professor Singer admitted his participation in the group, but invoked his Fifth Amendment right to silence when the committee demanded that he divulge the names of others who participated. He was arraigned on a contempt charge, and as a result Cornell University relieved him of his teaching duties while allowing him to remain in his job as a researcher.

Kiki became protégé and research assistant to Cornell professor of government Robert Cushman, who was supervising the university's Studies in Civil Liberties program funded by the Rockefeller Center. Professor Cushman impressed upon his students that McCarthy's committee was violating the constitutional rights of Americans and essentially conducting a widespread witch hunt, thereby estranging America from its most basic values.

Kiki first felt the desire to become a lawyer when she understood that the lawyers representing the accused in the McCarthy hearings—while of course working for profit—were also trying to repair the wounds in the society. She also tied her interest in law and justice to her Jewish education and heritage, noting that demand for justice runs through the entirety of Jewish tradition. Because she liked reading, thinking, and laying out arguments, it seemed to her that law was a better career match for her than teaching high school.

Meanwhile, she and Marty were growing together as soul mates. They felt equally enraged at McCarthy's attempts to ruin the career of a Cornell professor because he had been a member of a communist group as a student. They shared walks through the Arts Quad and drives past the lake. Kiki learned to play golf. She was a frequent guest at Marty's home on Long Island. Marty's mother, Evelyn, took a liking to Kiki, and took Kiki—who after all had recently lost her own mother—under her wing. One summer, Kiki worked as a clerk in one of Marty's father's department stores. It was there, on the streets of Long Island, that Kiki encountered for the first time a test she had trouble passing: Her driving test. She had to take the test five times before she passed.

Marty and Kiki decided they wanted to go into the same

Cornell University Arts Quad.

profession so they could understand each other's work and support each other. "The idea," Marty explained, "was to be in the same discipline so there would be something you could talk about, bounce ideas off of, know what each other was doing."[12] Business was out because the Harvard Business School didn't accept women and Marty wanted to go to Harvard. So they decided to become lawyers, even though Marty suspected Kiki had already made up her mind that this was what she wanted. Nathan was dismayed when he learned that his daughter wanted to go to law school. The legal profession was all but closed to women, so there didn't seem much sense in Kiki trying to become a lawyer. Teaching, to him, was a much more logical choice. Moreover, his own business had never recovered since Celia's death, and he knew he wouldn't be able to support her should she be unable to find a job.

Kiki believed that Celia had wanted her to be a high school history teacher simply because a possibility like law had never occurred to her. Kiki felt confident that if Celia were alive and saw such a possibility open to her daughter, she would have encouraged her. One of Kiki's cousins, Jane Gevirtz, later came across a letter Kiki had written in 1953 revealing self-doubts about her aptitude for law, but explaining that she was determined to see if she could get into law school despite being told from all sides that it was "more appropriate for a woman to be a teacher."[13]

Nathan felt better about the idea of law school after Kiki and Marty announced their engagement. Since she would have a man to support her, it didn't matter as much if she would be unable to work in her chosen profession.

Marty graduated and was accepted to Harvard Law School. Kiki, who was ready to shed her childhood nickname and become Ruth, still had one year left at Cornell. She came up with an idea: She would take her fourth year of college in the Cornell Law School, then join Marty at Harvard, where they'd both be second-year students. She proposed this idea to the dean at Harvard, who told her this would not work because she would get no credit at Harvard for courses taken at Cornell. Ruth had no desire to go through the first year of law school twice, so instead, after Marty left for his first year of Harvard—now driving a green Pontiac instead of his gray Chevrolet—Kiki spent her last year at Cornell taking art and music classes. Later she said it was the year she most enjoyed her studies.

Ruth graduated with high honors in government, with distinction in all subjects. She was elected to Phi Beta Kappa, and because she was the woman with the highest academic average, she graduated as class marshal. She was admitted to Harvard Law School and offered a generous scholarship.

She and Marty were married in Marty's parents' living room in Rockville Centre, New York, the same month she graduated from Cornell. The ceremony was performed by the rabbi from the synagogue Celia and Nathan had belonged to for years.

The wedding was small, with only eighteen guests, a number representing the Hebrew symbol for life. Ruth and Marty would use the money saved by having a small wedding for a European honeymoon: a car trip through France, Italy, and Switzerland.

Ruth's soon-to-be mother-in-law gave her advice about how to have a happy marriage. Just before the ceremony, Evelyn sat her down and said, "Ruth, remember in every good marriage it helps to be a little hard of hearing."[14] She then presented Ruth with a pair of earplugs. Ruth said that whereas she didn't particularly need those earplugs in her marriage, they definitely came in handy later with law faculty colleagues.

3

AXIOMATIC TRUTHS
ABOUT WOMEN

The female lawyers who came before proved the difficulty of defying cultural expectations. Indeed, the qualities in a successful lawyer—the ability to think rationally and analytically, the ability to engage in public speaking, possession of a certain toughness, and the ability to occupy a position of authority as an officer of the court—ran directly contrary to the common view that women were fragile, emotional, and hence unsuited for public life. The women who came before showed something else as well: those who had the gumption, the stamina, and the intelligence to work around barriers often found themselves in positions of much greater significance than if the barrier hadn't been there in the first place.

Myra Bradwell was born Myra Colby in 1831. As was typical of upper-class girls in the middle part of the nineteenth century, Myra attended the Elgin Female Seminary in Illinois, a finishing school intended to train girls for their future roles as wives and mothers and offer a broad education in literature and the arts. After finishing her education, Myra taught at the seminary for a year. While teaching, she met James Bradwell,

Myra Bradwell, February 12, 1831.

who came from a family of poor English immigrants, and was financing his education by doing manual labor. Myra's family had no intention of allowing her to marry a manual laborer, so Myra and James eloped. Myra's brother pursued them with a shotgun, but was unable to stop them. They were married in Chicago on May 18, 1852.

Myra's inclination to rebel didn't stop with a runaway marriage. After James completed his education in 1855 and was admitted to the Illinois bar, Myra decided she wanted to work with him in his law practice. There were two ways to become a lawyer: Attend law school or study law under the supervision of a practicing lawyer. As a woman, Myra wasn't permitted to attend law school, so she studied with James. She was thirty-eight years old when she passed the Illinois bar exam with high honors and became the first woman in the United States to apply for a license to practice law. She submitted her application in the usual way, accompanied by a court certificate attesting to her good character and the results of her examination showing that she possessed the requisite qualifications.

The Illinois Supreme Court denied her request on the grounds that the laws that applied to her as a married woman would prevent her from practicing law. Under the law in Illinois, as derived from common law, a woman had no legal existence apart from her husband:

> By marriage, the husband and wife are one person in law: that is, the very being or legal existence of the woman is suspended during the marriage, or at least is incorporated and consolidated into that of the husband; under whose wing, protection, and *cover*, she performs everything.[15]

A married woman could not own property in her own name, enter into contracts, sit on juries, vote, run for office, or even apply for credit without her husband's permission, limitations that—according to the Illinois Supreme Court—would interfere with Myra's ability to practice law. How, for example, could she freely enter legal agreements with her clients if she needed her husband's permission each time she wanted to enter a contract?

Myra challenged the decision. She admitted she was married, but insisted that she nonetheless had the right as an American citizen to practice law. The Illinois Supreme Court issued its final response, relying on the fallback position that the Illinois legislature did not intend women to practice law, so the court had no authority to grant a license to a woman. The court concluded that even if not forbidden to do so by law, it would deny her application because:

God designed the sexes to occupy different spheres of action, and that it belonged to men to make, apply, and execute the laws was regarded as an almost axiomatic truth.[16]

Myra brought her case to the U.S. Supreme Court. She invoked the newly ratified Fourteenth Amendment of the U.S. Constitution, which guaranteed all persons equal protection of the laws. Her argument was a simple one. The Fourteenth Amendment of the Constitution plainly decreed that no state may deny any *person* equal protection of the laws. She was a person. The Illinois law deprived her of equal protection by refusing to allow her to practice law on the basis of her gender. Therefore, the Illinois law violated the Constitution and must be overturned.

She must have known she was on shaky ground. The Thirteenth, Fourteenth, and Fifteenth Amendments, known collectively as the Reconstruction Amendments, were ratified immediately after the Civil War to give the newly freed slaves the full rights of citizenship. Indeed, the U.S. Supreme Court ruled against her, holding that the Fourteenth Amendment didn't apply because the intent of the Reconstruction Amendments had nothing to do with whether women could practice law. Justice Bradley's concurring opinion echoed the sentiments of the Illinois Supreme Court by describing the different spheres and destinies of men and women:

Man is, or should be, woman's protector and defender. The natural and proper timidity and delicacy which belongs to the female sex evidently unfits it for many of the occupations of civil life. The Constitution of the family organization, which is founded in the divine ordinance as well as in the nature of things, indicates the domestic sphere as that which properly belongs to the domain and functions of womanhood. The harmony, not to say identity, of interest and views which belong, or should belong, to the family institution is repugnant to the idea of a woman adopting a distinct and independent career from that of her husband. [17]

And Justice Bradley's oft-quoted conclusion:

The paramount destiny and mission of woman are to fulfill the noble and benign offices of wife and mother. This is the law of the Creator. And the rules of civil society must be adapted to the general constitution of things, and cannot be based upon exceptional cases.[18]

Even after being told by the U.S. Supreme Court that women were not included as persons under the Fourteenth Amendment, women refused to give up. One woman after another read the Constitution, saw the word "person," believed she should be included, and tried unsuccessfully to argue in court that even if the original framers hadn't intended to include women, it was time for that to change.

In 1872, when Virginia Minor tried to register to vote in the upcoming presidential election, the St. Louis district registrar, Reese Happersett, refused to allow her to register because she was a woman. She wanted to sue, but she couldn't without her husband's permission. Her husband gave permission, so she sued on the grounds that the Fourteenth Amendment guaranteed equal protection of the laws to all persons, and she was a person; therefore, she should be allowed to vote. Her case went all the way to the U.S. Supreme Court.

The Court ruled against her, holding that while women were citizens and persons and as such owed allegiance to the United States, so were children, and nobody would expect a child to be given the right to vote.[19]

Meanwhile, Myra Bradwell—denied the right to practice law—established the *Chicago Legal News*, which became one of the most influential and widely read law journals in the Midwest. In a column called "Law Relating to Women," she argued for legal and political equality for women. Her paper provided support for women trying to obtain law licenses in their own states. She became active in the woman's suffrage movement, joining with other suffragists to form the American Woman Suffrage Association in Cleveland. That same year, Elizabeth Cady Stanton and Susan B. Anthony founded the national woman's suffrage movement. In 1890 the two groups merged to become the National American Suffrage Association. That same year, the Illinois Supreme Court, acting on its own motion, granted Myra a license to practice law. She lived to see her efforts come to fruition when women were granted the right to vote in 1920 with the ratification of the Nineteenth Amendment.

Colonial men might have also believed that women were unfit for such professions as the practice of law, but when the country was undeveloped and sparsely populated, and when there weren't enough men to do the work, it often happened that the most capable person—and sometimes the *only* capable person—was a woman.

Margaret Brent, born in 1601, known to her contemporaries as "Mistress Margaret Brent, Spinster," was America's first woman lawyer—in a loose sense of the word, of course because there wasn't yet a United States of America and what could be termed the legal profession was unregulated and unlicensed. Margaret was born in Gloucestershire, England, into a well-to-do Catholic family, members of the landed gentry. In 1638, at the age of thirty-seven, Margaret—an unmarried woman—came with two of her brothers and her sister, also unmarried, to the colony of Maryland in search of religious freedom. Margaret, it turned out, had a head for business. Because she was single, she was allowed to own property. She went into the tobacco business with a grant of land from the governor of Maryland, Leonard Calvert, and by hiring indentured servants. She became wealthy lending money to new immigrants. She often appeared in court to collect debts and manage her business affairs.

Governor Calvert came to trust her, and on his deathbed, appointed her as his executrix, which put her in the unusual position of managing state affairs and finances. After Governor Calvert's death, his brother, Lord Baltimore, then residing in England, inherited Maryland and became governor. Margaret paid Governor Calvert's debts, as he requested, and discovered that there wasn't enough money to pay the soldiers he'd hired to protect the colony. The soldiers were angry and threatened mutiny if they weren't paid. Margaret therefore went to the Provincial Court and asked that she be named the absent Lord Baltimore's attorney. Her request was granted. She used her power as Lord Baltimore's attorney to sell some of his cattle to get the money to pay the soldiers, thus preventing a rebellion. Lord Baltimore was furious when he learned what she'd done, but the Assembly—Maryland's legislative governing body—came to her defense, assuring Lord Baltimore that she had preserved Maryland's safety.

Emboldened, she went before the all-male Assembly and

asked for the right to vote as a property owner and as Lord Baltimore's attorney. The Assembly denied her request on the grounds that she was a woman. So she and her sister moved to Virginia, where she acquired a large tract of land and lived until her death in 1671.

The American frontier, in folklore and legend, was a land of cowboys, wide-open spaces, and high-noon gunfights. While there was a measure of truth to the legends, there were also new opportunities for women because often there were not enough men able to do necessary work.

Susanna Wright, born in England in 1697, was a Quaker woman on the Pennsylvania frontier, and the most literate and educated of her neighbors. She therefore wrote wills, deeds, indentures, and other contracts. She served as an arbitrator in property disputes and joined Benjamin Franklin in speaking out against attacks on Native Americans.

In the nineteenth century, women found it easier to become lawyers in states closer to the frontier, where the establishment was a little less established, and professions less regulated. Arabella Mansfield, in Iowa in 1869, was the first American woman admitted to the bar. The Iowa code stated that the bar exam was limited to "any white male person," but she was permitted in nonetheless. Back east, that same year, Lemma Barkaloo was denied admission to Columbia Law School in New York. The administrator said he would not be a part of "degrading" women to the practice of law. So she moved west to St. Louis, Missouri, and was admitted to law school at Washington University, where she became the nation's first female law student. She quit law school after a year, passed the Missouri bar, and began practicing in 1870, just months before her death of typhoid fever at approximately the age of twenty-two. One obituary said she died of mental fatigue.

In 1869, thirty-nine-year-old Belva Ann Bennett Lockwood, a teacher and founder of one of the first woman's suffrage groups, applied to three law schools—Columbia College, now George Washington University, Howard University, and Georgetown. She was denied on the grounds that her presence would distract the male students. In 1870 she drafted a bill that made it illegal to pay women less than men in civil service positions. In 1872, her bill was passed. In 1871, she was at last admitted to a law school as one of fifteen women entering the

Belva Ann Bennett Lockwood, circa 1870.

first-year class of National University School of Law, which is also now part of George Washington University. She finished her coursework, but none of the women were allowed to go through graduation or receive diplomas. She wrote to President Grant and eventually received her diploma, but she was the only woman in her class to do so. In 1906, she became the first woman to argue before the Supreme Court. She represented the Cherokee Nation in a lawsuit alleging that the U.S. government violated a treaty. She won, securing a judgment of $5 million for the Cherokee Nation.

Jane Foster was a student at Cornell Law School from 1915 to 1918. She excelled at her studies, served as editor of the law review, and was elected to the Order of the Coif, an honor society for outstanding law school graduates. After graduation, no firm would hire her. With the help of one of her professors, she finally found work, not as a lawyer but as a legal assistant. She worked as a legal assistant from 1918 until 1929, watching as one man after another advanced to partner. With strong recommendations from Cornell Law professors and her employer, she tried again to find work as a lawyer, but never succeeded. The Wall Street firm of White & Case wrote to the law school's dean, telling him that White & Case steadfastly refused to take women on their legal staff, and he was certain they would continue to adhere to that policy.

Unable to find work as a lawyer, Jane instead used her financial skills in the stock market. She purchased stock in companies such as the Computing-Tabulating-Recording Company, the company that was to become IBM. She amassed a fortune that allowed her to donate generously to the Cornell Law School. In the 1950s—while Ruth Bader Ginsburg was an undergraduate at Cornell—Jane returned to her hometown in Ohio and cared for her aging mother. She never practiced law.

Before 1920, there was perhaps an excuse for excluding women from the practice of law. Without a voice in making laws, how could women enforce or interpret them? But the passage of the Nineteenth Amendment, giving women the right to vote, did not open the courtroom or law school doors to women. A 1922 Barnard College graduate recalled,

> At the time I was ready to enter law school, women were looked upon as people who should not be in law schools. I wanted very much to go to Columbia, but I couldn't get in. I went over to see Harlan Stone, Dean Stone, who was later Chief Justice of the United States, and asked him to open the law school to women. He said no. I asked why. He said, we don't because we don't and that was final.[20]

One major firm in Houston prided itself on hiring women lawyers through the 1920s, but the women were given work as librarians or clerks, and were never given real legal work. The Depression made the situation worse. Women lawyers who interviewed or asked for work at firms were asked how they could possibly be considered when so many men with families to support were out of work. Even though women had little chance of being hired as anything other than secretaries or librarians in law firms, women continued to go to law school, often excelling. A few lucky women did find legal work, but they never expected advancement. They certainly didn't expect to make partner. One major law firm, Sullivan & Cromwell, did in fact hire five women lawyers in the 1930s, but no woman made partner in the firm until 1982.

Women went to law school in greater numbers during World War II because wartime enrollment for men was down.

During the war and man shortage in the country, many women were able to find work, not only in the legal field but in all fields that were typically dominated by men. But at the end of World War II, women were expected to return to the home and give the jobs to the returning veterans. In the 1950s, women were occasionally hired by the prestigious firms, but they were the exceptions, frequently hired as a token woman to show that the firm was progressive.

Some firms said they didn't want to hire women for fear that the women would get married, have children, and leave. Many simply believed that a woman's responsibility was in the home. Others were afraid women could not keep up the pace, or would have emotional outbursts, resulting in bad relationships with courts. One female graduate of Harvard Law School in the 1950s offered other women a warning: "Beware of firms specifically looking to hire a woman lawyer. They want you for work they cannot get any man to do."[21]

People often asked Ruth Bader Ginsburg why she went to law school. Those asking the question were perhaps expecting an idealistic response, like the famous answer given by Oliver Hill, one of the NAACP lawyers who helped bring about school desegregation. Oliver Hill said, "I went to law school so I could go out and fight segregation."[22]

"I became a lawyer for personal, selfish reasons," Ruth said. "I thought I could do a lawyer's job better than any other. I have no talent in the arts but I do write fairly well and analyze problems clearly."[23]

4

RUTHLESS
RUTHIE

Harvard Law School would have to wait. Shortly after Ruth and
Marty's wedding, Marty was called to duty in the reserves and
sent to Fort Sill, Oklahoma, to serve as an artillery officer. He'd
joined the Reserve Officers Training Corps (ROTC) program
while an undergraduate at Cornell, thinking that if he was going
to be drafted, it would be better to serve as an officer.

Fort Sill, Oklahoma, was nestled in the plains just south of
the Wichita Mountains in Comanche County, in the southwest
part of Oklahoma. The fort was built at the time of the
Indian Wars. The adjacent town of Lawton had been founded
fifty-three years earlier, when the Kiowa-Comanche-Apache
Reservation—the last of the Indian lands in Oklahoma—was
opened up by the federal government for settlement. The lands
were offered by lottery, with sixty-five hundred homesteaders
selected to receive plots. By the time the Ginsburgs arrived,
the town had a population of about thirty-five thousand and
boasted a newly built high school and hospital.

The first day Marty reported for duty, his training officer
asked him how much artillery experience he had. "I will level

with you," Marty said. "The first artillery piece I have seen in my life is the one I see through your window, on the back of that jeep."[24]

"Son," his training officer replied, "that's an automatic fence post digger."[25] An inauspicious beginning to a military career if ever there was one.

Marty and Ruth lived in the married officers' quarters. Later, Marty said the two years they spent in Fort Sill were a gift and a blessing: They were able to build their life and marriage far away from family and the pressures of school. Marty quipped that, compared to the pressures of law school and their later careers, his job in Oklahoma required him to focus approximately four hours each week, which gave him plenty of time to devote to his marriage.

It didn't take long for Marty to discover an area, in addition to driving a car, in which Ruth fell short of her usual standards of perfection: She was a terrible cook. In fact, her cooking became a running joke throughout their marriage. One memorable evening early in their marriage, she placed a lumpy mass of food on the table and her new husband—perhaps unwisely— asked, "What is it?" She replied, "It's tuna fish casserole."[26] Later he said that the casserole was as close to inedible as a freshly prepared meal could be.

Ruth freely admitted that she had no interest in the kitchen. Eventually she mastered seven meals, all of which came from a cookbook called the *60-Minute Chef*, meaning that nothing in the book took longer than sixty minutes from the start of preparation to the table. She favored frozen vegetables and grilling meat after defrosting it. One of Ruth's cousins, Richard, evidently well aware of Ruth's talents—or in this case lack thereof—and apparently taking pity on Marty, had given the newlyweds as a gift the *Escofier Cookbook: A Guide to the Fine Art of Cookery.* The day after being presented with the memorable tuna casserole Marty opened the cookbook and began learning. The former chemistry major discovered his talent for cooking. "Hell," he told a friend, "it's just like chemistry."[27] Later he joked that he learned to cook as an act of self-defense.

Ruth's first job in Oklahoma was as a clerk-typist at the engineer supply office in Fort Sill. Next she took the civil service exam and scored well enough to land a high-level position with the Social Security Administration office in nearby Lawton. Ruth was not afraid to bend the rules where necessary in the interests of justice. She disapproved of her boss's policy of refusing Native Americans applying for pensions because they didn't have birth certificates to prove their ages, even though they were clearly old enough. Native Americans born more than sixty years earlier were never issued birth certificates. In denying them pensions, Ruth felt her boss was abusing his powers. She quietly rebelled, approving the pensions of elderly Native Americans based on nothing more than fishing licenses.

In January, Ruth learned she was pregnant. She made the mistake of revealing this information at work. She'd been scheduled to travel to a training session, but her supervisor said that because of her pregnancy, she could not travel; therefore, she could not remain at her current level. She was demoted three pay levels. Another colleague, who was also pregnant, kept her pregnancy a secret as long as she could. The other woman was not demoted and traveled to the training seminar. This irked Ruth, but the idea of challenging the unequal treatment of women in court did not occur to her. That was the way things were, so she accepted it. Anger was not an emotion in which the carefully controlled Ruth indulged.

When the time came for the baby to be born, Marty and Ruth decided they preferred a hospital they were familiar with instead of the hospital provided by the army. Ruth, therefore, returned to New York to stay with Marty's parents and have her baby there. Jane Carol Ginsburg was born on Long Island on July 21, 1955.

Ruth always put beautiful music on the Victrola while feeding Jane because she wanted Jane to associate food with beautiful music. Marty read up on child development and learned that the first year of a baby's life was when a child's personality and deepest attachments were formed. He made the decision to spend a lot of time with his infant daughter—and he followed through—something not typical of a man in 1955. The pattern of their marriage was now set: Responsibilities would be shared equally without regard for traditional gender roles. At this time Ruth began formulating her dream for the world: "That a child should have two caring parents who share the joys and often the burdens," which, she insisted, required "a man who regards his wife as his best friend, his equal, his true partner in life."[28]

The Ginsburgs became, in effect, a nineties family in the fifties.[29]

Jane was one year old when Marty's compulsory time in the army was over. Two more years were optional. Marty had no interest in remaining in the reserves.

Ruth had to reapply for admission to Harvard Law School. Once more, she was accepted. This time, though, Harvard withdrew her scholarship and instructed her to submit her father-in-law's financial statement. She and Marty decided not to make a fuss over it. As Marty said with a laugh, "Nobody could see anything wrong with it, except us."[30] Fortunately, Marty's parents were supportive enough of Ruth's desire to go to law school—and generous enough—that they were willing to pay her tuition at Harvard. In fact, her father-in-law said he would be *happy* to pay her tuition. He supported her emotionally as well as financially, telling her that going against gender expectations by becoming a lawyer while the mother of a small child would be difficult, but if she really wanted to do it, she should.

Later, in an interview with Philip Galene of the *New York Times*, Ruth said that she sympathized with Harvard's decision not to offer scholarship funds to a person with family money, but she doubted a man would have been required to submit *his* father-in-law's financial statement. "Or his *mother*-in-law's statement," interjected Gloria Steinem, who was participating in the conversation.[31]

So, in 1956, the Ginsburgs moved out of the married officers' housing and headed to Cambridge, Massachusetts, where both Marty and Ruth enrolled at Harvard Law School, Marty entering his second year, Ruth beginning her first. They hired a grandmother-type nanny to stay with Jane during the days, and arranged their schedules so that one of them could be home each day at 4:00 p.m., when it was time for the nanny to leave.

There were nine women in Ruth's entering class of about five hundred. Because the first woman had been admitted in 1950, women in Harvard Law School were still a genuine novelty. Dean Erwin Griswold hosted a dinner early in the term for all nine of the women. After dinner, he brought the women into his living room and had each of them sit next to a distinguished professor who had been invited to be the woman's escort.

What the dean did next deeply rattled Ruth. He asked each woman to tell their escorts what they were doing in law school occupying a seat that could have been held by a man. Ruth was so shaken by the question that she knocked over an ashtray, which clattered to the floor. The answer she came up with was that her husband was in the second-year class and it was

Austin Hall, a classroom building of the Harvard Law School.

important for a wife to understand her husband's work. She didn't add that he had a similar reason for being there—so he could understand *her* work. One woman present had the nerve to respond to the question with a question of her own that she intended to be tongue-in-cheek: with almost five hundred Harvard men and nine women, she asked, "What better place to catch a man?"[32]

Ruth didn't think the dean's question was intended to wound. She believed he was just trying to address the faculty who didn't believe women should be admitted and take the place from deserving men, so—as she understood the dean's motives—he wanted the women to tell their stories so they could be reported to doubting members of the faculty.

After her first day of classes, Ruth experienced a pang of self-doubt. In her class was Anthony Lewis, who later became a Pulitzer Prize–winning *New York Times* columnist and reporter. After Anthony Lewis performed brilliantly, she went home and told Marty, "If they're all that smart, I won't make it."[33] But it was soon clear that Ruth took to law school. After the large lecture classes of her undergraduate years, where she had mostly been a passive learner, she loved the Socratic method used in law classrooms, where professors asked questions instead of providing answers, and learning involved a constant dialogue. In her view, a person who had been educated in the Jewish traditions of Talmudic scholarship as she had was comfortable with the method of intellectual probing and answering questions with another question.

The nine women in the class were divided among four sections, which meant most of the women were in a lecture hall with only one other female classmate. This put a kind of pressure on the women because if a woman was called on, she worried that a wrong answer would reflect badly not only on her but on all women. So the women were always on their toes, always well prepared. Later, a law professor at Columbia remarked that he longed for the good old days when there were only a few women in his law classes because if things were going slowly and he wanted a crisp answer, he could always call on a woman. "Nowadays," he remarked, "there's no difference; the women are as unprepared as the men."[34] Other sections in the Harvard Law School held "Ladies Day," when only women were called on, while they were ignored the rest of the year, but Ruth and the other woman in her section were spared that ordeal.

Ruth's favorite class was Civil Procedure, taught by Benjamin Kaplan, the grand master of the Socratic method, which he used to keep his students alert. If a student gave a poorly thought out answer, he would rephrase the answer for the benefit of the entire class. He stressed the purpose of procedure—to secure the just and speedy resolution of controversies. Ruth fell in love with the subject matter, so often considered dry, as she came to understand that procedure was the vehicle for fairness and justice, with rules that must be carefully neutral "precisely because they apply equally to your friends and your enemies."[35] The late 1950s, when Ruth was in law school, was the heyday of the legal-process movement, when scholars like Columbia's Herbert Wechsler argued that neutrality and justice were achieved through procedure. Under this theory, judges and courts should never rule based on their own biases or preferences, but should dispassionately analyze the competing interests in a case and make judgments that were procedurally consistent.

Early on in the semester, Marty predicted—and even bragged—that his wife would make law review, an honor he hadn't achieved. His classmates responded by questioning his judgment. No woman had yet made law review, and certainly nobody expected it of a tiny wisp of a woman like Ruth, who, according to one male classmate, didn't look particularly impressive. She wasn't likely to be taken for a scholar, at least according to the 1950s' stereotyped views of scholars. She was so attractive that when a professor called on Mrs. Ginsburg there was "an audible and collective groan of male disappointment in the room."[36]

Along with the nine women, there was one African American student in Ruth's first-year class. While it didn't occur to Ruth that anything was particularly amiss in this lack of diversity—it was something everyone was accustomed to—she did wonder why the number of women had decreased rather than increased since 1950. She and a few of her female classmates posed this question to a member of the faculty, who assured them that, in selecting from the applicants, the law school gave weight to "anything strange, unusual, singular about an applicant. Using that criterion, a bull fiddler gained a plus, so did a woman."[37] Eventually she concluded that the small number of women in law school in the 1950s was the result of "self-selection" since so few opportunities in law were available to them.[38]

Being a woman at Harvard Law School in the late 1950s brought small annoyances. There were two classroom buildings with plenty of men's restrooms, but there was only one women's restroom, located in the basement of one of the classroom buildings. This proved very inconvenient, to say the least. Women were always dashing back and forth between the buildings. Women were not admitted in the faculty club dining room. The old periodical room at Lamont Library was closed to women, a rule that caused Ruth trouble one evening when she needed an article. A man barred her way. She offered to stand outside the door if he would bring her the periodical she needed, but he refused, so she had to leave and return with a man who could get her the article she needed. Women were not permitted to live in the dormitory, a striking difference to Cornell, where women were required to live in the dorms. The difference, for Ruth, spoke to the arbitrariness of the rules.

Partway through Ruth's first semester of law school, the Ginsburg family was dealt a blow: Marty was diagnosed with a virulent form of testicular cancer. His chances of recovery were not good. Later Ruth said there were no known cases of survivors, but she and Marty never lost hope that he would recover. Treatment required two operations and weeks of radiation therapy, with the treatment to take place primarily during the second semester. As a result, Marty was able to attend classes for only two weeks of the second semester.

In a law school known for its cut-throat competitiveness, his classmates pulled together to help out. Ruth gathered together a group who she thought would take the best notes. They inserted carbon paper in their notebooks to make copies for Marty. One classmate even had his girlfriend type up the notes to make it easier for Marty to study. Ruth herself often typed up the notes for him as well. Classmates from his Corporate Reorganization seminar would visit Marty and discuss the finer points of corporate law. While Marty was undergoing radiation, he was awake only from midnight into the wee hours of the morning. During these hours, he rested on the couch and dictated to Ruth a paper on corporations. Ruth carried the burden of her own coursework, caring for Jane and Marty, and coordinating Marty's note takers. That was when she learned to work all through the night.

The school was less helpful than the students. Ruth went to the administration and asked a question: If her husband passed his exams, could he have his class rank and grades based on his work during the other two years? The answer was no. Whatever grades he got while he was sick would factor into the average, but the school would include a note in his file that he was sick. Rules were rules, and that was it. Ruth went home and told Marty a white lie. She told him that all he had to do was pass, and his class standing would be based on his first and last years. As a result, Marty went into his exams at ease and relaxed. As it turned out, he earned the highest grades of his law school career. With customary modesty, he gave all the credit to his brilliant note takers. He also joked that the only reason he was a decent law student was because Harvard Law School didn't field a golf team.

By the end of the school year, it was clear Marty's operations had been a success. He would have a full recovery, and would be back in school full-time for his final year—but it would be five years before the doctors would be able to say for sure that the cancer had been eliminated. If there was any doubt that after finishing school Ruth would pursue a career of her own—or if she simply needed an excuse to follow her own career path—this settled the issue. They didn't know how long Marty would live, so Ruth must be prepared to support herself and Jane.

Unbelievably enough, given the pressures Ruth faced during her first year of law school, she finished her first semester with top grades. Based on her grade-point average, she finished her first year as one of the top ten students in a class of five hundred—and she became the first woman to make *Harvard Law Review*. She gave credit to Jane for her excellent grades. "I went home, played with Jane, had dinner, and then I was ready to go back to the books. It was the pause that refreshes."[39] She felt she was less apprehensive about her schoolwork than her classmates because she had something in her life that was more important than the law.

By Ruth's second year of law school, she and Marty established their routine: No matter how busy they were with work or studying, they would have dinner at home together. Occasionally, when the nanny was not available but Ruth needed to work in Gannet House, the building where the law review offices were housed, Ruth simply brought Jane with her, and Jane crawled around as Ruth worked. Each evening, after Jane went to sleep, both Marty and Ruth studied late into the night.

The minor annoyances Ruth experienced as a result of gender continued into her second year. The law review held a banquet. She was allowed to invite her father-in-law and her father. She was not allowed to invite her mother-in-law, though, because the banquet was just for men—even though Ruth insisted that aside from her husband, her mother-in-law had been her greatest personal supporter. Ruth herself was the only woman allowed in. She was allowed to bring Marty, but the men on law review could not bring their wives.

Many of Ruth's classmates looked at her with awe. In the words of one classmate, "While the rest of us were sulking around in dirty khaki pants and frayed button-down Oxford shirts, missing classes and complaining about all the work we had, you set a standard too high for any of us to achieve: you never missed classes; you were always prepared; your Law Review work was always done; you were always beautifully groomed; and you had a happy husband and a lovely young daughter."[40]

Other classmates were harsher in their opinions. One classmate revealed that Ruth was known as Ruthless Ruthie. Years later, another classmate, while presiding over a Rotarian induction ceremony, recalled that he and his friends had known Ruth "by her law school nickname, 'Bitch.'"[41] After she was nominated to the U.S. Supreme Court, she received an apology from the classmate, in the form of a fax, assuring her that he and the Rotary Club would ban such sexist and scatological statements. Ruth read the fax, and, with her usual calm, responded with, "Better bitch than mouse."[42]

As Marty approached graduation, he was offered a job with a top New York law firm, Weil, Gotshal, & Manges. The Ginsburgs had no intention of splitting up the family, so, in a search for alternatives, Ruth went to the dean, Erwin Griswold, with a proposition. "If I successfully complete my third year at Columbia Law School," she asked, "will I be able to earn a Harvard degree?"[43] He said absolutely not. She had her rebuttal argument ready: She pointed out that one student had transferred to Harvard Law after completing her first year at the University of Pennsylvania Law School. She received a law degree having done only two years at Harvard—and the first year is generally considered the most important. In Ruth's case, she would have done the most important year at Harvard.

Shouldn't she, then, receive a Harvard Law degree? The dean said no. More specifically, she had not made a case of "exigent personal circumstances" as to why she should be granted permission.[44]

After Ruth achieved national prominence, Harvard deans tried repeatedly to give her a Harvard Law degree—but she always refused. One Harvard dean called her each year, pressing her to accept a Harvard degree. The careful and meticulous Ruth Bader Ginsburg, who always made sure the I's were dotted and the T's crossed and that every fact had been checked and double-checked, was not about to retroactively alter history. One time when Elena Kagan, then dean of the law school and now a Supreme Court justice herself, called Ruth—who was then Justice Ginsburg—and urged her to accept a Harvard Law degree, Marty, with his usual good humor, advised Ruth to hold out for an honorary degree. Once, in an exchange of letters through the campus newspaper with Marty, the spokesperson for Harvard even responded with humor, saying, "Just think what else she might have accomplished had she enjoyed the benefits of a Harvard degree." Marty responded with: "It's a nice thing to have a degree from the Harvard Law School. On the rare occasion I run across it, I treasure every Latin word.[45]

5

THE SPIRIT
OF LIBERTY

Ruth signed up for summer job interviews with every firm that
didn't bar women. When she interviewed with the New York
law firm of Paul, Weiss, Rifkind, Wharton, & Garrison, it was
obvious to her that the partner who interviewed her, Lloyd
Garrison, wasn't much interested in what she had to say. After
she'd barely said two sentences, he hired her on the spot. She
soon learned the reason: The law firm had already decided they
wanted a woman. Ruth was the Harvard woman with the highest
grades, so they'd already decided to hire her. End of story. No
need to waste time on an interview. The custom was for firms
to make full-time job offers to its summer associates at the end
of the summer. Ruth believed that her work that summer at
the firm was up to their usual standards. She was surprised and
disappointed when she was not offered a job. Later she found
out that the firm had hired a full-time female associate, so she
supposed they no longer needed her. The woman they hired,
Pauli Murray, was a feminist who worked hard for women's
rights. Later she and Pauli became friends.

When Ruth applied to transfer to Columbia Law School,
Dean Warren of Columbia accepted her and welcomed her.

Soon the word went around the Columbia Law campus that the smartest person on the East Coast was transferring in, so everyone could anticipate dropping down one rank.

In her new class at Columbia, Ruth was one of twelve women. Her classmates viewed her as serious and smart, a woman who did things with a minimum of fuss. "She was extraordinarily intelligent, but low-key and reserved," said Marie Garibaldi, a Columbia classmate who went on to become a state Supreme Court justice. "She was thoughtful and deliberate in her responses to professors' questions, but she was never arrogant about her intelligence."[46] Others found her aloof and reserved. One classmate said, "Due to the demands on her time . . . I don't think anyone became really close friends with Ruth."[47] After all, with Marty working in a major Wall Street firm and eager to make partner, she was mostly responsible for the home and Jane, as well as her studies.

At Columbia, as at Harvard, Ruth pulled it off: Her first round of grades put her at the top of the class, and she was offered a place on Columbia's law review, giving her the unusual distinction of having made law review at both Harvard and Columbia. She signed up for Herbert Wexler's noontime seminar in federal courts and the federal system, considered one of the most difficult in the law school. She was the star student. Wexler had a habit of asking his students long, complicated questions. When it was Ruth's turn to respond, she paused before answering, then gave an equally long, complicated answer. Then, after another pause, she would politely add factors Wexler had left out.

With graduation approaching and time to look for a job, Ruth signed up for interviews. Major law firms posted sign-up sheets for students who wanted to interview with their firm. Only two firms invited her to interview, Cadwalader, Wickerhsam, & Taft, and Casey, Lane, & Mittendorf. Her mother-in-law had given her a black interview suit, and when she wore it she felt she looked "very much like a young lawyer."[48] She was disappointed when neither firm offered her a job. "In the fifties, traditional law firms were just beginning to turn around on hiring Jews," Ruth explained later. "But to be a woman, a Jew and a mother to boot—that combination was a bit too much."[49] She remarked that after being shunned by so many law firms, she looked in the mirror to see if she had two heads.

Some of the reasons given for refusing to hire women seemed downright silly and even ironic to Ruth. For example, U.S. attorney's offices refused to hire women as prosecutors. The excuse was that women were too soft to be able to confront hardened criminals. But Legal Aid, the organization most often entrusted with defending the accused, was full of women even though the defense lawyer was positioned more closely to hardened criminals. Ruth concluded that the difference was that Legal Aid lawyers were paid paltry salaries compared to prosecutors. Other excuses were simply annoying. One that Ruth heard was, "We hired a woman at this firm once and she was dreadful."[50] Never mind plenty of male hires hadn't worked out, either. Others said they wanted to feel comfortable enough in the workplace so they could just kick off their shoes if they wanted—and they didn't feel they could do that with women around.

The most interesting and prestigious positions available to new law school graduates were judicial clerkships lasting a year or two—and they always went to the very top students. Professor Albert Sachs, then a Harvard Law professor and later dean of the law school, recommended Ruth as a clerk to Supreme Court Justice Felix Frankfurter. Justice Frankfurter had been the first Supreme Court justice to hire an African American law clerk, so both Professor Sachs and Ruth had high hopes that Justice Frankfurter would hire her. A legend, which has now been debunked, was that after Justice Frankfurter received the call from Professor Sachs recommending Ruth, he asked whether she wore skirts and then said, "I can't stand girls in pants." He may not have made the snarky comment, but he refused to hire Ruth. He admitted to being impressed with her academic credentials, but he said he wasn't prepared to break the tradition of hiring only men as clerks.

Columbia professor Gerald Gunther, who had been Ruth's professor in a course on federal courts and who played an active role in helping Columbia's top students secure judicial clerkships, took Ruth on as a special case. He called every judge on the second circuit, and the eastern and southern districts of New York. He recommended her to judges as "a brilliant student" who "demonstrated extraordinary intellectual capacities." He described her as "modest, thoughtful, penetrating, fair and open-minded."[51] The answer? No. Even judges open to taking a chance on a woman were frightened of hiring the mother of a young child. What if the child was sick? How could Ruth work the long hours often expected of a clerk? What about Sundays and weekends? It would seem that Ruth's grades and academic performance would have alleviated these concerns. After all, if she managed to earn top grades in two top law schools as the mother of a toddler, why wouldn't she be able to perform the demanding duties of a clerk?

The judge Ruth most admired and most wished to clerk for was Learned Hand, an extraordinarily influential judge. Appointed to the Court of Appeals for the Second Circuit by Calvin Coolidge, he was known for his rulings in the field of civil liberties. Her mentors tried to get her a clerkship with

Learned Hand, circa 1910.

Judge Hand, but he declined, saying that he had a foul mouth and so he didn't want a woman around because he didn't want to have to curb his swearing.

Professor Gunther finally got her a clerkship with Judge Palmieri of the U.S. District court for the Southern District of New York by means of a promise and a threat. A Columbia Law graduate then working in a Wall Street law firm promised that if Ruth didn't work out, he would step in and take over. The threat was this: Gunther told Judge Palmieri, "And if you don't give her a chance, Columbia will never again send you another law clerk."[52] The combination of threat and promise did the trick. Judge Palmieri hired Ruth for a two-year clerkship.

Gunther knew Ruth would not fail—and she didn't. To prove herself, she worked harder than any other law clerk in the building, staying late whenever it was necessary, coming in to work on Saturdays, and bringing work home. Shortly after she began work, she was in the courtroom when two lawyers were arguing over the merits of a particular motion. After hearing arguments, Judge Palmieri was about to rule on the motion when Ruth passed him a note asking if he could delay ruling because she believed there was a Supreme Court case directly on point. Ruth turned out to be right. Both lawyers had overlooked the case, and the judge hadn't thought of it. Ruth had saved the Judge Palmieri from error. He was duly impressed.

While working with Judge Palmieri she learned the need for flexibility, and the truth of one of Learned Hand's famous sayings—"spirit of liberty is the spirit which is not too sure that it is right."[53] At one point, she felt absolutely sure she knew the answer to a question: Does a federal district court have authority to transfer a case, although the transferee court lacked both subject matter and personal jurisdiction? She and Judge Palmieri discussed the question, and came to the same conclusion: The court was powerless to do anything but dismiss the case. The second circuit affirmed the dismissal on appeal. The case went to the Supreme Court. The Supreme Court reversed, saying that Ruth and her judge got it wrong. The Supreme Court explained that we have only one federal court system, so dismissal would not be appropriate because the litigants would have no other venue for their grievances. Many times over the coming years Ruth reflected on the Supreme Court's analysis, and she came to understand her error.

As it turned out, Learned Hand and Judge Palmieri lived near each other, so Palmieri often drove Judge Hand home from court, with Ruth riding in the back seat. Judge Hand would swear, sing indelicate songs, and say whatever popped into his head, however crude. "How can you carry on this way with me in the car, and yet you wouldn't consider me to be your law clerk?" Ruth asked once. "Young lady," Judge Hand responded. "I am not looking you in the face."[54]

By the end of Ruth's two-year clerkship, Judge Palmieri was so impressed with her that the very next year, he hired another woman.

6

AN AMERICAN
LAWYER IN SWEDEN

After a successful clerkship, and rave recommendations from Judge Palmieri, law firms were now willing to hire Ruth. She was about to accept a job with Marty's Manhattan firm when Professor Hans Smit contacted her and asked if she'd meet him for lunch at the Harvard Club. Smit held law degrees from both Amsterdam University and Columbia. He had recently joined the Columbia faculty to work on an international civil procedure project funded by the Carnegie Foundation to do basic research on foreign systems of procedure and propose improvements of U.S. rules on transnational litigation. One goal was to make U.S. rules more accommodating to lawyers abroad who wanted to find evidence in the states, or access American courts. The project had grants to study procedure in France, Italy, and Sweden. Finding scholars willing to travel to France and Italy wasn't hard. Sweden was another matter.

To meet Smit, she had to enter the Harvard Club through a red side door reserved for women. Not long into their conversation, he asked, "Ruth, how would you like to co-author a book about civil procedure in Sweden?"[55] An odd idea, she thought. In fact, in that moment, she couldn't quite recall where Sweden was on the map in relation to Norway.

But she'd always had a strong interest in civil procedure, and she liked the idea of traveling abroad and living on her own in Sweden. She'd never lived alone, having married young, going from the college dormitories to a home shared with her husband. The deciding factor was that she liked the notion of being an author of a book. She was also impressed that Smit not only was willing to hire a woman to work on his project, but also offered to pay her the same salary that men were being paid by the major law firms at the time.

She accepted the job, and began work in September of 1961. "I was rather shy when I came on board,"[56] she said, but Hans Smit helped by taking on the role of mentor, encouraging her, and helping her feel at ease. Her first task was to become familiar with the language. Columbia provided a language tutor, a former dancer from the Swedish ballet who offered Ruth both excellent language instruction *and* ballet gossip. She retained enough Swedish all her life to be able to watch Ingmar Bergman movies without subtitles and to translate the Swedish code of civil procedure into English.

In late spring of 1962, she boarded a plane for Sweden, leaving Jane with Marty so she could finish out first grade. Ruth's first stay in Sweden would last four months. In a few weeks, when Jane was out of school, Jane and Marty would join her. She did much of her work at the University of Lund, and produced works of impressive scholarship. *Civil Procedure in Sweden* offers a history of Swedish procedural law, the sources of Swedish procedural law, an outline of Swedish legal education, the structure of a Swedish lawsuit, and chapters on the expense of litigation and collection of judgments, concluding with a chapter on international cooperation. In 1969, the University

University of Lund, Main Building.

of Lund awarded her an honorary law degree for her contributions to the book.

Lessons in comparative civil procedure were not Ruth's main takeaways from her time abroad. In Sweden, for the first time, she felt the stirrings of what we'd now call feminism. The women's movement came to Sweden early. Ruth was startled to see that a relatively large percentage of law students—between 20 percent and 25 percent—were women. She was also impressed by the fact that the University of Lund had an excellent daycare center for children of students and faculty, something just about unknown then in the United States. There were even female judges. Most startling of all, she went to a proceeding in Stockholm and saw that the presiding judge was eight months pregnant.

Inflation in Sweden meant that most families required two incomes. A Swedish writer, Eva Moberg, published a column in a Swedish daily paper, asking, "Why should women have two jobs and men only one?"[57] The idea was that the woman might have a job to help with living expenses, but she was still the one expected to shop for children's shoes and have dinner on the table at seven o'clock. How fair was that? Moberg's argument—that women would not achieve equality simply from entering the workforce, and men would have to enter what was traditionally considered the woman's sphere before there would be equality—was one that Marty and Ruth had already worked out for themselves. The whole debate was still a few years away from reaching the United States. Ruth was fascinated by the responses from different women. Some women were queen bees—they could handle everything, thank you very much. Others felt it was time for men to do their share of the housework, a revolutionary idea in 1962.

While she was there, Swedish and American headlines exploded with the controversy of Sherri Finkbine and her abortion. The American actress known as Miss Sherri on the Phoenix, Arizona, version of a franchised children's television show, *Romper Room*, found herself embroiled in controversy when she became pregnant with her fifth child while taking thalidomide, a drug that, if taken by a pregnant woman, caused a condition known as phocomelia, in which the limbs of the fetus do not form, resulting in severely deformed children. Finkbine's doctor strongly recommended that she obtain an abortion. She scheduled an abortion, despite legal barriers: Arizona permitted abortions only if the life of the mother was in danger. The district attorney immediately threatened to prosecute the institution and any hospital staff who participated in the procedure. When the hospital canceled the procedure, Sherri's doctor requested a court order to proceed with the abortion, but the order was denied.

International media coverage made Sherri Finkbine a major name. When she received death threats, the FBI had to step in to offer protection. Initially the Finkbines traveled to Japan, hoping to secure an abortion, but the Japanese would not issue a visa. The Finkbines then flew to Sweden with a stop in Copenhagen. To obtain an abortion in Sweden, Sherri had to initiate legal proceedings and appear before a panel that considered the social, medical, and spiritual consequences of an abortion. The panel approved her abortion. By then she was at the end of her first trimester. The obstetrician who performed the abortion reported that the fetus had no legs, only one arm, and genitalia that were growing abnormally. As a result of the abortion, Sherri's husband was fired from his job as a high school teacher, and she was fired from her job as the host of *Romper Room*.

Sherri Finkbine arrives in Copenhagen on her way to Sweden, August 8, 1962.

That was also the summer Ruth read Simone de Beauvoir's *The Second Sex*. She found the book "overwhelming, staggering."[58] All the new information she was taking in—the Finkbine scandal, Eva Moberg's article, and Beauvoir's eye-opening book—she simply absorbed and tucked away for later.

At the end of Ruth's first year on the project, she was promoted to associate director. She would return once more to Sweden the following summer accompanied by both Jane and Marty, who planned to take vacation time from his firm.

Just as her stay in Sweden showed Ruth new possibilities, coming home reminded her of the American Dream. In an interview she explained that after a prolonged stay in Sweden and becoming accustomed to people whose complexion was the same, she rode the New York subway and was struck by the amazing diversity in the United States. American diversity reminded her of the motto *E pluribus unum*, "Of many, one," an idea she preferred to the melting pot because Americans could keep their individual identities while being American.[59]

Meanwhile, Marty had made partner at his firm of Weil, Gotshal, & Manges, where he discovered a love and aptitude for the tax code. He mastered the art of structuring a financial deal to minimize taxes. His father used to say about lawyers that they were "no" people—they would always say no, you can't do it, or it costs too much to comply with the law. Marty, optimistic by nature, enjoyed structuring financial deals for maximum tax benefit because it made him a "yes" person.

In 1963, at the conclusion of her work on the project, Ruth was again planning to work for Marty's firm when a Columbia professor, Walter Gellhorn—who was something of a one-person placement office for law school faculty positions—asked Ruth to come see him in his office. When she arrived, he asked, "Ruth, what is your name doing on this Harvard list when you're a Columbia graduate?"[60] At first she had no idea what he was talking about. Then she remembered that Harvard had sent her a form with instructions to fill it out if she was interested in a career teaching law. She'd filled it out and sent it back, but thought no more of it because at that time, there were only fourteen women teaching law in the entire country.

In that moment in Walter's office, she jumped to the wrong conclusion. "Walter," she said, "is Columbia interested in *me*?"[61] He said not Columbia, but Rutgers, the State University of New Jersey School of Law. Rutgers was looking to fill a vacancy left by their professor of civil procedure, Clarence Clyde Ferguson, who left to take the position of dean at Howard School of Law. Rutgers tried to replace him with another African American man, but having failed in that quest, they were looking for a woman. Rutgers, one of the few law schools willing to hire a woman, already had a female professor on the faculty, Eva Hanks.

Ruth always thought she'd like to teach law—but she thought she'd rather practice for a few years first. There were so few law teaching positions available to women, though, that she thought she better take one while she had the chance. So she interviewed with the hiring committee at Rutgers. Before she was offered the position, a member of the faculty asked Eva Hanks if she'd be upset if they hired another woman. Professor Hanks, evidently finding the question strange, asked, "Why would I mind?" The colleague said, "Because you will no longer be the only woman on the faculty."[62] She just looked at him and assured him that it was quite all right.

When Willard Heckel, the dean at Rutgers, offered Ruth a faculty position, he warned her that because Rutgers was a state school with limited resources, she would have to take a cut in salary. She expected that—but when she heard the amount she was being offered, she was surprised. She asked about the salary of a male professor who had graduated law school the same year as her. The dean admitted they were paying him more. He said, "Ruth, he has a wife and two children to support, and Marty has a good paying job with a law firm."[63]

7

A STEEL
BUTTERFLY

At Rutgers, Ruth mostly taught constitutional law, civil procedure, and conflict of laws. Alex Brooks, the professor who headed the hiring committee, described her as "very quiet, almost withdrawn."[64] Eva Hanks—who became a good friend, taking Ruth under her wing, and filling her in on the quirks of the faculty—had a different view. In Ruth, she saw someone with "an inner strength," and "an inner light."[65] Another colleague described her as a steel butterfly.

Students saw her as quiet, intense, and ultra-focused. She was not the sort of teacher to worry about entertaining her class. When students were inclined toward a knee-jerk reaction, she would present the opposing side as strongly as she could to force them to think more deeply and defend their views, but she didn't pretend to be neutral when she wasn't. Her students, for example, had no doubts about where she stood on the Bill of Rights and civil liberties.

At the end of Ruth's first year of teaching, the students performed skits making fun of the faculty members. The actress playing Ruth read civil procedure while a male student approached from behind, unzipped her dress, and pulled it down to her ankles. Standing in a slip, "Professor Ginsburg" kept on lecturing, entirely oblivious to the fact that she was being undressed.

Gone now was the cheerful party-girl baton twirler of James Madison High. She read on the subway and prepared for classes while commuting on the PATH train. She wore her hair pulled back in a no-nonsense pony tail tied with a scarf. Her clothing was muted and professional.

Ruth approached parenting with the same deliberate thoroughness she approached everything else. When Jane was eight years old, Ruth got tickets for the family to see Mozart's *Cosi Fan Tutte* at the Metropolitan Opera. To make sure Jane would enjoy the show, she played the record for months ahead of time, going through the libretto with Jane so that by the time she went to see the performance, she knew all the lines. In honor of the occasion, Ruth had a velvet jumper made for her, which she wore with a new pair of patent-leather shoes. "I wanted her to remember it as something special," Ruth said.[66] Most weekends, they visited exhibitions and children's shows in the city. When Jane went to sleep-away camp, Ruth wrote to her every day. "She just sort of has this way of being meticulous and attending to detail that in a way is quite daunting to even think about keeping up with," Jane said later.[67]

Marty bragged to his law partners of the rare occasions he was able to make his wife chuckle. Jane, who decided that Mommy's sense of humor needed improvement, documented in a booklet the occasions when "Mommy Laughs." Ruth may have been serious, but she wasn't without emotion. She wept freely at the opera. Close friends said in private life she was warm, good-humored, and kind. A glass of wine could make her positively giddy. Among her pastimes were golfing, waterskiing, and reading mysteries.

Jane described the disciplining styles of her parents this way: "When I did something bad, which happened often, my dad would yell, but my mother would be real quiet and I'd know she was very disappointed in me."[68]

Not long after Ruth joined the Rutgers Law faculty, she got to talking to other women teaching at the university and they decided to do something about the situation of unequal pay. Title VII of the Civil Rights Act of 1964 guaranteeing freedom from sex discrimination in hiring wasn't on the books yet—it didn't go into effect until the year after Ruth began teaching—but the Equal Pay Act of 1963 was in effect. When the female professors, led by Ruth, tried to learn what the university paid the men, the administration said, "That's secret information. All kinds of jealousies would result if we published them."[69] So Ruth and the other woman on the faculty brought an equal pay case against the university and discovered that their suspicions had been correct. Ruth wasn't alone—the women as a class were paid considerably less than their male counterparts. It took several years before the case was settled, with each female faculty member securing a substantial raise.

During her second year of teaching, in the spring semester of 1965, Ruth discovered she was pregnant again, a surprise and a miracle after Marty's testicular cancer. Her employment with Rutgers was based on a contract that had to be renewed yearly. Remembering well what happened when she'd informed her employer at the Social Security office of her first pregnancy, she was genuinely afraid that if she told the dean she was pregnant, her contract would not be renewed. So she went rogue: She borrowed clothing from her mother-in-law and hid her pregnancy. The timing of her pregnancy—the semester ended just before the start of her third trimester—allowed her to hide her pregnancy from her faculty colleagues. As she put it, the baby was very cooperative. She didn't reveal she was pregnant until she had her signed contract in hand for another year's employment. After the last class that semester, she drove home from New Jersey to New York with three of her colleagues and announced that there would be one more in her family when she returned in the fall. James Steven Ginsburg was born September 8, 1965, shortly before the fall semester began.

Later Ruth disclosed that she felt "some discrimination" as a woman during her first few years at Rutgers.[70] While she didn't elaborate when interviewed for the *New York Times,* one of her male colleagues, Alex Brooks, responded defensively. "I think what she didn't recognize, or refused to recognize, was that everyone did welcome her, but she didn't welcome everyone. She pretty much kept to herself. Efforts to include her were usually met with resistance." Ruth, with her usual tact and reticence, didn't respond or point out that her salary had been lower because she was a married woman whose husband had a good job, which, in her view at least, counted as discrimination.

Ruth's work habits from law school carried over to her time at Rutgers. During her first three years of teaching, she published seven articles, mostly on Swedish procedure, and saw her two books on Swedish civil procedure through the publication process. In 1966, she was named to the editorial board of the *American Journal of Comparative Law.* The following year, she was named to the European Law committee of the American Bar Association's section of International Law and Practice. She joined the Foreign Law Committee of the New York Bar, and was a member of the Citizen Union, an organization designed to promote good government in New York, and the Children's

International Summer Villages, an organization for bringing together children from around the globe for a summer camp experience.

Because Marty was putting in the long hours necessary for making partner in a major law firm, and because Ruth's job as a professor was more flexible, she was still doing the lion's share of the work in maintaining the household.

In 1966 she was promoted to associate professor. Meanwhile, Marty was well on his way to becoming one of the top tax lawyers in New York City. His income allowed the family to live in a luxurious apartment at Sixty-Ninth Street and Lexington Avenue. Their home was large enough for both Ruth and Marty to have separate offices—a long way from her humble beginnings in Brooklyn. Their children attended the finest private schools. They had a beautiful piano. Sometimes during parties, Ruth would sit down and play.

When James was two, the daily routine of family life and work was upset by a family emergency that almost became a tragedy. One day, while James was home with the housekeeper, he got into a cabinet and tried to drink Drano. Fortunately the liquid got no farther than his lips and face, where it caused severe burning instead of the certain death that would have come from ingesting it. The housekeeper rushed him to the hospital. After several excruciating days, the doctors told his parents that he'd be fine, but he would need reconstructive surgery to repair the damaged tissue. The surgery was successful and the burn scars were almost entirely erased. Among the questions Ruth had to answer from reporters was whether she felt guilty to be working while tragedy almost struck her son. It seemed to Ruth that the mistake had been failing to put the Drano out of James's reach, not committing the sin of being a working mother and being gone when the accident happened. She always commended the housekeeper for her exemplary response to the emergency.

In 1968, the number of women entering law schools increased dramatically because the draft laws were changed, eliminating the deferment for law students. Men who wanted to avoid Vietnam went into teaching instead, or became conscientious objectors, or headed for Canada, creating places for women. Even when the major law schools began admitting women in greater numbers it was accompanied by comments that irked Ruth. During the height of the Vietnam War, Harvard University's president said, "We shall be left with the blind, the lame, and the women."[71]

The women now entering the law schools were part of a new generation that came of age during the tumultuous 1960s. Unlike Ruth and her classmates, who rolled with the sexist punches and sought to defy gender stereotypes by quietly doing good work—the young women now, empowered by the social revolution of the 1960s, had the nerve to stand up and boo when professors made sexist comments. The entire decade had seen a new wave of feminist activism. Betty Friedan's *The Feminist Mystique* was widely read. The attitudes of this generation of feminists were captured by the protests of the Miss America pageant in 1968 and 1969, when angry women parodied what they saw as a degrading and oppressive tradition that reduced women to sexual objects.

Ruth, like many college professors in the 1960s, faced unique challenges in teaching a generation that was asserting itself as never before, relying on the First Amendment to engage in all kinds of expression. She taught a class once at Rutgers while a male student was outside her window thumbing his nose at her. She calmly continued with her class.

She approved when two female New York University law students got the idea to form a women's rights group. One of the women was Janice Goodman, a first-year law student who, prior to entering law school, organized against discrimination in Mississippi with the Democratic Party. One day she was standing in a bookstore in a line next to a second-year student, Susan Deller Ross, and they got talking about scholarships and shared their irritation that a certain prestigious—and generous— scholarship was available only to male students. Ross said to Goodman, "Don't you think we should do something about that?"[72] They then created the Women's Rights Committee, the first women's group at any law school. When they circulated a petition to open the scholarship to women, opponents pointed out that allowing women to receive the scholarship would make certain traditional rituals impossible, such as the custom of scholarship winners throwing water balloons at each other while running naked through their residence. The women's group then stunned the faculty by threatening to sue their own law school if the scholarship was not opened to women. Within days, New York University opened its scholarship to women.

The women of New York University Law School next asked for a course on women and the law, but they met with resistance and mockery. One professor suggested the school's next step would be to teach the law of the bicycle. But the women persisted, and the university hired a part-time teacher to teach the course. Once the women of New York University Law School had their own course started, they took their program on the road. Rutgers School of Law, just a few stops away along the PATH train from Manhattan, was their next destination. Rutgers was the natural next stop because Rutgers had something that New York University—and indeed, most law schools—lacked: two women on the faculty.

When the students approached Ruth and asked her to offer a course at Rutgers on women and the law, she took up the task. To put together the course, she spent the better part of a month in the library, reading every federal case and article about gender equality published since the birth of the nation, a task easily done in a month because there were so few. Among the laws she found were that "The husband is the head of the family. He may choose any reasonable place or mode of living and his wife must conform thereto"—a law derived from Napoleon's code.[73] Reading through these cases, for the first time, she felt something like the stirring of real anger. "How have people been putting up with such arbitrary distinctions?" she wondered. "How have I been putting up with them?"[74] Nonetheless she said her awakening was a gradual process. It wasn't as if one morning she saw a bright light.

8

SPECIAL
TREATMENT

When Ruth went to the library to read everything she could find on women and the law, what she found was that the law reflected and reinforced traditional gender roles and stereotypes. Most statutes and court decisions she found rested on the belief that the natural place for a woman was as a nurturer in the home, while a man belonged in the work world.

She also understood that discriminatory laws were often justified and rationalized as necessary to protect women—but in fact they often protected men from female competition. For example, an Oregon law passed in 1903 prohibited women from working more than ten hours in a single day. Under this law, Curt Muller, a laundry owner, was charged with allowing Mrs. Gotcher to work more than ten hours and was fined $10. Muller sued, arguing that the law violated Mrs. Gotcher's Fourteenth Amendment right to due process by preventing her from freely contracting with her employer. Louis Brandeis, who later became a Supreme Court justice, represented the state and defended the law on the grounds that women needed protection by virtue of their physical differences from men. The Supreme Court agreed with Brandeis, holding that the state could—and should—protect women with appropriate legislation. In the words of the court, women need special treatment because

> That woman's physical structure and the performance of maternal functions place her at a disadvantage in the struggle for subsistence is obvious. This is especially true when the burdens of motherhood are upon her. Even when they are not, by abundant testimony of the medical fraternity, continuance for a long time on her feet at work, repeating this from day to day, tends to injurious effects upon the body, and, as healthy mothers are essential to vigorous offspring, the physical wellbeing of woman becomes an object of public interest and care in order to preserve the strength and vigor of the race.

> . . . history discloses the fact that woman has always been dependent upon man. He established his control at the outset by superior physical strength, and this control in various forms, with diminishing intensity, has continued to the present. As minors, though not to the same extent, she has been looked upon in the courts as needing especial care that her rights may be preserved. Education was long denied her, and while now the doors of the schoolroom are opened and her opportunities for acquiring knowledge are great, yet, even with that and the consequent increase of capacity for business affairs, it is still true that, in the struggle for subsistence, she is not an equal competitor with her brother.[75]

It seemed to Ruth that laws prohibiting women from working more than eight-hour days made sense when they were passed, back when sweatshop days were often twelve hours in length. But over the years, unions enacted protective changes, and the workweek for everyone was reduced to eight hours. An employer who wanted more hours would have to pay time-and-a-half or double time for additional hours. If an employer had two alternatives, a woman who could not work more than eight hours or a man who could, the employer would hire the man.

Laws also penalized married women who failed to take their husband's name, codifying the ancient notion that a woman had no legal existence apart from her husband. A married woman in 1926 neglected to change her car registration to her husband's name after she was married. One day her car was struck by a train. The court, however, barred her from suing for damages because her car registration was not filed properly under her husband's name. The court, in fact, declared her a "nuisance on the highway" for not properly registering her car.[76]

One satirist characterized the contemporary opinion of women in the law this way:

> It is probably no mere chance that in our legal textbooks the problems relating to married women are usually considered immediately after the pages devoted to idiots and lunatics. . . . The view that there exists a class of beings, illogical, impulsive, careless, irresponsible, extravagant, prejudiced, and vain, free for the most part from those worthy and repellent excellences which distinguish the Reasonable Man, and devoted to the irrational arts of pleasure and attraction, is one which should be as welcome and as well accepted in our Courts as it is in our drawing-rooms and even in Parliament.[77]

After World War II, two women challenged a Michigan law that denied bartender licenses to women unless the woman was the wife or daughter of the male owner of a liquor establishment. The women argued that the law violated the equal protection clause of the Fourteenth Amendment, claiming that the statute was "an unchivalrous desire of male bartenders to try to monopolize the calling."[78] The state of Michigan argued that a bartending woman could give rise to social and moral problems that the state would then have resolve or police. Michigan also argued that the law protected women from the sorts of hazards that might confront a woman bartender.

When deciding whether laws that discriminate between groups of people violate the equal protection clause, courts balance the government's need for the law against the liberty interest of the citizens. The test that courts use is called the rational basis test: If there is a rational basis for making the distinction—if discriminating between groups of people is rationally related to a legitimate government interest—the courts uphold the law. Under this test, the Supreme Court concluded that the state's desire to prevent women from entering an immoral or inappropriate profession provided a rational basis for the law. Felix Frankfurter—the justice who had refused to interview Ruth for a clerkship because she was a woman—wrote the opinion for the majority of the court, saying that even if women "now indulge in vices that men have long practiced," lawmakers were allowed to make distinctions between men and women and were not required to bend its laws to reflect "sociological insights or shifting social standards."[79]

Women's equality was helped along by the Equal Pay Act of 1963, which explicitly prohibited sex discrimination in pay, while allowing for such exceptions as merit systems, or systems rewarding production. The biggest boon, though, came when gender discrimination in employment was prohibited by the Civil Rights Act of 1964. Initially Title VII of the Civil Rights Act declared that

> Title VII prohibits employment discrimination based on race, color, religion, and national origin.

While the bill was being debated on the house floor, Representative Howard W. Smith of Virginia, chairman of the Rules Committee, rose up and offered a one-word addition to Title VII, "sex," resulting in,

> Title VII prohibits employment discrimination based on race, color, religion, sex, and national origin.

The suggestion that gender equality in employment should be added, which struck many people as ludicrous, prompted several hours of humorous debate, later known as Ladies Day at the House. When the bill came to a vote, it passed 168 to 133—with the word "sex" included.

It was long assumed that Representative Smith, who vehemently opposed the Civil Rights Act, inserted the word "sex" as a way of sinking the bill on the grounds that the very idea of giving equal employment status to women was just so absurd the bill would naturally be voted down. Recently scholars, however, have offered an alternate—and more likely—interpretation, arguing that Smith added the word upon pressure from an extremely well-organized group of women from the National Women's Party, working in collaboration with Representative Martha Griffiths.[80]

Representative Martha Griffiths worked to pass the ERA.

However it happened, there were now two important pieces of federal legislation forbidding gender discrimination in employment and wages. But there remained an overwhelming number of laws that, while not in conflict with the new legislation, nonetheless reinforced the idea that the woman should remain in the home and the man should make all important decisions. Under the tax laws, for example, if a woman's earnings approached that of her husband's, the couple would retain more of their income if the couple lived together without marriage.[81] A deduction for childcare was available for divorced parents, but a married couple could claim a childcare deduction only if the adjusted gross income of the couple was close to subsistence level.[82]

Ruth found it particularly irksome that a property law textbook published in 1968 declared that, "after all, land, like woman, was meant to be possessed."[83]

9

CATCHING
FIRE

About the time Ruth was putting together her course on women and law, a woman named Nora Simon wrote to the ACLU complaining about her treatment by the army. She and her husband were both serving in the army, she as an army nurse. In 1969, they had a child. Soon after the birth of their child, their marriage ended in divorce, and they put the child up for adoption. Nora's husband was permitted to continue to serve in the army. Nora was banned from all military services because of her pregnancy. She was discharged despite the fact that her work in the army had been exemplary and in 1970, the height of the war in Vietnam, the army badly needed nurses. According to army regulations, her past pregnancy constituted a "nonwaivable moral and administrative disqualification" to reentry.[84] Absurdly enough, under the regulations, had the child died, Nora would have been eligible for reenlistment.

In her letter to the ACLU, Nora described the discrimination she faced, stressing that she wanted to be of assistance to her country, which she loved and respected. Her letter was shuffled around various ACLU offices, and at last made its way to the

New Jersey branch of the ACLU, where a Rutgers law student, Diana Rigelman, one of the students who had urged Ruth to offer a course on women and law, happened to be employed that summer. She saw Nora Simon's letter, and immediately thought of Ruth. Diana, who had also been a student in Ruth's course on civil procedure, viewed Ruth as precise, scholarly, and professional. She recommended Ruth to the head of the New Jersey branch of the ACLU as a lawyer who might be willing to take the case, and who might be viewed by the military as a female lawyer with clout.

In July of 1970, the executive director of the New Jersey ACLU, Stephen Nagler, called Ruth, introduced himself, described Nora's case, and asked if she'd be interested in taking it. Among the reasons he gave for asking Ruth was that she taught civil procedure, so she'd understand how courts operated. Ruth was pretty sure nobody else wanted the case because "sex discrimination was regarded as a woman's job."[85] Because such work wasn't considered serious, she knew if she spent her time on gender equality issues, she ran the risk of not being awarded tenure. She agreed to take the case partly because she wanted litigation experience. She also liked the idea of taking on women's issues under the umbrella of the ACLU, which handled all sorts of human rights and civil liberties issues. Speaking with the voice of the ACLU instead of an all-women's group meant men and women would be working side by side for women's equality.

Within two weeks, she sent a letter to the director for Equal Opportunity in the Armed Forces at the Pentagon, offering simple logic mixed with passionate concern:

> Since Miss Simon is no longer married, and has
> effectively relinquished her parental right to the

child to whom she give birth, it seems clear that her current situation meets the concern evidenced in the exception recognized by the Army: she has no child dependent upon her for care or support. Her legal status is in all respects that of a single woman without issue.[86]

Meanwhile, other complaints from women were trickling into the ACLU, cases often referred to Ruth, including complaints from workers who felt it was unfair that they lost their jobs after becoming pregnant. Pregnant teachers were given what was known as a maternity leave, but the leave was without pay and without benefits, including health care, and without guarantee that the teacher be able to return to her job. Pregnant teachers were essentially told, "We'll call you back if we have a need for you."[87] Ruth remarked that, after all, "children must be spared the thought that their teacher had swallowed a watermelon."[88]

Another complaint typical of those coming into the ACLU was from a woman who worked for Lipton Tea, a company that offered an excellent health care plan to employees. The woman was married, and her husband's employer's plan was inferior, so she wanted the Lipton Tea plan for herself, her husband, and her children, but was told that the family insurance coverage was available only for men. For Ruth, these new complaints represented a new "spirit in the land that said: Maybe the way things are isn't right."[89]

While Ruth was waiting for a response from the Pentagon about Nora Simon's case, she met up with Melvin Wulf, a former fellow camper from Camp Che-Na-Wah. Melvin, also a lawyer, was the national director of the ACLU. They'd never known each other well, but he followed her career because his sister Harriet kept in close touch with one of Ruth's cousins. One day he was invited to speak at Rutgers Law School, so he took the opportunity to knock on her door and rekindle their friendship. They talked about Swedish civil procedure, and she told him about Nora Simon's case. He wasn't particularly impressed with the low-level cases she was handling with the ACLU. As Wulf later characterized their conversation, that was the day he began the process of "plucking Ruth Bader Ginsburg from obscurity."[90]

A month and a half passed without a response from the Pentagon, so while the Ginsburg family was on vacation in Hawaii, Ruth redrafted her letter to the Pentagon into a legal complaint, which she sent to several people, including the secretary of defense and the general counsel for the U.S. Army. In mid-October, she received a response from the Pentagon: Miss Simon was welcome to rejoin the army.

After such an easy victory, she was eager to try again, but now she wanted the right case, a case she could take all the way through the courts.

She and Marty were working at home in their separate offices at about nine in the evening. Marty was reading the tax advance sheets—pamphlets containing recently decided judicial decisions—when he came across a case then making its way through the courts. He perked up and walked into Ruth's office.

"You've gotta read this," he told her.[91]

"Marty," she said wearily, "you know I don't read tax cases."

"You've gotta read *this*."

He dropped the tax advance sheets on her desk, returned to his own office, and waited. He knew he'd just handed her the equal rights test case she was looking for—Charles Moritz's tax case.

Charles Moritz was a single man who'd never married.

He lived in Denver and worked as an editor for the western division of Lea and Febiger, a Philadelphia-based company. He maintained an office in his home, but his job required extensive travel around the eleven western states. For ten years, from 1958 to 1968, his elderly mother lived with him. By 1968, when his mother was eighty-nine, she was confined to a wheelchair, suffering from arthritis, lapse of memory, arteriosclerosis, impaired hearing, and other disabilities. She was unable to care for herself, but refused to enter a nursing home. To provide for her care, Charles hired a caretaker.

Had Charles been a woman or a divorced man, the tax code would have permitted him to deduct the expenses of caring for his mother. The deduction was known as the babysitter deduction. As a single man, the deduction was unavailable. The tax deduction, if granted, was worth only $600, so the cost of a lawyer would have eaten up anything he might have been awarded by the court—assuming he won—so he represented himself in tax court. Given the wording of the statute, he had little chance of winning, but he brought his case anyway because it struck him as unreasonable and unfair. He wrote his own legal brief, which Ruth described as the "soul of simplicity." He wrote, "If I had been a dutiful daughter, I would get this deduction for the care of my mother. I am a dutiful son, and I don't get the deduction. That makes no sense."[92] The court informed Moritz that it had no choice but to enforce the code as written, so Charles Moritz was denied his deduction.

What made the case perfect was that Ruth wouldn't have to ask for much. The court needed only to repair an under-inclusive piece of legislation, changing a "good daughters" benefit to "good sons and good daughters." It was not a case that would rock many boats, but it would make a point.

Ruth walked into Marty's office, told him it was a great case, and suggested that they work on the case together. Marty could do the tax part of the case, and she could do the equal protection part. The next day, Marty called Charles Moritz at his home in Denver and told him that he and his wife wanted to handle his case—and they'd do it pro bono. When Charles realized that Marty claimed to be a tax partner in one of the snazziest law firms in Manhattan, and that his wife was a law professor, he thought it was a joke. Why on earth would a Manhattan lawyer and a law professor want to handle a case worth only $600? Charles told Marty he didn't appreciate getting crank calls.

To prove he wasn't joking, Marty offered to send Charles a letter on his letterhead, explaining why he and his wife thought the case was important. In exchange for free legal representation, the Ginsburgs asked one thing from Charles: The only settlement he would accept would be a 100 percent concession, which Marty guaranteed he'd get, and that the settlement agreement must be entered in federal court. Not surprisingly, Moritz agreed to these terms.

For help with travel and other expenses, the Ginsburgs turned to the ACLU. Ruth wrote to Melvin Wulf, told him about the case, and asked for help with the expenses. Recalling one of their Gilbert and Sullivan productions at Camp Che-Na-Wah in which Mel had sung, "tight little, light little, trim little, slim little craft," she told him that the Moritz case would be "as neat a craft as one could find to test sex-based discrimination against the Constitution."[93] Wulf agreed that the ACLU would finance their litigation.

Ruth wrote a docketing statement for Moritz, summarizing the issues and law, and sent it to Melvin Wulf. He was impressed and wrote back:

Dear Ruth/Kiki:

Your proposed docketing statement meets the high standards to be expected of one who was early exposed to the rigorous discipline of Che-Na-Wah.

Mel[94]

When the government received the docketing statement, it offered to settle for much less than the full amount. In keeping with his agreement with the Ginsburgs, Moritz declined. With no settlement reached, the Ginsburgs left town for a two-day work vacation to draft their argument on behalf of Charles Moritz. Here Ruth laid out the equal rights argument that would become the blueprint of her future legal campaign on behalf of women's rights.

Because it was well settled that anyone who wanted to challenge a law as violating the equal protection clause of the Constitution had to show there was no rational basis for the law, Ruth made the argument. It was, indeed, hard to find a rational basis for a law that gave a dutiful daughter a deduction not but not a dutiful son. Nonetheless, she knew the problem with her argument: The rational basis test was so easy to meet that almost anything short of a serious miscarriage of justice would pass. In fact, as Ruth liked to say, in the hundred years since the ratification of the Fourteenth Amendment, the U.S. Supreme Court "had never met a gender classification that it didn't like."[95] The Court always found a way to rationalize a law that distinguished on the basis of gender, usually by relying on stereotyped views of men and women.

It occurred to Ruth that sex distinctions should not be put into the same category as innocuous distinctions, such as distinctions based on property value, or the size of a city's population. It seemed to Ruth that gender distinctions were *not* innocuous—they were invidious, the word used to describe race-based distinctions. She thought they should require more than a rational basis test.

So she took a bold step. She asked the Court to treat gender distinctions the way it treated racial distinctions. Laws that discriminated on the basis of race required stricter scrutiny, which meant courts must give a more in-depth analysis and uphold only those laws that satisfied a compelling government interest. Once the Supreme Court applied strict scrutiny to racial laws, it became easy to strike them down as unconstitutional.

Ruth fully understood what she would be up against in trying to convince male judges that gender discrimination should be treated the same as racial discrimination. She'd seen how defensive men became if anyone suggested that their attitudes were harmful. They considered themselves good husbands and fathers, keeping their wives in clean, bright homes. What she saw as harmful gender discrimination they saw as treating women well by putting them on a pedestal. She wanted to teach the justices that the very notion of "sugar and spice and everything nice" limited the opportunities and aspirations of their daughters. One way to do that was to show how seemingly benign gender classifications harmed men as well as women.

At about this time, colleagues noticed a change in Ruth. No longer completely drawn into herself, she was gripped by something almost like passion. She was meeting people, talking freely to colleagues about the unfairness of gender discrimination. She still spoke with an aching precision, always appearing completely measured and controlled. But there was a marked difference in her manner, a new glow and purpose. "She sort of caught fire," one of her colleagues commented.[96]

10

THE TIMES THEY
ARE A-CHANGING

When Ruth devised her overall strategy for achieving equal rights for women, she borrowed and adapted the strategy the NAACP had used to persuade the courts to outlaw racial segregation. She also knew to tread gently when comparing gender discrimination to racial discrimination. Women who stood up for their rights risked mockery. Blacks risked their lives.

The NACCP strategy was, indeed, a brilliant blueprint for how to achieve social justice through the courts—and why sometimes there is simply no other way. In the 1930s, when the NAACP legal team, under the leadership of such luminaries as Thurgood Marshall, Oliver Hill, and Spottswood Robinson, decided to take on racial segregation, they had a seemingly insurmountable obstacle: In 1898, the U.S. Supreme Court, in *Plessy v. Ferguson*,[97] held racial segregation legal as long as the separate facilities were equal.

Women seeking the vote had an easier road. When the Supreme Court held that the equal protection clause of the Fourteenth Amendment did not guarantee women the right to vote, suffragist groups organized and began the work of amending the Constitution, a cumbersome process requiring a two-thirds majority in both the House of Representatives and Senate, followed by ratification by two-thirds of the state legislatures. In 1918, both the Democratic and Republican parties openly endorsed female enfranchisement. In January 1918, the amendment passed the House with two-thirds majority. In June 1919, it was approved by the Senate and sent to the states for ratification. On August 18, 1920, Tennessee became the thirty-sixth state to ratify the amendment, giving the amendment the two-thirds majority of state ratification necessary to make it part of the U.S. Constitution.

The NAACP lawyers knew they had no hope of persuading elected officials to get behind integration. This was particularly true of elected officials from the South, but racism was not confined to the South, and in the 1930s, the reality was that the majority of elected officials answered to constituents, and would thus never vote for integration.

Getting the Supreme Court to overrule itself was also not easy. Among the obligations of the Supreme Court was to create and follow precedent, which was necessary for stability and predictability in the law and the culture. Many states built entire legal and social systems relying on *Plessy v. Ferguson*, which made it precisely the kind of case the Supreme Court was reluctant to overrule.

Nonetheless, NAACP lawyers knew their only hope was in the federal courts, where judges were appointed for life and thus did not answer to constituents. Their task was to educate the justices about the evils of segregation, so they carefully selected cases to allow for a step-by-step process of educating the courts. They started their campaign for integration with the schools—public institutions paid for with public money—leaving for later the thornier problem of integrating privately owned businesses, like stores and restaurants. Knowing elementary schools would be hardest because Southern whites would fight tooth and nail to keep their children from mixing with black children, the NAACP strategy was to start with colleges, graduate schools, and law schools, where there would be less resistance.

After making progress integrating colleges and professional schools, they turned to public school districts, where they began by suing school districts on the grounds that the facilities were unequal, and therefore unconstitutional under the rule in *Plessey v. Ferguson*. At first they had the idea that if school districts were held to the law, requiring them to maintain two separate but entirely equal school systems, the sheer waste through duplication would overtake the hatred. The hope was that communities would be motivated to combine the schools from purely economic considerations. This turned out to be entirely wishful thinking. Communities, particularly in the South, were willing to pour large amounts of money into keeping segregation legal.

Spottswood Robinson told a story that illustrated the attitudes in the South during the late 1940s. He was in Cumberland County, Virginia, trying to get the school district to replace tar paper shack classrooms for black children, when a school board official said, "We'd like to help you fellas, but you're pushing too fast, and we just don't have enough money."[98] Mr. Robinson said, "Look, I know how you could do it overnight— all you have to do is let the colored kids into Cumberland High School." A school board member then jumped to his feet and shouted, "The first little black son of a bitch that comes down the road to set foot in that school, I'll take my shotgun and blow his brains out."

The NAACP approach with the courts was not to push for too much too fast to avoid rulings against them that would

*Spottswood Robinson, a civil rights attorney who worked on
Brown v. Board of Education and later became a federal judge.*

make the road harder. They first brought the most sympathetic
cases, with facts that were easy to digest and understand. At last,
when they believed the time was right and the Supreme Court
justices truly understood the evils of segregation, they brought
a bundle of cases to the U.S. Supreme Court under the name
Brown v. Board of Education.[99]

The Court's 1954 decision in *Brown v. Board of Education,*
holding that racial segregation was unconstitutional, was among
the most far-reaching and momentous decisions in American
Supreme Court history, sending waves of joy and shock and
anger rippling through the country. There were calls throughout
the South to impeach Chief Justice Earl Warren, and furious
accusations that the court had overstepped its authority and
was legislating from the bench.

Although *Brown v. Board of Education* was limited to
desegregating schools, the implications were clear. If it was

unconstitutional for schools to be segregated, what about buses? What about lunch counters and restaurants? If blacks could no longer be segregated, why not put an end to discrimination in hiring and housing? And what about all those laws all over the South making it difficult for blacks to vote? And why shouldn't blacks be put on juries, right alongside whites? Indeed, the very next year, Rosa Parks refused to give up her seat on a bus—and the modern American civil rights movement began.

The civil rights movement paved the way for the women's movement, and in fact, the two were always entwined. Prior to the Civil War, the legal subjugation of slaves was justified in the courts by analogy to the legal status of women. Both slaves and wives were subject to the paternalistic "head of the house."[100] Just as there was the myth of the happy slave, a woman was presumed to be happiest when under the control of someone more powerful than herself. An 1852 *New York Herald* editorial asked,

> How did women first become subject to man as she now is all over the world? By her nature, her sex, just as the negro is and always will be, to the end of time, inferior to the white race, and, therefore, doomed to subjection; but happier than she would be in any other condition, just because it is the law of her nature. Women themselves would not want this law reversed.[101]

One of the earliest and most famous advocates for both racial and gender equality was Sojourner Truth. Born into slavery in 1797, she escaped with her infant daughter and became an abolitionist and vocal advocate for women's rights.

The women's movement was so deeply entwined with the civil rights movement that when the concept of women's liberation arrived in the South, it was greeted as yet another northern idea intended to destroy deeply held Southern traditions by upending a centuries-old patriarchal way of life. Southern culture of the nineteenth and early twentieth centuries—as explained by scholar Susan Cahn—prized the notion that white women were pure and chaste and in need of male protection, while black women were viewed through the stereotyped lenses of sexual promiscuity and immorality. There was the opposite stereotype as well: the sexless, devoted family servant, as characterized by Mammy in *Gone with the Wind.* The very notion of a sexual revolution happening in close proximity to a sudden mixing of the races created what Cahn called a moral panic among white Southerners.

Women who worked for civil rights in the 1950s and early 1960s naturally segued to fighting for women's equality in the late 1960s. Anna Pauline Murray, known as Pauli Murray, was born in 1910. Her mother died of cerebral hemorrhage when she was four. Her father, a graduate of Howard University, taught in a high school. He suffered the long-term effects of typhoid fever and was committed to a state hospital, where he was murdered by a guard. After graduating high school with distinction, Pauli went to New York, where she worked as a teacher. She published articles, poems, and a novel, *Angel of the Desert.* In 1938 she worked with the NAACP in an attempt to enroll in the all-white University of North Carolina, during which time she developed a lifelong friendship with Eleanor Roosevelt. Fifteen years before Rosa Parks, Murray refused to sit in the back of the bus and was jailed.

After graduating from Howard University and winning the prestigious Rosenwald Fellowship, she applied to Harvard Law

Pauli Murray.

School, but was rejected because of her gender. So she enrolled at Boalt Hall, now the University of California Berkeley School of Law. She said, "I entered law school preoccupied with the racial struggle and single-mindedly bent upon becoming a civil rights lawyer, but I graduated an unabashed feminist as well."[102] She moved back to New York City, and soon became critical of the way men dominated the civil rights movement.

Dorothy Kenyon came from an entirely different background of money and privilege. She graduated from Smith College and spent a few years as a social butterfly before becoming sensitized to the problems of poverty and injustice. She entered New York University Law School in 1914 with the goal of pursuing social justice through the courts. Her commitment to liberal and racial issues caused Senator Joseph McCarthy to go after her in the 1950s. Under fire from McCarthy, she acknowledged

*Dorothy Kenyon answering Joseph McCarthy's
accusations that she supported communists, 1950.*

her support of progressive causes, but denied that she was disloyal to America, or a communist. Despite her protests, his accusations ended her public career.

Through the 1940s and 1950s, Dorothy Kenyon and Pauli Murray tried repeatedly but failed to secure legal rights for women, bringing suits such as one to protect teachers in Connecticut who lost their jobs after having children. Then a change occurred. In the early 1960s, when the modern civil rights movement was well underway, there were those who began to take women's rights seriously. In 1961, President Kennedy established a Committee on the Status of Women. Women were entering the workforce in large numbers that were expected to continue growing. President Kennedy appointed

Pauli Murray to his Committee on Civil and Political Rights. Along with Betty Freidan, she was one of thirty co-founders of the National Organization for Women (NOW), which she labeled the "NAACP for women."[103]

In 1966, Pauli Murray and Mary Eastwood published an article called "Jane Crow and the Law," an article Ruth used in developing her course on women and the law. This was the article that planted the seed that would become Ruth's litigation strategy. In this article, Murray and her co-author drew the striking parallels between discriminatory attitudes toward women and blacks, and said that sex discrimination could be better understood if compared with race discrimination. They suggested that the legal status of women could be improved by following the path paved by the movement for racial equality, and argued that the "classification by sex" doctrine was inherently discriminatory and should be shelved alongside the doctrine of "separate but equal."

At last, in 1966, Dorothy Kenyan and Pauli Murray won an important victory for the ACLU, a case called *White v. Crook*[104] that challenged an Alabama statute exempting African Americans and women from all races from serving on juries. A complicated procedure used in Alabama resulted in juries consisting exclusively of white men. Dorothy Kenyon and Pauli Murray succeeded in having the law struck down as unconstitutional.

In June 1967, a new phrase—"women's liberation"—was coined at a conference of Students for a Democratic Society. Within months, women's liberation groups formed in Chicago and New York. Dorothy Kenyon demonstrated with much younger women for women's liberation, and continued preparing briefs for the NAACP and the ACLU. Women's leaders were often the targets of jokes and mockery. On July

14, 1971, on page 28 of the *New York Times*, the headline read, "Women's Caucus Target of White House Jokes." According to the article, four militant women leaders formed a Women's Political Caucus: Gloria Steinem, Betty Friedan, and Representatives Bella Abzug of Manhattan and Shirley Chisholm of Brooklyn. President Nixon, Secretary of State William P. Rogers, and Henry Kissinger pointed out that the four looked like a burlesque. Nixon then wanted to know what was wrong with burlesque. Rogers referred to Gloria Steinem as "Henry's old girlfriend."

When Ruth Bader Ginsburg took up the cause of gender equality in the late 1960s, she said she "stood on the shoulders" of Dorothy Kenyon and Pauli Murray, continuing the work they had begun.[105] She considered what happened in the United States in the 1970s to be a "revived" feminist movement.[106] She felt that the difference between her and such women as Kenyon and Murray was that when they spoke about women's rights, the nation wasn't yet ready to listen.

11

A DRY PROCEDURALIST
OR A RABBLE ROUSER?

Outwardly Ruth did not fit the stereotype of a 1960s or 1970s feminist. A secretary in the typing pool of Marty's law firm tells an amusing story of her first impression of Ruth. Anita Esquedero began typing Ruth's manuscript entitled *Sex-Based Discrimination* when Marty brought her chunks of the handwritten manuscript. Anita was horrified by the material, which contained arguments about abortion. The words "male" and "female" were used in ways she'd never seen. The subject seemed entirely nonsensical to her. One day Marty told her that his wife was coming in for a visit. Anita thought, "Good, God, here she comes. The weird one."[107] In walked a petite, soft-voiced woman with her hair sleeked back and tied with a green scarf. Anita didn't think she could be the same woman. Anita was expecting someone who looked a little more masculine. She expected a cigar. Later, after months of typing, Anita returned to Spain for a visit. At a large party, her husband introduced her as his woman, using common Spanish phrasing. She realized she'd been "converted through typing" Ruth's manuscript when she said proudly, "I am *not* your woman. I am a *person*. My name is Anita." From the other side of the room, the host's eighty-year-old grandmother boomed, "Viva America!"

Ruth's students also misjudged her. One of her students, who had always read her reserve as coldness, was surprised the day she walked into Ruth's seminar, completely unprepared because of illness. She expected a stern rebuke from the professor she thought was icy and severe. Instead, Ruth greeted her with kindness.

While other feminists were out marching and protesting, Ruth sat quietly in her office reading through legal cases, watching for the perfect test case to join with Charles Moritz's tax case. The perfect case would have sympathetic clients, archaic laws steeped in outdated stereotypes, and a low-cost resolution that wouldn't push the needle too far. She had her eye on a case that was just then making its way through the courts—the case of Skip Reed, a nineteen-year-old Idaho boy who committed suicide. She'd learned the Reeds' story while researching her Women and the Law class. The case was being handled by the ACLU. She learned from a notice in *U.S. Law Week* when the Reed case had been granted review by the U.S. Supreme Court.

Skip's parents separated and then divorced when he was a toddler. Initially he lived with his mother, Sally, who earned her living caring for disabled people in her home. When Skip became a teenager, his father, Richard, sued for custody, arguing that a teenage boy needed a father. According to Sally, Skip's father was an abusive husband and father who deserted the family. Furthermore, because Skip struggled with depression and had spent time in a juvenile corrections facility, Sally believed the last thing he needed was to live with a father like Richard. In court, Sally bitterly opposed Richard's demand, but the court awarded him partial custody.

On March 29, 1967, during a visit in his father's home in Ada County, Idaho, Skip was found dead in his father's basement after shooting himself with one of his father's rifles. Sally sought to be named the administrator of Skip's estate, then valued at about $1,000. Several days later, Richard's father filed a competing application for the same appointment.

The probate court held a joint hearing on the two petitions and ordered that Richard's father be named executor. Under Idaho law, the court had no choice. After an intermediate-level appeal, the case went to the Idaho Supreme Court, which held that under section 15-312 of the Idaho Code, if more than one person equally entitled to administer an estate files a petition, "males must be preferred to females."[108] The Idaho Supreme Court held that the equal protection clause of the Fourteenth Amendment did not preclude legislatures from classifying on the basis of sex as long as a rational basis existed, and it was perfectly rational for the state legislature to conclude that in general men were better qualified to act as administrators than women. The court acknowledged that this generality might not always be true, but it wasn't irrational. In issuing its order, the probate court made no attempt to determine which of the parents might be more capable or the more appropriate administrator. When Sally lost, she wanted to take her case to the Supreme Court. She and her lawyer, Alan Derr, turned to the ACLU for help.

Ruth thought it was the perfect case to argue for strict scrutiny of sex discrimination laws. The facts were simple, and the motive behind the statute was easy to dissect and evidently based on traditional stereotypes. The law made clear that ability didn't matter; the mother was denied administration of her son's estate based solely on her gender, which, for Ruth, made the point crystal-clear that the distinction was invidious. As a fallback position, should the court not accept application of a strict scrutiny standard, it should be easy enough to show that there was no rational basis for the gender distinction. After the ACLU persuaded the Supreme Court to take Sally's case, Ruth wrote to Melvin Wulf, asking how he had done it. She also wanted to know what arguments the lawyer on the case planned to make on Sally's behalf.

In response, Melvin sent her the papers filed thus far, and invited her to call him to discuss tactics. She read the documents, and saw that the ACLU lawyers had made the standard argument that the Idaho statute giving automatic preference to a man over a woman had no rational basis. She sent Melvin a copy of the final brief she had drafted for Moritz, with its more ambitious argument that gender distinctions should be treated like racial distinctions subject to stricter scrutiny. Then in her cover letter on Rutgers letterhead, she asked him to make her co-counsel on the case:

> Dear Mel,
> Some of this should be useful for Reed v. Reed. Have you thought about whether it would be appropriate to have a woman co-counsel in that case???[109]
> Best regards
> Ruth

When Mel did not immediately answer, Ruth mailed a copy of the Moritz brief to Norman Dorsen, a professor of law at NYU and volunteer general counsel of the ACLU. Dorsen wrote back, stating that the Mortiz brief was one of the best legal presentations he'd seen in a long time, and—even though she was proposing an utterly new challenge to the U.S.

Constitution—he couldn't see how it could lose. Dorsen sent a copy of his letter praising her brief to Melvin, who promptly called Ruth and asked her to be his co-counsel on the Reed case.

Ruth's plan was to take Charles Moritz's tax case and Sally Reed's Idaho case to the Supreme Court at the same time, as companion cases, one with a man harmed by gender discrimination, the other a woman. But the course of litigation seldom runs smooth. In the fall of 1971, the time came to argue Charles Moritz's tax case in the Tenth Circuit Court of Appeals in Denver, so it was unlikely the Moritz case would be ready to appeal to the Supreme Court in time to join it with the Reed case.

In Denver the evening before the argument for Charles Moritz's case, Charles took the Ginsburgs out to dinner. He had to hire a caretaker for his mother. The next day, in court, the government argued that there was a rational basis for the gender distinction in the statute allowing dutiful daughters to claim the benefit but not dutiful sons. The government also argued—among other things—that Charles wouldn't be entitled to the deduction anyway because he never proved himself capable of caring for his mother, so there was no evidence that the nurse was a substitute for himself. Ruth pointed out that this argument was based on the stereotype that a woman was presumed to be a capable caretaker, but a man wasn't.

While waiting for court's ruling on Moritz's case, Ruth and Mel recruited young lawyers and her best students to work on the research and writing team for *Reed v. Reed*.[110] On the brief-writing team were Mary Kelley and Janice Goodman, the two NYU students who had asked Ruth to teach a course on women and law, Anne Freedman, from Yale, who had helped spread the idea of offering courses on women and law, and Diana Rigelman, who had worked with Ruth on Nora Simon's case.

The young women wrote a brief and sent it to Ruth. They

expected her to make a few minor changes and check the footnotes. Instead, she gave the brief a major overhaul.

Ruth opened the brief by stating that Idaho's law,

> mandating subordination of women to men without regard to individual capacity, creates a "suspect classification" requiring close judicial scrutiny.[111]

Echoing the language used to declare racial segregation unconstitutional, she described the legal condition of women as "separate but unequal,"[112] and went on to suggest parallels to the quest for racial equality by suggesting that

> the time is ripe for this Court to repudiate the premise that, with minimum justification, the legislature may draw "a sharp line between the sexes."[113]

She next drew similarities between gender and racial distinction, pointing out that membership in each category was beyond the individual's control, and both were based on highly visible characteristics upon which legislators found it easy to draw stereotypical distinctions. She asked the court to consider how it would react to a statute that preferred whites to blacks or Christians to Jews, and suggesting that statutes preferring men to women should fare no better. She preempted the response that legal gender distinctions often protected women by putting them on a pedestal by claiming that

> Laws which disable women from full participation in the political, business and economic arenas are often characterized as "protective" and beneficial. Those same laws applied to racial or ethnic minorities would readily be recognized as invidious

and impermissible. The pedestal upon which women have been placed has all too often, upon closer inspection, been revealed as a cage.[114]

To counter the stereotyped views of women as frail and in need of protection, she quoted Sojourner Truth's extemporaneous speech delivered at the Ohio Women's Rights Convention in 1851:

That man over there says that women need to be helped into carriages, and lifted over ditches, and to have the best place everywhere. Nobody ever helps me into carriages, or over mud-puddles, or gives me any best place! And ain't I a woman? Look at me! Look at my arm! I have ploughed and planted, and

Sojourner Truth, circa 1870.

gathered into barns, and no man could head me!
And ain't I a woman? I could work as much and
eat as much as a man—when I could get it—and
bear the lash as well! And ain't I a woman? I have
borne thirteen children, and seen most all sold off
to slavery, and when I cried out with my mother's
grief, none but Jesus heard me! And ain't I a woman?

Part of Ruth's brief was directly addressed to Justice Felix
Frankfurter, who had written the opinion in *Groesaert v. Cleary*,[115]
the case that upheld the Michigan law forbidding women to
own bars. In the *Groesaert* decision, Frankfurter acknowledged
that recent history had brought "vast changes in the social and
legal position of women," but said that

The Constitution does not require legislatures to
reflect sociological insight, or shifting social standards,
any more than it requires them to keep abreast of the
latest scientific standards.[116]

Now, in urging Frankfurter to change his position, she
dropped in a reminder that in *Brown v. Board of Education*, he *did*
take the position that the Constitution does require legislatures
to reflect sociological insight and shifting standards. To
persuade the justices to take a "living constitution" approach,
she reminded Felix Frankfurter that he had recently quoted the
great justice Oliver Wendell Holmes:

It's revolting to have no better reason for a rule of
law than that it was laid down at the time of Henry
IV. It is still more revolting if the grounds upon
which it was laid down have vanished long since,

and the rule simply persists from blind imitation of the past.[117]

Her alternative argument—the only argument the ACLU lawyers had been prepared to make before she stepped in—was that "the statutory classification based on the sex of the applicant established in Section 15-314 of the Idaho Code is arbitrary and capricious and bears no rational relationship to a legitimate legislative purpose."[118]

One scholar commented that her brief might as well have been called the Kitchen Sink Brief because she'd put so much into it, from poetry to social commentary. She thought of it as the Educate the Nine Justices of the Supreme Court Brief.

On the cover, along with her own name, Mel's name, and Alan Derr, the Idaho lawyer who had represented Sally Reed at the trial level, Ruth added the names of Dorothy Kenyon and Pauli Murray because she wanted to honor their contributions and ideas, which had influenced and given shape to hers.

When Mary Kelley, Janice Goodman, Anne Freedman, and Diana Rigelman saw what Ruth had done to their brief, they were amazed. Their tiny, primly dressed, and ultra-careful professor had *chutzpah*.

The brief, while clearly and powerfully written, was nonetheless much like Ruth herself: utterly reasonable in tone, measured, professional, and entirely rational in presentation. Even with a few literary quotations and Sojourner Truth's speech, the brief was understated. Not a single word came across as shrill or emotional. Everyone who read it agreed that it was brilliant.

The ACLU team were not the only ones surprised by Ruth's brief. Reporter Nina Totenburg, who was then new to the

Supreme Court beat and trying to get her footing, discovered she could understand what was going on in court if she read the briefs—so she did. When she read Ruth's brief in *Reed v. Reed,* she felt confused. "Hmm," she mused. "I thought the Fourteenth Amendment was for freed slaves and for blacks. How does that apply to women?"[119] She flipped to the front of the brief, and saw that it had been written by a Rutgers professor. She went to a phone booth, called the professor at Rutgers, and asked her question. Ruth explained that the Fourteenth Amendment says no *person* shall be denied equal protection of the laws. "The last time I checked," Ruth told her, "women were people."[120] Ruth then spent one full hour delivering a lecture on women and law. Afterwards Nina Totenberg emerged from the phone booth at the Supreme Court a bit dazed.

The government's response to Ruth's brief, written by an Idaho government lawyer, was predictable. The government claimed the law was valid because it had a rational basis: The state of Idaho recognized that all species protected the female, and it was an obvious fact that men were better at business than women, so men would in general make better executors.

The New York City Human Rights Commission asked permission to show their support for the ACLU position by filing what was known as an amicus brief—the term used to designate supporting briefs by interested parties, literally meaning a brief submitted by a friend of the court. Their amicus brief pointed out that the Human Rights Commission had been receiving a flood of complaints from women claiming unfair gender discrimination.

Then, suddenly, an obstacle arose, threatening to deprive Ruth and the ACLU team of victory. The Idaho lawyer who had represented Sally Reed at the trial level, Alan Derr, decided he wanted to do the Supreme Court oral arguments himself.

Mel Wulf wanted Ruth to argue the case. For one thing, Mel suspected the arguments in the brief would prompt the justices on the bench to engage in sexist banter, and he believed having Ruth at the podium would hinder this sort of thing. He and the others on the ACLU team also believed, quite simply, that Alan Derr was not up to the task. Melvin Wulf, perhaps rather snobbishly, asked Derr if he felt he was ready to play in the big leagues with a big-league brief, but Alan Derr stood his ground and enlisted the support of Sally Reed herself. It was Alan Derr's case, so there was nothing anyone could do. Derr would submit the brief written by Ruth and her team, but he would be the one to argue the case before the Supreme Court.

Alan Derr may not have been up to the task of a Supreme Court oral argument, but nobody doubted that his heart was in the right place. As a serviceman in World War II, serving in China, he'd been disturbed by the institutionalized discrimination against African Americans. After the service, while in college, he'd worked to end discrimination in fraternities against African American students. Raising a daughter inspired him to expand his beliefs about equality for all to women.

On October 19, 1971, Allan Derr, standing at the podium in front of the nine justices of the Supreme Court, opened his oral argument by telling the justices of the U.S. Supreme Court,

> [W]e are here today to ask you do to something that this Court has never done since the Fourteenth Amendment was adopted in 1868 and that is to declare a state statute that distinguishes between— that classifies between—males and females as unconstitutional.[121]

Telling the Supreme Court it was being asked to do something it had never done before was a terrible idea, as anyone with the vaguest understanding of how the Supreme Court operates should know. Ruth had advised Alan Derr to open his arguments by comparing Sally Reed's case to *Brown v. Board of Education*, in which the Supreme Court *did* reverse direction on the Fourteenth Amendment. Alan told Ruth he liked her advice and that he would follow it, but in his own words. He'd either entirely missed the point of Ruth's analogy or he simply blundered.

Things got worse for Alan Derr as his allotted time went on. He stammered and had a difficult time answering in complete sentences. When Justice Douglas interrupted and pointed out that the Supreme Court had decided a similar case about bartenders in Michigan, Derr said, "That case was decided, Your Honor, on a premise that we feel is no longer tenable," and then went on to explain why it was wrong. Telling the Supreme Court it was wrong lacked diplomacy and finesse, to say the least. About women, he said, "We admit they're different," and then went on to make the incomprehensible statement that "but we do feel as a result of this rational relationship test is almost as they enter it is separate but equal test."

When the government lawyer took his turn at the podium, he argued that the Idaho statute served the purpose of keeping court and administrative costs low. By simply choosing men over women, courts could avoid lengthy hearings to decide the relative merits of more than one relative who wanted to administer the estate.

Justice Harry Blackmun, who gave grades to lawyers as if they were students in his class, awarded Alan Derr a D+ and said it was the worst-argued case he'd ever heard. If the ACLU had any hope of winning, the hope rested with Ruth's brief.

12

WOMEN
WORKING

On the evening of November 22, 1971, Ruth was returning home from Rutgers on the train when she saw a man reading *The New York Post*. The banner headline caught her eye: "High Court Outlaws Sex Discrimination." That was how she learned that Sally Reed won her case, and that the Supreme Court struck down the Idaho probate code giving preference to men over women on the ground that there was no rational basis for such discrimination against women.

Despite the win, Melvin Wulf was disappointed. He had hoped the court would buy Ruth's argument that gender distinctions should be treated like racial distinctions requiring heightened scrutiny. Instead, the court entirely ignored Ruth's strict scrutiny argument, and simply applied the rational basis test. Under this test, the court found the statute lacked a rational basis and thus violated the equal protection clause of the Fourteenth Amendment.

Ruth shared the widespread feeling that the case was an astounding victory and a turning point in the history of women and law. For the very first time ever, the Supreme Court struck down a statute as unfairly discriminating against women in violation of the Fourteenth Amendment. She had fully expected to make the argument perhaps a dozen more times before the court ruled in her favor. Whereas Mel was dismayed by the caution of the court, she approved. She understood the court was reluctant to move too quickly, and she approved of judicial restraint, even when the practice worked against her. She often quoted Justice Benjamin Cardozo, who said, "Justice is not to be taken by storm. She is to be wooed by slow advances." There would be other cases and other opportunities to try to push the needle a little farther. She found it encouraging that the Supreme Court had not addressed her argument comparing gender inequality to racial inequality because this meant they hadn't ruled it out. The question was left open for another day, for another case with another set of facts. To those who wanted the change to come quicker, the court's step was a small one. But to Ruth and the public at large, the case heralded a whole new direction. The process of educating the justices on the realities of gender discrimination had begun, and was off to a good start.

Ruth always insisted her victory was simply a matter of good timing. "When I graduated from law school in 1959," she said, "it was not possible to move legislators or judges toward recognition of a sex-equality principle. The idea was unfamiliar and therefore unacceptable."[122] But by 1971, when the phrase "women's liberation" was no longer shocking, and women were moving into the workforce and professions in significant numbers, the idea was no longer unfamiliar. "A court," she explained, "is a reactive institution."[123] She liked quoting the constitutional scholar Paul Freund, who said, "the Court should never be influenced by the weather of the day but inevitably they will be influenced by the climate of the era."[124]

The consensus among the legal community was that full credit for the victory went to Ruth's brief. In fact, it was about this time that Harvard finally thought Ruth "worthy of a Harvard degree."[125] That was when she received her first call of many to come from Harvard deans urging her to accept a belated degree. The first request came from Albert Sacks, who had been one of her mentors while she'd been at Harvard. The problem? The granting of a Harvard degree was contingent upon her renouncing her Columbia degree. "I have only one *earned* degree," she told him.[126]

In the wake of the Supreme Court's decision in *Reed v. Reed*, Congress went through the provisions of the U.S. Code and changed many of the laws that classified overtly on the basis of gender, which demonstrated for Ruth that the decision was timely. The Court's ruling did not spark resistance or resentment in Congress, and the rewriting of the laws that followed was essentially a conversation between the court and Congress.

In October of 1971, the ACLU board voted to add women's rights as a new priority. On December 4, Ruth and a group of women asked the ACLU to create a Women's Rights Project that would press the strategy begun with *Reed v. Reed*. Some of the ACLU governing members were reluctant to get into sex-equality law, preferring to keep their focus on upholding the First Amendment, which had always been at the top of the ACLU agenda. At last the ACLU board agreed to form a Women's Rights Project, and committed $50,000 and made Ruth the director. She wanted a co-director. In particular, she wanted Linda Feigan, a lawyer who had served as legislative vice president of NOW, and was working to launch the first issue of *Ms. Magazine* with Gloria Steinem. Mel Wulf called Linda Feigan and offered her the job. She was honored and intrigued, but hesitated to leave just as *Ms. Magazine* was getting off the ground.

The first issue of Steinem's *Ms. Magazine* appeared on the

newsstands in the spring of 1972. The cover featured a woman with eight arms, each performing a different task, including typing, frying an egg, ironing, and holding a mirror. The issue featured such articles as "Letty Pogrebin on Raising Kids without Sex Roles," a write-up about Sylvia Plath, and "Women Tell the Truth about Their Abortion." The magazine, initially published as an insert in *New York Magazine*, was an instant hit. In eight days, three hundred thousand copies sold. Ruth read the first issue and became a devoted reader of the magazine. In time, she came to count Gloria Steinem as a friend.

Ms. Magazine, Spring 1972.

Later that year, Linda Feigan came to work with Ruth with a "blessing from Gloria."[127] Ruth and Linda converted an unused part of the ACLU office to their headquarters, where they hung a sign that said, "WOMEN WORKING."[128] The Women's Rights Project accepted funding from diverse sources, including—ironically enough—the Playboy Foundation. The result was that an early mailing from the project went out in envelopes bearing the symbol of the Playboy bunny. One woman called and shouted at Ruth over the phone, "Do you know what's on those envelopes? The bunny!"[129] Ruth remained calm. The caller struck her as an angry feminist. She had little sympathy, and didn't identify with such rage.

The new Women's Rights Project had three stated missions—to educate the public, to influence legislation, and to achieve equal justice through the courts. In Ruth's words,

> We wanted to open all doors, for men and for women. Nobody should be blocked from an opportunity because he was male, or she was female. So the idea was to get rid of the overt gender-based classification. That was the starting point. To have law books that did not make lump classifications based on mother/father son/daughter.[130]

Not everyone was happy with the result in *Reed v. Reed*. Many critics believed that judges interpreting the Constitution must be bound by the meaning at the time the Constitution was drafted, according to the intention of the drafters. For a strict originalist, the framers of the Fourteenth Amendment didn't intend "people" to include women, so that was the end of it. The theory was that deviating even slightly from the original intent of the drafters would create uncertainty and instability because values change, and anyway, people rarely agree on contemporary values.

Ruth responded to such criticism by saying that she, too, was an originalist—but a different kind of an originalist. She was true to the original *spirit* of the document. The actual Constitution had certain blind spots that proved to be a blot on our history, including the fact that liberty did not apply to slaves and that "We the People" left out a lot of people. "People" in the Constitution originally meant white, property-owning men. The belief was that male property owners were more trustworthy as voters because they would not be overly influenced by their masters, whether that meant a person's owner or employer, or the man as master of the house. Non-whites, including Native Americans, and women were not included.

Ruth's view of the history of America was that through the years, the democratic process progressively opened up to more and more people. The Civil Rights Act and the Voting Rights Act were steps toward putting an end to the notion that only white landowning men could be trusted to vote with integrity. The originalists' desire to roll back the clock to the eighteenth century and return to a time when the ruling elite was white and male struck her as absurd. She believed that if Thomas Jefferson were alive today, he would believe that women should be given equal stature to men. She held to the great jurist Cardozo's belief that the framers' expectation was not that the Constitution would govern for a passing hour, but for the expanding future.

The Constitution contains a great many phrases like *due process* and *equal protection*, phrases that are morally charged and deliberately vague, serving as a sort of legal Rorschach test: a person sees in these phrases whatever preconceived notion of liberty that person brings to the Constitution. Does liberty mean the freedom to enter any public place even if your skin is dark? Or does liberty mean the freedom to prevent dark-skinned people swimming in your neighborhood pool? These two conceptions of liberty are in conflict. Both sides believe they are the defenders of liberty.

As a practical matter, holding the 1970s to eighteenth-century values simply made no sense to Ruth. The last thing she wanted was for women—herself included—to be forced to live the life of an eighteenth-century housewife.

The obvious solution was to amend the Constitution. Indeed, immediately after the suffragettes succeeded in passing the Nineteenth Amendment and securing the right to vote, they got started on their next task—achieving equal status under the Constitution. The proposed Equal Rights Amendment was straightforward:

> Section 1. Equality of rights under the law shall not be denied or abridged by the United States or by any State on account of sex.
>
> Section 2. The Congress shall have the power to enforce, by appropriate legislation, the provisions of this article.
>
> Section 3. This article shall take effect 2 years after the date of ratification.

The National Women's Party introduced the Equal Rights Amendment to each session of Congress beginning in 1923 until at last, in 1972, it was ratified by Congress and the work of getting the states to approve the amendment began.

The task of getting the amendment approved by the states was complicated by a particular fact: Not all women *wanted* to be liberated. Some groups of women, in fact, became the strongest opponents of the Equal Rights Amendment. The

Alice Paul with the National Women's Party introduced the ERA to Congress. 1915.

conservative reaction was led by the now iconic Phyllis Schlafly and her followers, who thought the Equal Rights Amendment would end women's privilege and destroy the American family. Phyllis Schlafly, a lawyer and author, has been credited with starting the American conservative movement, which initially she called the pro-family movement. She called her project to stop the Equal Rights Amendment STOP ERA, which stood for Stop Taking Our Privileges. During the decades since, she backed such Republican candidates as Barry Goldwater in 1964 and Donald Trump in 2016.

In her view, American women were blessed to live in a Christian country where notions of chivalry held. Her belief was that as America grew wealthier and more powerful, life was improving for women, who she believed were indeed the weaker sex. She believed women were lowering themselves to equal rights, giving up special privileges. Phyllis Schlafly was not without a sense of humor. At a rally in Houston she said, "First of all, I want to thank my husband, Fred, for letting me come." Then she added, "I always like to say that because it makes the libs so mad."[131]

There was other opposition to the Equal Rights Amendment as well. Religious groups lined up behind Phyllis Schlafly on the grounds that equal rights were an attack on the traditional family. States-rights advocates said the ERA was a federal power grab. Business interests, including insurance companies, opposed the amendment because they were afraid it would cost them money.

As women's rights became a real possibility, anger heated up. All too often, women were angry at other women. A feminist lawyer in Miami, Florence Kennedy, went on a talk radio show and said she thought it would be a good idea for someone to hit Phyllis Schlafly in the mouth. Betty Friedan called Phyllis Schlafly a traitor to her sex and an Uncle Tom. Critics called her a hypocrite—she praised stay-at-home wives, and wanted legislation that would make it harder for women to work, while she herself worked full-time as a lawyer and activist.

Ruth's opinion was that Phyllis Schlafly and her followers were raising a "parade of horribles."[132] Some of these horribles ranged from the absurd—the claim that under the ERA, wives would lose their right to be supported within the family unit and the traditional family would be outlawed—to the silly—restrooms in public places would no longer be permitted to be separate. This last was called the "potty problem," and started the discussion of whether men would want to use the women's facilities or whether women would want to use men's. A real concern, particularly during the Vietnam War, was the fear that the ERA meant women would be drafted. Proponents of the amendment tried to assure the public that equal rights did not mean women would be drafted, or restrooms would be combined.

For Ruth, equal rights were simply about opportunity and choice for everyone. She felt inspired by the song "Free to Be . . . You and Me," from a 1972 hit children's album created by Marlo Thomas.[133] Thomas assembled the finest musical, stage, and literary talent of the era—including Diana Ross, Harry Belafonte, Mel Brooks, Shel Silverstein, Carl Reiner, and others—to create a catchy album with an underlying message that resounded deeply for Ruth. In Thomas's dreamland where "you and me are free to be you and me," Ruth liked to think a girl could be a rocket scientist and a boy might grow up to be a househusband, without any stigma attached. She also understood that until men could—and would—perform what was considered traditionally women's work without social stigma, there would never be complete equality. "Free to Be ... You and Me" embodied gender-neutral parenting and a gender-neutral world—a radical idea in 1972.

13

FREE TO BE
YOU AND ME

Bernice Sandler was tired of being discriminated against because she was a woman. As a part-time lecturer in psychology and counseling at the University of Maryland, she applied for a tenure-track position, but was told she wouldn't be hired because she came on "too strong for a woman."[134] She continued to apply for jobs, but was rejected. One university hiring committee told her she was not really a professor, just a housewife who went back to school. In January of 1970, she and a few others filed complaints against every college with federal contracts, all 250 of them. Sandler encouraged women to contact their representatives in Congress. As a result, Representative Edith Green, a Democrat from Oregon, introduced a bill requiring gender equality in education. Sandler and other women testified about not being hired because of their gender. After passage in the House, the bill, which came to be known as Title IX, went to the Senate, where Senator Birch Bayh, a Democrat from Indiana, helped the bill through by reassuring people that beauty pageants would still be allowed to award scholarships, and that women would not be allowed to play on football teams. In June of 1972, President Nixon signed the bill into law. President Nixon's administration was already active in promoting affirmative action. They'd started with the highly nepotistic construction trades, in which women were almost entirely unrepresented. Construction workers generally got their start as apprentices if a father or uncle was a member of the union, and construction contracts were given to insiders. Nixon's labor secretary proposed a way to break the nepotism by having government contracts go to those who would pledge to set hiring goals and timetables. These goals and timetables were determined by asking the question, If there was no discrimination, how many members of a minority—where "minority" included women—might be expected to be hired? The contracting company then determined that number, and set a goal to achieve it. It was understood that the numbers were not absolute. There were often legitimate reasons the goals could not be reached. But those who desired government contracts had to at least make an effort to hire minorities.

In the wake of Title IX, Nixon's Department of Health, Education, and Welfare began targeting colleges and universities receiving government money—and most colleges and universities received at least some. The head of the agency, Stan Pottinger, visited colleges and universities, encouraging them to fulfill their affirmative action obligations and reminding them that if they didn't, they stood to lose their government contracts.

Suddenly every law school wanted to hire a black or female professor. Columbia Law School sought to add two members to their faculty, an African American and a woman. Columbia already had women on its law faculty, but no tenured professors. In fact, in its entire history, Columbia Law School had never hired a woman for a full-time post higher than a lecturer or a part-time post higher than adjunct professor.

Newspaper articles often left out the fact that affirmative action was behind the sudden scramble to hire women and minority law professors. One law school dean was quoted by the *New York Times* as saying, "A major reason for this new effort is the increased number of women now coming out of law school."[135] When asked why there were currently so few women teaching in law schools, another dean said the "lack of available women in the past was the reason for the present paucity of female faculty members."[136] Michigan Law School dean Theodore St. Antoine gave another reason for the sudden scramble to hire women in law schools: the realization that "law is a profession that a woman can handle as well as man."[137] Michigan dean St. Antoine acknowledged that, because of the scarcity of women in law, most law schools were often trying to hire the same women.

One of the women in sudden demand was Ruth, who had top academic credentials and had just made national headlines by writing a winning Supreme Court brief in a landmark case. Harvard invited her to spend the fall semester of 1971 as a guest professor, where she became the first woman to teach in the Harvard Law School. The hiring committee at Harvard contemplated offering her a faculty position, but they hesitated, wanting one more round of interviews. Columbia, though, grabbed her first and agreed to her terms: She would devote half her time to the Women's Rights Project, and half to teaching and other faculty responsibilities. Columbia did not put Ruth, who was then thirty-nine years old, through much in the way of interviewing. As she put it, "I was not subjected to any examination or asked to show and tell. The faculty simply held a party in my honor to say welcome home."[138] She thus became the first full-time tenured faculty member in Columbia's law school.

It wasn't as if law schools were actively hiding the fact that federal money rewarding affirmative action hires was the motivation behind hiring women and minorities. Shortly after Ruth was hired, the president of Columbia, William McGill, was asked by a newspaper reporter, "How is Columbia doing with its affirmative action?"[139] He responded by saying it was no coincidence that the two most recent appointments to the law school were a woman and an African American man. "I was the woman," Ruth said. "I never would have gotten that invitation from Columbia without the push from the Nixon administration."[140] She also said she met no resistance when she arrived at Columbia as an affirmative action hire—although she preferred to call it "the end of negative action."[141]

The dean at the Rutgers Law School was resentful when Ruth left for Columbia, accusing her of putting her own ambition above the university that had hired her. Another Rutgers law professor who taught at the school since 1965 said that "her eyes were elsewhere. She was eager to move on to another school." [142] While Ruth never denied that the prospect of teaching at one of the nation's top law schools was appealing, there were also practical matters. She lived in Manhattan's Upper East Side. Marty was working in a Manhattan law firm. The ACLU offices of the Women's Rights Project were set up in Manhattan. Plus, she had two children at home, so she must have been relieved to teach closer to home and give up a daily commute on the PATH train to New Jersey.

If Ruth turned out to be a bit of a sex-equality firebrand on the faculty, Columbia shouldn't have been surprised. Almost immediately after taking up her new position, she wrote a letter to President McGill of Columbia University, reminding him that they'd already met at Dalton School—both had children in the school—and enclosing information about Rutgers's plan for recruiting more female professors.

During her very first month at Columbia, the university experienced a bit of drama. Columbia wanted to cut back expenses by reducing the housekeeping department, so it sent layoff notices to twenty-five maids, but no janitors. The jobs of janitor and maid were similar, the primary difference being that maids were women. Ruth weighed in on the dispute by quietly and calmly speaking out against the layoffs, which she characterized as unfairly falling on women. The university settled the matter by not laying off anyone at all.

At about this time, Professors Herma Hill Kay and Kenneth Davidson were discussing the idea of writing a law casebook on sex discrimination. Herma was a law professor at UC Berkeley, and Kenneth was a professor of law at SUNY Buffalo. Both, like Ruth, had received requests from students to offer courses in women and the law. Herma persuaded a practitioner to offer such a course, and Kenneth had offered one himself, but there were no appropriate textbooks in existence. They wanted a collaborator with an expertise in constitutional law as applied to women. The obvious choice was Ruth Bader Ginsburg. They pitched the idea to her at a NYU symposium that Ruth had helped to organize. She agreed, and the collaboration resulted in a 1974 casebook for a stand-alone course in women and the law called *Sex-Based Discrimination: Text, Cases, and Materials.*

Also about this time, Benjamin Kaplan, Ruth's civil procedure professor from her first year at Harvard Law School, was appointed to the Massachusetts Supreme Judicial Court. When he was appointed, he'd been serving as reporter to the U.S. Judicial Conference Advisory Committee on Civil Rules. He contacted Ruth and asked if she would take up his not-yet-completed work of drafting the American Law Institute's *Restatement (Second) of Judgments*. She felt flattered to be considered fit for the job by a legal scholar she had long admired, but she knew such a task would consume her waking hours for the coming decade. She therefore politely declined the invitation so she could continue to devote her time to reforming the law of equal protection.

She continued her habit of working almost nonstop, often very late into the night, sometimes with "a box of prunes and a pot of coffee."[143] She called herself a night owl. Marty called her a bat. In addition to teaching, and performing legal work through the Women's Rights Project, she was named to the Association of American Law Schools Executive Committee. She was elected to the board of editors for the *American Bar Association Journal*, and to the board of governors of the Society of American Law Teachers. She wrote articles and gave speeches about the importance of passing the Equal Rights Amendment. One of her students said there was a rumor that Professor Ginsburg never slept.

On November 22, 1972—exactly one year after the Supreme Court decided *Reed v. Reed*, the Court of Appeals of the Tenth Circuit ruled on Marty and Ruth's tax case. Charles Moritz won. The court found that the tax code provision that allowed a dutiful daughter but not a dutiful son to deduct expenses of caring was an "invidious discrimination and invalid under due process principles."[144] As precedent, the court cited the recent Supreme Court case of *Reed v. Reed*. Charles Moritz received his $600 deduction.

The U.S. solicitor general at the time was Erwin Griswold, the former Harvard Law School dean who, when Ruth entered law school, asked the women to justify why they were taking a place that could have been given to a man. Unhappy with the appellate court's ruling in Moritz's case, Griswold petitioned the U.S. Supreme Court to review the Moritz case. He was concerned that appellate court ruling "casts a cloud of unconstitutionality upon many federal statutes."[145] In an appendix, which he labeled Appendix E, he carefully listed all the provisions in the U.S. Code that distinguished on the basis of gender and might be rendered unconstitutional, should the Supreme Court affirm the ruling in Moritz's case. The list contained eight hundred federal statutes. The Supreme Court declined to hear the Moritz case on appeal, letting the lower court ruling stand.

Griswold's appendix turned out to be an unexpected gift to Ruth and her team. "There it was," Ruth said, "all laid out for us."[146] The task for her team was to take down those laws, one at a time, either through Congress or the courts.

Now that Ruth had earned the nickname of a women's rights pioneer, she decided she didn't like any of the current phrases to describe women's fight for equality. She didn't particularly like "women's liberation," or "women's rights," or even "sex discrimination." She preferred "the constitutional principle of the equal citizenship stature of men and women."[147] Precise, yes. But not likely to catch on as a popular slogan or bumper sticker, and definitely lacking pizazz. So for the time being, she went with the commonly used "sex discrimination."

The sheer amount of work Ruth did in her position as director of the WRP and as a law professor at Columbia created a shift at home. Marty now put her career first. Previously she had been the everyday cook, while Marty had been the weekend and special occasions cook. As Ruth likes to tell the story, once Marty started doing more of the everyday cooking—and after Jane returned home from a trip to France—Jane noticed a distinct difference in their cooking skills. Dad's meals were so much better than Mom's that Jane decided Mom should be banished altogether from the kitchen. Mom was happy to comply. Marty joked that both their children decided to banish their mother from the kitchen because the children had good taste.

In an interview, Jane explained that in their home, all responsibility was divided. She described the division of labor this way: "My father did the cooking and my mother did the thinking."[148] Marty, upon hearing this, joked that the truth should no longer be a defense against defamation.[149]

Ruth, it seemed, was always working. During car trips to Marty's golf club or to visit Marty's parents on Long Island, Marty would drive and Ruth would read, often advance sheets. The family discussed Ruth's cases at the dinner table. Ruth herself used the word "bad" to describe her own work habits. By "bad," she meant she had a hard time stopping for breaks. Sometimes Marty would say, "If you would leave off and come to bed, in the morning the issues will be clearer."[150] She knew he was right. Sometimes she'd feel like she was in a maze, then she'd go to sleep thinking about the way out, and when she woke up in the morning, she'd see the path.

The children were so accustomed to having two professional parents that they were often oblivious to the fact that their family was an anomaly in the early 1970s. Jane, who attended the prestigious Brearley School, a girls' day school, wondered why people asked her what her father did, but didn't ask what her mother did. Some expressed pity for Jane that she had a mother who worked. James was ten years younger than his sister, so by the time he was in grade school, at the end of the 1970s, working women were more common, but were still unusual.

Ruth felt irked the day she tried to enroll James in Sunday school at Temple Emanu-El on Fifth Avenue. Jane, ten years older, had finished her Jewish education. The rabbi didn't want an application written by a married woman, but he told her she could go ahead and fill out the membership as if she were her husband. The idea was that a single or divorced woman could join, but if a woman was married, the application should come from her husband. "Well, I haven't consulted him," she said. "I don't know if he wants to be a member of Temple Emanu-El."[151] Despite the annoyance, she wanted James to have a Jewish education. Instead of joining, she offered to make a contribution to the temple equivalent to membership if the rabbi would enroll James in Sunday school.

Ruth enjoyed telling another story that for her exemplified life for a career mother during the years of James's childhood. The word she used to describe her son was "lively." School officials at the Dalton School used less flattering phrases, like "hyperactive." The teachers and school officials were constantly calling her at work, insisting that she come to the school to meet with the classroom teacher, the principal, or even on occasion the school psychologist to hear about James's latest misadventure. One day, she was in her office at Columbia, feeling particularly weary after being up most of the night, writing a brief, when she received another call from the principal inviting her for a conference about James. She said, "This child has two parents. Please alternate calls. This time, it's his father's turn."[152]

Marty showed up for the next meeting at the school, where he was greeted by three stony-faced adults who told him the nature of James's latest transgression: He had taken the elevator—it was a manual elevator, and the operator was on a break. One of James's classmates dared him to take his classmates to the top floor, whereupon he loaded a group of kindergarteners into the elevator and took them to the top floor. Upon being told that James had taken the elevator, Marty asked, "Well, how far could he take it?" After that, the calls became much less frequent. With her usual wry humor, Ruth suggested that either the principal was put off by Marty's humor, or James suddenly became a model citizen—or, more likely, the teachers and principal didn't feel comfortable bothering a busy man with such matters.

Meanwhile, Ruth discovered a way to calm down her son: Take him to a concert. As early as kindergarten, he gave music his rapt attention. She tried to give him piano lessons, but the teacher she hired, Miss Czerny, just didn't work out for him. Miss Czerny was a descendant of Carl Czerny, the author of the Czerny exercises. James did not take to such a disciplined approach. Ruth, in trying to figure out the problem, concluded that with a mother, a big sister, and a female housekeeper, it was all too much. Fully aware of the irony, she called the Julliard School and asked, "Do you have a young man who teaches piano?"[153] The idea worked. With a young male teacher as a role model, James developed a lifelong love of music and gave his exhausted parents an easy way to calm him down. Ruth began taking him to see the Little Orchestra Society at Hunter College, and when he was older, the New York Philharmonic.

One of Ruth's students remembered Ruth bringing James to a faculty event. She said she'd never seen a child that active in her life. He liked math, so to get a little peace and quiet during walks across town, Ruth would give him complicated math problems to solve in his head. Later he said, "I grew up playing Scrabble with my mom."[154]

The children always seemed a bit defensive when asked about having a working mother. When newspaper reporters asked the children about their home life, they gave answers intended to assure people that while busy, their mother never neglected her domestic duties. "The family was always home for dinner," James later explained. "And a night did not go by when my mother did not check to see that I was doing my schoolwork. She was always there when I wanted her to be—and even when I didn't."[155] Jane, too, reported that her mother checked her homework and made her do it over until it was perfect. "Her day off was not my favorite," she said.

Kathleen Peratis, a lawyer in private practice in New York who worked closely with the ACLU, said Ruth and Marty were warm parents and fairly relaxed in their parenting style, "not doing a lot of fretting and obsessing about kid things and teenage things."[156] Jane agreed with this, saying that her mother was good with children because she didn't overly dramatize them.

14

THE ABORTION
QUESTION

Ruth had no trouble selecting her next client, Susan Struck, a woman forced by the government to choose between an abortion or her job.

Susan was born in Louisville, Kentucky, in 1944. Her mother once told her she regretted giving up her job in real estate to raise a family. Susan had no intention of following in her mother's footsteps. The women's movement, with its protests and slogans of sisterhood, didn't appeal to her, but she wanted independence, so she became a nurse. She loved ships, airplanes, and uniforms and craved adventure, so, on April 8, 1967, at the age of twenty-three, she joined the Air Force. The recruiter warned her that she would be discharged if she got pregnant. She thought that was "the dumbest thing I ever heard."[157]

After basic training, while stationed at David Monthan Air Force Base in Tucson, Arizona, she bought a Camaro, drank beer, and smoked cigarettes. She loved her life as an Air Force nurse, but wanted the excitement of war, so she asked to be sent to Vietnam. After arriving at the Phu Cat Air Force Base, she went to a party and was immediately swarmed by men, plying her with pickup lines. Her favorite aircraft was the F-4, so it wasn't surprising that the man she fell for was an F-4 pilot. When he asked her for a date, she responded with, "Where should we go? The ammo dump?"[158]

When Susan learned she was pregnant, her commanding officer gave her a choice: Get an abortion, or leave the Air Force. At that time, the armed services were one of the few places where abortion was legal. Susan refused an abortion on the grounds that she was Catholic, although admittedly, a lapsed Catholic. She wanted to give her child up for adoption and remain in the Air Force.

According to Air Force regulation, when an officer became pregnant, a board of officers was convened to hear the case. On October 6, 1970, Susan appeared before the board and asked if she could use her accumulated leave to have the baby, arrange for the adoption, and then return. The board refused her request. A few weeks later, on October 26, the secretary of the Air Force reviewed the findings of the board and directed that Susan be discharged as soon as possible. Her discharge orders were effective as of October 28, 1970.

With the help of the ACLU in Washington state, Susan obtained an order from the U.S. District Court for the Western Division of Washington staying her discharge for twenty-four hours so she could present her case for a restraining order. The next morning, the judge denied the restraining order. That very afternoon, the ACLU lawyers asked the Court of Appeals of the Ninth Circuit for an order staying the discharge until her case could be heard in the federal district court.

Meanwhile, Susan returned home to have her baby and arrange for the adoption. She gave birth to a girl, who she called L.B., which stood for "Little Baby-san" or, if she was in a different sort of mood, "Little Bastard."[159] She selected the adoptive parents, Julie and Art, who agreed to Susan's terms: the baby would be raised Catholic, and Susan would be allowed to visit. On December 10, 1970, the adoption was finalized. Julie and Art named the baby Tanya Marie.

As part of the court proceedings, Colonel Max B. Bralliar, commanding officer of the Minot Air Force Base, reported that Susan "demonstrated excellent ability in the performance of the managerial aspects of the work units and an excellent knowledge and application of nursing care principles," and that she was highly dedicated with a "professionally correct and mature attitude."[160] On June 4, 1971, the district court ruled against her, so she appealed to the U.S. Court of Appeals for the Ninth Circuit. Five months later, the Ninth Circuit affirmed the district court's order. She filed a petition for rehearing, but was again denied. One of the judges, however, changed his mind and dissented for two reasons: first, because men with temporary periods of disability were not discharged, and second, because he found it irrational that only the natural mother, not the natural father, was declared unfit for service after the birth of a child. With the dissent, the ruling was 2-1 against Susan.

It was time to ask the U.S. Supreme Court to hear the case. This was 1972, shortly after Ruth formed the Women's Right Project, so the case found its way to her office. She thought Susan's case was perfect for pushing the strategy she'd begun in *Reed v. Reed.* Here was a gender distinction that made absolutely no sense. Once the baby was adopted and Susan was legally no longer a mother, there was no reason to deem her unfit for military service on the grounds that she had refused an abortion and carried a baby to term. Even better, the facts—an Air Force captain forced to choose between an abortion and her job— were ideal for opening a dialogue with the Supreme Court about a woman's right to control her own reproductive organs. Ruth and Joel Gora, ACLU Legal Office staff counsel, spent long hours in June and July preparing a petition for certiorari for Susan Struck, hoping to get the Supreme Court's attention.

Very few legal issues have been as heated or divisive as the laws concerning contraception and abortion, or have been as central to the women's movement in America.

Contraceptives were largely illegal in the colonies. After the United States was formed, most states enacted laws prohibiting the advertising, sale, and distribution of contraceptives. As a practical matter, while there were a large number of convictions under the anti-contraceptive laws, contraceptives and information about birth control were widely distributed. Ironically, many states outlawed contraceptives, but permitted early-stage abortion.

In the mid-nineteenth century, Anthony Comstock, a politician known for his adherence to Victorian standards

Anthony Comstock, circa 1913.

of morality, decided to do something about what he saw as the problem of vice. In his view, contraceptives allowed for adultery and the spread of venereal diseases. By force of will, he was able to get a bill through Congress called "Suppression of Trade in, and Circulation of, Obscene Literature and Articles of Immoral Use." The act specifically defined information about contraceptives as obscene. Anthony Comstock was appointed special agent of the Post Office, with the authority to track and destroy illegal mail, and bring offenders to justice. Within a few years, twenty-four states passed equally harsh laws against contraceptives. Connecticut passed the most restrictive chastity laws in the country, making it a crime for even a married couple to use contraceptives.

Margaret Sanger took it as her mission to overturn the Comstock laws. One of eleven children, she was born to a mother who was perpetually pregnant. Margaret trained as a nurse and married an architect. Using contraceptives, she limited the number of her own children to three. Working in New York's Lower East Side sensitized her to the plight of women who "wore themselves out with continuous childbirth." Because they were denied safe and effective contraceptives and safe abortions, women passed suggestions among themselves, including "herb teas, turpentine, steaming, rolling down stairs, inserting slippery elm, knitting needles, and shoe hooks."[161]

After watching a desperate young woman die from a self-induced abortion, Margaret made up her mind to do something. Her resolve was strengthened after caring for another woman who nearly died after a difficult birth. The woman knew another pregnancy would kill her, so she asked the doctor if there was some way she could prevent another pregnancy. The doctor said, "You want to have your cake and eat it too, do you? Well, it can't be done."[162] He advised her to tell her husband to sleep on the roof.

Three months later, Margaret's telephone rang. The woman's husband called to tell Margaret that his wife was once again pregnant. Evidently he hadn't wanted to sleep on the roof. Margaret rushed to their house to find the woman in a room surrounded by her young children. Margaret was unable to save her. She soon slipped into a coma and died. That was it—Margaret could not take any more. She instituted training for women on reproduction, birth control, and sexuality, and tried to spread information about birth control the only way she could, by writing a column in a socialist newspaper.

Margaret Sanger, 1922.

She was soon arrested and charged with violating the Comstock Act. If found guilty, she could be sentenced to forty-five years in prison. The district attorney who charged her with criminal activity claimed that her crime—disseminating information on birth control—was the moral and legal equivalent of throwing bombs and committing murder. To avoid conviction and prison, Margaret fled to Canada, where she continued writing about the need to educate women about birth control. Eventually she returned to the United States to stand trial, defending herself by saying that no woman could call herself free unless she could control her own reproduction and decide when—and if—she became a mother. Because of an outpouring of public support on her behalf, she was not convicted. She opened a controversial birth control clinic that grew into today's Planned Parenthood.

In 1936 the Comstock Laws were amended to allow doctors to disseminate contraceptives to patients. Over the next few decades, the Comstock laws were further limited. A landmark Supreme Court case, *Griswold v. Connecticut*, struck down Connecticut's law making it illegal for any person to use contraceptives.[163] Griswold, the director of Planned Parenthood League of Connecticut, was brought to trial for giving information to married couples about contraceptives. In a controversial ruling, the Supreme Court held that the Connecticut law infringed on a married couple's constitutional right to privacy. The hitch was that there is nothing explicitly in the Constitution about privacy. The Supreme Court, however, held that the various guarantees within the Bill of Rights created penumbras, or zones, that established a right to privacy.

In 1950, when Sanger was in her eighties, she took the step that probably did more to change the lives of twentieth-century women than any other: She raised $150,000 for the research to develop a safe and effective birth control pill. In 1960, the first oral contraceptive, Enovid, was approved by the U.S. Food and Drug Administration, although it would be a few more years before the pill would be widely available. It was probably not a coincidence that the wide availability of the pill coincided with the sexual revolution of the 1960s.

The last of the Comstock laws were not struck down until 1972, when the Supreme Court decided a case called *Eisenstadt v. Baird*, finding that unmarried couples had the same rights to contraceptives as married couples.[164]

One of the ironies of the laws surrounding reproduction in the early twentieth century was that while birth control and abortions were illegal, there were an abundance of laws allowing the government to forcibly sterilize citizens. In 1924, Virginia passed a law allowing for the sterilization of inmates in institutions supported by the state. Carrie Buck was considered feebleminded—a common word at the time for disorders of the mind. Carrie, who was committed to the State Colony for Epileptics and Feebleminded, was the daughter of a "feebleminded" mother who lived in the same institution. Both Carrie and her mother were judged to be promiscuous on the grounds that both had children out of wedlock. When Carrie was eighteen years old, the state sought to have her sterilized on the theory that as long as she was capable of bearing children, she was a menace to society because she would likely bear similarly feebleminded children. The U.S. Supreme Court upheld the right of Virginia to forcibly sterilize Carrie, thereby legalizing eugenics.[165]

Soon after the Supreme Court's ruling in *Buck v. Bell*, a dozen other states passed their own sterilization laws. The largest percentage of forced sterilizations was carried out in the South.

Although all races and both genders were forcibly sterilized, it wasn't long before the victims were primarily female. Initially, the sterilized girls were generally white, single, and sexually active, with a low IQ. Susan Cahn, a professor of women's history, explains this by stating that sexually active poor white women procreating in large numbers threatened the social order in the South because of the embarrassment of sexually promiscuous whites failing to live up to stereotyped views of whites as morally superior and hence fit to be the ruling class. Promiscuous white girls inverted the usual ideas—prevalent everywhere but particularly so in the South—that white women embodied a special purity. Promiscuous was understood to mean having a baby without being married.

Authorities, in selecting those to be sterilized, often conflated feebleminded with promiscuity, and in fact, promiscuity was taken as proof of feeblemindedness. In the words of the doctor and administrator of a state-run institution for the feebleminded,

> It is well known that feebleminded women and girls are very liable to become sources of unspeakable debauchery and licentiousness which pollutes . . . the minds and bodies of thoughtless youth at the very threshold of manhood.[166]

The problem was how to understand promiscuous white girls who did not *appear* feebleminded. The theory arose that promiscuous white girls must have borderline intelligence—while not visibly feebleminded, they must have low intelligence because nothing else explained their behavior, and hence, they were good candidates for forced sterilization.

By the 1940s and 1950s there was a shift, particularly in the

South, with authorities more often targeting African American females as candidates for forced sterilization. The reason for the shift was that for the first time, welfare became widely available to African Americans. In response, there arose the stereotype of the welfare mother, typically characterized as an African American woman deliberately cheating the state by bearing too many children. Ronald Reagan is credited with exploiting the pejorative phrase "welfare queens," which he applied to women on welfare who—according to implication—were too lazy to work, choosing to have babies as a means to increase their government income.

In an effort to locate candidates for sterilization, state social workers entered black communities and attempted to learn the names of women who might "benefit" from sterilization. The black communities mounted a silent resistance, refusing to cooperate and provide names. So state governments disguised what they were up to. If a poor woman or pregnant teenager went to a public clinic for birth control, prenatal care, or an infection, a public health worker might evaluate her as a prospect for sterilization and refer her to the welfare department. Some authorities purposely misled individuals about the nature of the operation they were about to perform, saying that a medical condition required treatment. Many surgeons used events like childbirth or appendectomies to perform sterilizations—often without permission. One notorious obstetrician automatically and without permission sterilized a woman after her third child. Another—the only obstetrician in Aiken County, South Carolina, who accepted Medicaid—required welfare patients to agree to sterilization after childbirth or he would refuse them as patients. Many women were told they had to undergo sterilization or risk losing their jobs or welfare benefits.

About the time Ruth Bader Ginsburg founded the Women's

Rights Project, complaints about women being forced to undergo unwanted sterilizations became so numerous that the ACLU formed a division called the Reproductive Freedom Project. Eventually this division handled issues of contraceptives and abortion as well.

The first abortion rights advocates were doctors—male doctors to be precise—because in the early part of the twentieth century, very few women were part of the medical profession. Those opposed to abortions on moral grounds accused doctors of being businessmen and profiting by performing abortions. In fact, doctors first began advocating for safe and legal abortions because they were alarmed by the large numbers of women who died each year as a result of botched illegal abortions. As of 1970, illegal abortions were the leading cause of maternal death in the United States, whereas legal abortions performed by a medical professional were extremely safe. A frequent estimate was that badly botched abortions resulted in about five thousand maternal deaths each year. Most were married with children left behind at their deaths. The reality was that a woman desperate for an abortion would obtain one, and if she could not find a safe and legal abortionist, she would put herself at risk with an unlicensed abortionist. In response to the public health menace of so many unsafe abortions, jurisdictions such as New York, California, Alaska, Hawaii, and Washington, DC, repealed criminal sanctions for abortions, hence legalizing the procedure as long as it was performed by a licensed doctor. While there was much religious opposition to decriminalizing abortion, there were some religious leaders, including those in Catholic circles, such as Reverend Robert Drinan, dean of the Boston College Law School, who believed that abortion should be placed in the category of adultery—an act condemned by the Church as immoral but not criminally punished.

It wasn't until the 1960s that many feminists took up the cause of abortion, repeating Margaret Sanger's oft-quoted statement that no woman could call herself free unless she could control her own reproduction and decide when—and if—she became a mother. Ruth was always open about her personal views on abortion, perhaps born of her experience in Sweden watching the Sherri Finkbine case unfold. It was clear to Ruth that a woman with enough money to buy a plane ticket would be able to obtain a safe and legal abortion. Criminalizing abortion, therefore, simply meant restricting the choices of lower-income women.

Critics accused Planned Parenthood and the ACLU of practicing eugenics because of the rationalization that abortion and contraceptive laws—as a practical matter—fell only on the poor. Many African Americans, in fact, were afraid that the pro-choice movement would amount to another assault on the reproductive organs of black women by forcing them to have abortions. From the time of slavery through to the forced sterilizations of the twentieth century, black women knew how it felt for the government to control their reproductive organs. Scholar Dorothy Roberts argues that every indignity a woman suffers today when she is denied control of her reproductive organs can be found in the lives of slaves, who were often forced to reproduce to produce more slaves and who endured the indignity of being treated as procreative vessels.[167] Even the current debate pitting a mother's welfare against that of her unborn child was also expressed during slavery as the understanding that a slave woman's life was of less value than the babies she was expected to produce.

The philosophy of the ACLU and Planned Parenthood was that a woman should have complete control over her own reproductive organs without governmental interference, whether the woman wanted to prevent a pregnancy, end a pregnancy, or avoid forced sterilization. As Ruth put it, "No one is *for* abortion. People are for a woman's ability to decide what her life's course will be."[168]

Ruth and her colleagues at the Women's Right Project were pretty sure Captain Susan Struck's abortion case would be a winner. The facts were clear, and the plaintiff—a dedicated Catholic Air Force officer who didn't want an abortion on religious grounds—was sympathetic. Ruth's plan was to challenge the stereotypes about women underpinning the legislation, in particular the assumption that a woman who had borne a child was somehow unfit for service, and the notion that it was proper for the government to control a woman's reproductive choices.

Solicitor General Erwin Griswold also thought Ruth would win. To avoid a loss, he contacted the Air Force, and persuaded them to change their regulations. The Air Force responded by changing one detail in the regulation: The law still required the discharge of a pregnant officer, but allowed the pregnant officer to request a waiver. The Air Force, however, retained the unfettered discretion to grant or deny the waiver. The Air Force then granted Susan Struck an exemption to discharge, allowing her to return to her job. With this done, Griswold filed a motion with the Supreme Court asking for Susan Struck's case to be dismissed on the grounds that it was now moot.

Ruth felt frustrated by what she saw as a flagrant attempt on the part of the Air Force to dodge the question and avoid judicial scrutiny while keeping a law on the books that permitted them to unfairly discriminate against women. Hoping to keep the case alive, she asked Susan if she'd experienced any other discrimination. "I've always dreamed of being a pilot,"

Susan told her, "but the Air Force doesn't give flight training to women."[169] At that, both women laughed. They knew that expecting the Air Force to allow a woman to be a pilot was an "impossible dream."[170]

Meanwhile, another abortion case, *Roe v. Wade*, and its companion case, *Doe v. Bolton*, were then making their way through the courts. Jane Roe—whose real name was Norma McCorvey—wanted an abortion, but Texas law made it a crime for a doctor to perform abortion except to save a woman's life. She therefore turned to the ACLU for help.[171] Ruth had no hand in the legal work for *Roe v. Wade* because her work at the time was funded by the Ford Foundation, and while open to equal rights cases, the Ford Foundation refused to fund anything related to legalizing abortion.

The Supreme Court ruled against Texas in *Roe v. Wade*, giving a woman total control over her pregnancy during the first trimester, while restricting access to abortion in the later trimesters. For the first trimester, the court found that the decision of whether a woman should have an abortion should be left to the medical judgment of the woman's doctor. The court also imposed detailed prescriptions for how states could regulate abortion in each trimester of a pregnancy.

The constitutional basis for the decision was a woman's "right to privacy," a concept first developed by the court in *Griswold v. Connecticut*. For Ruth, the issue was about autonomy, not privacy. While Ruth wouldn't have objected to using the right to privacy as part of the court's justification, she felt it was inadequate as the entire justification. She would have preferred to cast the issue as one of equality under the equal protection clause of the Fourteenth Amendment.

Ruth also found the approach of putting the decision on

the doctor instead of the woman patriarchal and patronizing. The biggest problem for her, though, with *Roe v. Wade* was that the court made a broad ruling, saying flatly that a woman had a constitutional right to an abortion instead of simply deciding the constitutionality of the Texas law. In the ongoing debate among judges and legal scholars over whether courts should rule narrowly—sticking to the facts at hand—or whether they should offer broad opinions to provide context and guidance, Ruth was firmly on the side of narrow decisions, even when she thought the law was wrong and should be changed. Narrow decisions encouraged other branches of government to weigh in, which kept the shaping of the laws more democratic.

The Texas law before the Supreme Court was one of the harsher anti-abortion laws in existence in the country, so the court could have—and in Ruth's view, *should* have—simply struck down the excessive portion of the Texas law. At the time *Roe v. Wade* was decided, abortion laws were changing all across the country, with states removing criminal sanctions against doctors who performed abortions. The American Law Institute had issued a Model Penal Code suggesting that all criminal sanctions be removed for performing abortions, at any stage of pregnancy, if the mother's physical or mental health was at risk.

Because of the sweep of the Supreme Court's decision, the abortion laws of forty-six states were instantly and in one fell swoop rendered unconstitutional, even the most liberal of them. The result was an enormous backlash that entirely changed the political landscape. Prior to *Roe v. Wade*, Republicans were more likely than Democrats to favor decriminalizing abortion. Ruth believed the sweeping rule in *Roe v. Wade* created a "storm center," turning the issue into a political one, mobilizing the pro-life movement, and giving it a single focus.[172]

Ruth always regretted that Susan Struck's case hadn't been

the first abortion case to reach the Supreme Court because it better illustrated the wishes of a woman not wanting the government to control her reproductive choices. She would not have asked for all abortion laws to be overturned. She would have asked that the law forcing Susan Struck to choose between her job and an abortion be struck down on the theory that the woman had a right to control her own reproductive organs. A narrow ruling affecting only one statute would have allowed for a dialogue between the court, the legislature, and the public. Other challenges would have been brought—perhaps challenging the restriction that a woman needed her husband's permission, or that the procedure must be done in a hospital, or that two doctors needed to be consulted. A narrow ruling would have given states the latitude to create their own abortion statutes, step-by-step testing the limits of the Constitution, which for Ruth was preferable to the court handing down a sweeping rule like a thunderbolt.

15

PLEASE TAKE YOUR
FEET FROM OUR NECKS

Kathleen Peratis Frank at the Women's Rights Project was less restrained than Ruth. Kathleen wanted to bring a case requiring the enforcement of comparative worth—the idea of rating jobs by the skills required and forcing employers to pay the same salary for jobs of equal rating. The concept involved rating jobs commonly held by men and jobs typically held by women according to the skills required and the importance to society. Employers would then be forced to pay the same salary for jobs of equal rating.

"Too radical to win," Ruth said.[173] She preferred cases less disruptive to everyday American life, cases that made the point that discrimination harmed everyone, cases that inched the cause forward while educating judges and the public.

Kathleen filed the suit anyway, and lost. After that, she heeded Ruth's advice.

Ruth's next choice involved another Air Force servicewoman, Lieutenant Sharron Frontiero. Sharron's complaint arose while she was supporting her husband, who was attending college with the help of the GI bill. Under armed forces regulations, if a serviceman was married, he was automatically entitled to extra pay for housing. If a servicewoman was married, she was allowed extra housing pay only if she could prove her husband was dependent on her for more than half of his support. In Sharon's case, her $8,200 yearly income provided most of the couple's income, but her husband received $205 monthly from the GI bill, and his expenses were only $354. This meant he wasn't actually dependent on Sharron for more than half of his expenses. She therefore did not qualify for the extra housing allowance, even though she was earning most of the money that provided for the couple. Had their roles been reversed— had she been a man supporting a wife going to college on the GI bill—she would have been entitled to the extra pay.

Sharron and her husband were then living in Alabama. With the help of the Southern Poverty Law Center in Alabama, they challenged the Air Force regulations in district court, alleging that the law denied Sharron equal protection. They lost in the district court. The court concluded that there was a rational basis for a law that required a wife to submit proof that she provided more than half of her husband's support, while the husband was automatically given the extra pay on the grounds that men more often supported the family. As the court understood the problem, the "alleged injustice" of the gender distinction was the possibility that some men were getting a windfall—benefits when they were not actually supporting their wives—while a married woman was "denied a windfall."[174] The court held that requiring both men and women to show that their spouses were actually dependent on them would be extremely costly and require burdensome procedures, given that there were more than two hundred thousand servicemen throughout the armed forces. Because women were not unduly burdened by the requirement of proving they were the primary support of their husbands, the court held that the woman's due process rights were not violated. Because the statute was based on sound statistics—men were more often the primary provider of the family—the court denied that the statute was a relic of Victorian notions of "romantic paternalism."[175]

Sharron's lawyer, Joseph Levin, asked Mel Wulf at the ACLU for assistance in appealing to the U.S. Supreme Court. Ruth saw immediately that Sharron's case was perfect. The government's rationale—that the statute was necessary because it created administrative convenience—was contrary to the Supreme Court's ruling in *Reed v. Reed*, holding that administrative convenience wasn't a good enough reason for sex discrimination. What made the case particularly easy was that the case could be perceived as a straight equal pay case: Two people, both in the military at the same rank, but one was entitled to more money. As with Moritz's case, all that was needed was for the court to repair an under-inclusive statute. With two equal pay laws in effect, it wouldn't cause a tidal wave of opposition.

The ACLU accepted the case and agreed to fund the litigation on the condition that the ACLU would control the case, and if it went to the Supreme Court, Ruth would do the oral argument. Nobody wanted a repeat of the Alan Derr fiasco in *Reed v. Reed*.

Sharron and her trial lawyer, Joseph Levin, agreed, so Ruth wrote a petition for certiorari and jurisdictional statement asking the Supreme Court to review the case. She argued that the sex-based classification was unrelated to any biological difference between the sexes, and therefore arbitrarily and capriciously discriminated against women as a class, and should be subject to the same strict scrutiny applied to laws discriminating on the basis of race. In the alternative, she argued that there was no rational basis for requiring women to prove they were the primary providers without the same requirement for men.

The Supreme Court granted Ruth's petition. Then, in November of 1972, three months before oral argument, Joseph Levin changed his mind. He wanted to argue the case himself. The Southern Poverty Law Center had never before had the opportunity to appear before the highest court in the land, and now that the possibility was before them, he wanted to do it. Ruth and Mel did their best to hold him to his promise, even accusing him of chauvinism in taking the argument away from Ruth, but he held firm. His recollection was that he had made no such promise. His view of the situation was that his role had been usurped and he'd been reduced to a mere advisor on his own case. Moreover, he had a different idea as to how to approach the case. He did not want to argue for a strict scrutiny of the sex distinction in the law—he wanted instead to present the case under a modest application of the low standard of review from *Reed v. Reed*. He argued in his brief that under the standard applied in *Reed*, Lieutenant Frontiero was entitled to the extra pay because the statute was not in place to protect "physiologically weaker women."[176]

Ruth and Joseph agreed that he would have twenty minutes to present the appellant's argument. Ruth, then, would have ten minutes to put forward her argument for why statutes that discriminated on the basis of sex should be judged by a standard of strict scrutiny.

Ruth had kept in touch with Gerald Gunther, the professor who had secured her clerkship with Judge Palmieri. They'd been talking about her strategies and arguments. Just before oral argument in Frontiero's case, Gunther, who was then teaching at Stanford, published an article in the *Harvard Law Review* that proved influential: From the court's recent rulings in *Reed v. Reed* and other cases from the 1971 term, he argued that while the court was reluctant to apply a strict scrutiny to laws that discriminated on the basis of sex, there was a growing discontent with the rigid two-tier system, and the court was leaning instead toward an intermediate-level scrutiny for sex distinctions.

Supreme Court decisions profoundly affect the everyday lives of Americans, creating rules that define all aspects of life and culture, from marriage, family, and religion to guns and limits on police power. As Ruth herself said, "The controversies that come to the Supreme Court, as the last judicial resort, touch and concern the health and well-being of our nation and its people; they affect the preservation of liberty to ourselves and our posterity."[177]

The staggering power held by the nine justices of the Supreme Court comes largely from its power to interpret the Constitution. The Constitution, while a brilliant blueprint of government, cannot interpret itself—and it left out a few important details. Among them, the Constitution failed to designate whose job it should be to interpret the Constitution. Once the Constitution was ratified, different theories were floated. Some suggested that each branch of government should decide for itself how the Constitution should apply to its function. If Congress passed a law that the president believed unconstitutional, the president would direct his administration not to enforce it. If Congress believed a court ruling unconstitutional, they could disregard it. Support for this theory was found in certain of Thomas Jefferson's and Andrew Jackson's writings.[178] But that theory had obvious problems. What if the different branches were in conflict about how to read a constitutional provision? Another approach was that each branch is authoritative in certain areas. Political questions, for example, should be decided by the legislature, which again raises the possibility of conflicts among the branches.

In 1803, in *Marbury v. Madison*, Supreme Court Chief Justice John Marshall declared that the duty of interpreting the Constitution should fall to the Supreme Court.[179] It made sense, he argued, for the task of interpreting the Constitution to fall to a court, whose business was interpreting and applying laws. *Marbury v. Madison* thus established the principle of judicial review, whereby the Supreme Court has the task of determining whether laws passed by Congress pass constitutional muster. Ever since, the Supreme Court has been the final arbiter of the limits and meaning of the Constitution, with the power to strike down laws passed by Congress as unconstitutional, making the Supreme Court truly equal to the other two branches, and giving the nine justices an enormous amount of power.

Ruth believed that the power to interpret the Constitution was well vested in the Supreme Court on the grounds that elected officials "cannot always be trusted to keep society in tune with its most basic values."[180] This reality was painfully brought home to Europe after World War I, when the controls of government broke down in Germany, resulting in the Holocaust. To make sure such a thing never happened again, a number of European countries created constitutional courts modeled on the U.S. Supreme Court—courts that were detached, impartial, and removed from day-to-day politics, and judges who would never have to answer to a dictator.

The Supreme Court grants review in less than 3 percent of submitted petitions.[181] Petitions for review—or certiorari—are generally granted to the most pressing and controversial questions of the day. The party seeking Supreme Court review submits copies of a writ for certiorari according to very specific formatting requirements, explaining why the Supreme Court should grant review. Once a petition has been filed, the other side has thirty days to file a response. The Clerk's Office typically holds the petition until the opposition has been filed, and then distributes copies to each of the nine justices. In 1973, in order to cut back on the amount of work in reading through the petitions for Supreme Court review, Chief Justice Warren Burger set up a pool of clerks—top graduates from the top law schools—to make initial recommendations on which cases to hear and which to decline. While some justices elected to opt out and look through the petitions themselves, most came to rely on this first screening by the clerks. The nine justices then meet regularly for formal conferences on which cases to hear. The purpose of the secrecy—no clerks or court employees are permitted to attend the meeting—is to protect the privacy of the discussion. At a typical conference, the justices will discuss as many as one hundred cases. Four votes are all that are needed for the Court to grant review.

Ruth was nervous on January 17, 1973, the day *Frontiero v. Richardson* was scheduled to be argued in the Supreme Court.[182] "I didn't eat lunch for fear that I might throw up," she said.[183] But her colleagues and family had complete faith in her. She had been teaching law for almost a decade. Nobody who knew her doubted that she could do it.

She paid silent homage to her mother by wearing Celia's earrings and pin. She sat at the counsel table next to Brenda Feigen, listening as Joseph Levin presented his arguments. Behind her, in the section for spectators, was Marty. Unlike Alan Derr, Levin knew exactly what he was doing, expertly explaining his position and answering the justices' questions.

When his allotted time was up, Joseph Levin stepped

aside for Ruth to have a chance to explain why strict scrutiny was appropriate. Chief Justice Burger then called for "Mrs. Ginsburg." Some of her students wanted her to insist on being addressed as "Ms." instead of "Mrs.," but characteristically Ruth declined to make a fuss over it.

United States Supreme Court interior.

She opened by explaining that the discrimination in Sharron Frontiero's case was similar to Sally Reed's in that both derived from the same stereotype, that the woman was dependent and the man was the breadwinner. Shortly into her argument, her fears evaporated when she realized that the nine men on the bench in front of her—the most important and powerful judges in America and possibly in the entire world—were a captive audience. They had no choice for the next few minutes but to pay attention to what she said.

She told the justices that the lower courts were confused, to say the least, by what standard to use in sex discrimination cases because they were recognizing that something more was needed than the low-level rational basis test—but what? She asked the Court to clarify the standard. She also asked the Court to find that sex was a "suspect criteria," but then hastened to assure the court that this would not be a large or sudden step because, as Stanford professor Gunther pointed out in his *Harvard Law Review* article, some special suspicion of sex as a suspect classification was already present in the court's treatment of gender classification.

She wasn't interrupted once, which she found alarming. Were they even listening? Was she doing something wrong? She had no idea. She spoke clearly, slowly, and calmly, citing cases and statutes from memory. Joseph Levin, watching, thought she was brilliant. He hadn't wanted to make the strict scrutiny argument, but he felt she was impressive.

She finished by quoting Sara Grimke, a noted abolitionist and advocate of equal rights for men and women, who said, "I ask no favor for my sex. All I ask of our brethren is that they take their feet off our necks."[184]

When she finished, Samuel Huntington, the lawyer representing the government, went to the podium and presented his argument: He argued that there was a rational basis for the distinction because the statistics indicated that more men supported families than women. He also revealed that the armed forces had put before Congress a change in the statute giving the plaintiff exactly what she was asking for.

What Ruth didn't know was that Justice Blackmun gave her a grade of C+ with the comment, "Very precise female."[185]

As they left the courthouse, Marty joked that Ruth might be able to recite cases, statutes, and citations from memory, but she'd have trouble figuring out how to get back to New York on the shuttle. For Brenda Feigan, this went without saying. "She's just so focused on the law," Brenda said.[186]

The Court issued its decision on May 14, 1973, and at first glance it appeared to be a breathtaking victory for Ruth. The opinion written by Justice Brennan held that

> classifications based upon sex, like classifications based upon race, alienage, and national origin, are inherently suspect, and must therefore be subjected to close judicial scrutiny.[187]

The Court found implicit support for this approach in its earlier holding in *Reed v. Reed*. Under a stricter scrutiny, the statute denying Lieutenant Sharron Frontiero extra pay was unconstitutional under the Fourteenth Amendment. In justifying this departure from the traditional rational basis standard of review, Justice Brennan quoted extensively from Ruth's brief, using language she had borrowed from a California case, *Sail'er Inn, Inc. v. Kirby*,[188] and from the Supreme Court's opinion in *Bradwell v. Illinois*.[189]

There can be no doubt that our Nation has had a long and unfortunate history of sex discrimination. Traditionally, such discrimination was rationalized by an attitude of "romantic paternalism" which, in practical effect, put women not on a pedestal, but in a cage. Indeed, this paternalistic attitude became so firmly rooted in our national consciousness that, 100 years ago, a distinguished Member of this Court was able to proclaim: "Man is, or should be, woman's protector and defender. The natural and proper timidity and delicacy which belongs to the female sex evidently unfits it for many of the occupations of civil life . . . The paramount destiny and mission of woman are to fulfill the noble and benign offices of wife and mother. This is the law of the Creator."[190]

What appeared to be victory, though, fell short because only four justices signed on to this opinion: Justices Brennan, Douglas, White, and Marshall—considered the liberal wing of the court. Without a majority, the decision applied only to Sharron Frontiero's case without the reasoning becoming precedent. Two other justices, Chief Justice Burger and Justice Blackmun, signed a concurring opinion, agreeing that the statute was unconstitutional, but finding it unconstitutional under the rational basis test. Burger, Blackmun, and Stewart said they could not go along with "far-reaching implications" of subjecting all laws that distinguished based on gender to the same strict scrutiny used in race-based distinctions.

Justice Brennan, one of the court's liberals, had been Ruth's strongest advocate on the Court. Initially the justices who had decided to rule in favor of Frontiero wanted to follow the rule in *Reed v. Reed* without reaching the question of whether sex constitutes a suspect category requiring strict scrutiny. But Brennan had been strongly persuaded by Ruth's arguments and felt that laws that distinguished based on sex should be given stricter scrutiny. The problem was he could convince only three other justices to join him.

Justice Rehnquist—who would one day be Ruth's chief justice when she herself sat on the court—dissented. He alone of the nine justices wanted to rule for the government on the grounds that there was a rational basis for the statute.

So it was a victory, of sorts. Ruth had convinced four of the nine justices. One more, and she would have a majority. The task of persuading another of the justices would wait for another day and another set of facts. Meanwhile, Ruth and her staff at the Women's Rights Project responded to the victory by drafting memos that they distributed nationwide to ACLU affiliates, with suggestions for follow-up litigation and advice for changing statutes through legislative lobbying.

Shortly after the Supreme Court handed down its decision in *Frontiero v. Richardson*, Ruth's daughter Jane graduated from high school. She would enroll at the University of Chicago in the fall. Her ambition, listed in the Brearley School yearbook with her picture, was "To see my mother appointed to the Supreme Court." The line underneath read: "If necessary, I will appoint her."[191]

16

YOU CAN'T GET
BETTER THAN THAT

Stephen Wiesenfeld—Ruth's next client—and his wife Paula were married on November 15, 1970, and lived in New Brunswick, New Jersey. Paula was a high school math teacher at Edison High School, and Stephen, who had a master's in business administration and a master's in mathematics, was trying to start up a computer business at home. Paula was the primary wage earner, consistently earning more than Stephen, and always paying the maximum amount into Social Security. When she got pregnant, they decided that she would remain in her teaching job and Stephen would stay home and take care of the child. She had such a healthy and easy pregnancy that she was teaching into her ninth month. The day her baby was born, June 5, 1972, she was taken into the delivery room while Stephen waited. When the doctor came back out, he gave Stephen the shocking news: "You have a healthy baby boy, but your wife died of an embolism."[192]

Stephen, devastated, vowed that he would not go back to work, or work full-time, until Jason, the baby, was in school full-time. He visited the Social Security office in Brunswick,

New Jersey, and said that he wanted what were called "child in care" benefits—benefits available for a sole surviving parent to take care of a minor child.

Unfortunately, there was a problem. "These are mothers' benefits," the Social Security officer explained. "They are not available to fathers." Aghast, Stephen pointed out that Paula had paid Social Security taxes, just as a man would have. For seven years she had been gainfully employed. Shouldn't, therefore, her Social Security payments offer her family the same protection as those of a man? "Nope," the Social Security officer told him.

Frustrated, Stephen wrote a letter to the editor of the *New Brunswick Home News* on November 27, 1972, complaining about the sex discrimination he suffered. He concluded his letter with, "I wonder if Gloria Steinem knows about this."[193]

A woman on the Rutgers Spanish Department faculty, Phyllis Boring, who lived in Edison, New Jersey, not far from New Brunswick, saw the letter in the paper. She called Ruth, and told her about the letter. Phyllis thought that the young man should contact the ACLU. Ruth then asked Phyllis if she would contact the young man, see if he wanted legal help, and if so, suggest that he contact the ACLU. Phyllis called Stephen and asked him if he wanted to pursue the matter in court. He asked only one question. "How much will it cost me?"[194] When he learned that the ACLU would cover the cost, which would have been far more than any payments he might have collected in the event of a victory, he said he was interested. Phyllis introduced him to Ruth.

"Stephen's case so moved me," Ruth said. "He was devastated by his wife's death and he was really determined to bring up Jason himself."[195] His case was also perfect for showing how regulations based on the idea that men and women should occupy different spheres harmed both men and women. It was a story after Ruth's own heart, a story of threefold discrimination. The woman as wage earner had been discriminated against. The parent who wanted to care for his child, the man, was discriminated against. And the child, harmed by being denied the opportunity to be cared for by his sole surviving parent, was discriminated against. The case also demonstrated the harm in stereotypes: While often based in truth, people who didn't fit the mold were harmed.

One advantage to Stephen's case—aside from the sympathetic facts—was that getting a Supreme Court ruling in Stephen's case would not challenge the lifestyle of most people, nor were people likely to feel that Stephen's desire to raise his child himself as a widower was subverting the traditional social order. Also reassuring was that Stephen was *her* client. He had come to her, and he was in it on principle. She wouldn't have to worry about another lawyer insisting on doing the oral argument, or the case settling or being rendered moot.

Ruth has often been criticized for the fact that so many of her plaintiffs in her sex discrimination cases were men. Some of her critics assumed that she preferred cases with male plaintiffs because the judges were largely male, so they were more likely to sympathize with a male plaintiff. In fact, she preferred cases that pressed her idea that in order for there to be equality between the sexes, it wasn't enough for women to take on traditionally male roles—men must be willing to take on traditionally female roles. Leon Weiseltier, the editor of *The New Republic*, said Ginsburg's idea of using male plaintiffs to show that discrimination against women hurts everyone was "the classical Jewish way of arguing against intolerance—that you argue against exceptions from fairness not in the name of the particular exception but in the name of the general principle."[196]

Because Stephen was challenging a federal law, the case

would begin in the federal district court in New Jersey. After the decision in *Frontiero*, it was clear to Ruth that she'd never get five justices on the court to vote for strict scrutiny, so she modified her request. Instead of asking for strict scrutiny, she went for what she thought she'd get—a heightened scrutiny, the intermediate scrutiny Gunther had identified in his law review article, something more than the anything-goes rational basis test, but not quite the strict scrutiny used in race-based distinctions.

For help with the research and preparation of the case, she relied on students in her Equal Rights Advocacy seminar at Columbia Law School. Students in her seminar were permitted to choose from any of the cases Ruth was working on. Sandra Grayson, a student who chose to work on Stephen Wiesenfeld's case, said that working alongside Ruth was like fighting an uphill battle that you might actually win. Another of Ruth's students, Mary Elizabeth Freeman, understood immediately the strength of the facts in this case:

> [T]o pick a man whose wife died in childbirth, something that doesn't happen a lot in the latter part of the twentieth century, with a BABY—a child in arms that has, as its only parent left, a father who wants to take care of his kid, WIDOWS AND ORPHANS—you can't get any better than that![197]

Students helped with drafting and filing all the necessary papers—the complaint, the application for a three-judge court, a motion for summary judgment, and a response to the government's motion for summary judgment. The routine was that the students drafted, and then Ruth revised and rewrote, occasionally adding one of her zingers, as the students called them. When she appeared in court, students sat with her at the counsel's table.

To help her prepare for oral argument, her students held a moot court, fully researching all arguments and issues. Later Ruth commented that the questions she got from students were much harder than the questions posed to her by the actual justices of the Supreme Court.

As they worked on the case, Ruth got to know Stephen on a personal level, and found they had much in common. Both considered themselves pioneers of a lifestyle considered alternate in the early 1970s in which the husband and wife defied gender stereotypes. Stephen wanted to be a homemaker and caretaker, but the law and personal tragedy were against him. Ruth even advised him about hiring babysitters and nannies, telling him that she herself had gone through plenty of helpers and housekeepers over the years, so she knew from experience that eventually the perfect person would come along. Once that happened, he'd be set for a few years. Stephen opened a bicycle shop, put a playpen for baby Jason in a corner, and sold Fuji bikes. That same month, the Arab nations announced an oil embargo. With fuel prices soaring, there was a sudden demand for bicycles, and Jason's business so thrived that he was in danger of earning too much money to qualify for Social Security, which could render his case moot. He didn't want Ruth to have done all that work for nothing, so instead of taking a profit, he reinvested the money into his business.

Ruth had high hopes that this was a case she could win and take all the way to the Supreme Court. Then she was dealt a setback. One day in autumn, as she and her students were preparing to try Stephen's case in the district court, she opened a legal newspaper, *Law Week*, and learned that the Supreme Court would be hearing a different case on sex discrimination.

The facts of the case were appalling—the plaintiff, Melvin Kahn, objected to a law giving a small property tax break to widows that wasn't available to him, as a widower. To make matters worse, it was obvious the lawyer representing Melvin Kahn was using the exact arguments she'd been developing and presenting to the Supreme Court.

It was not the kind of case likely to appeal to the sympathy of Supreme Court justices, who would view the matter as a man trying to take money designated for widows. Unlike Wiesenfeld's Social Security benefit, Kahn's property tax exemption had nothing to do with his wife's earnings or ability to provide for her family. A simple property tax benefit for widows would likely stir the chivalrous impulses of the justices. In the special treatment versus unequal treatment argument, the justices were likely to think that widows were entitled to special treatment. The entire tax code, in fact, made provisions for widows and orphans. Going after special help for widows and orphans would do nothing to help achieve equality, and would give plenty of fuel to Phyllis Schlafly and the others who would point out that the feminists were taking away protections for women.

In Ruth's view, a case like Kahn's might have had a chance further down the road, once they'd made more inroads with the court. Taking such a case now to the Supreme Court was potentially disastrous in that it could generate bad precedent. As every lawyer knows, bad facts make for bad law. This was the kind of thing that never happened to the NAACP in the 1930s, 1940s, and 1950s because the NAACP had been the only show in town. Anyone who wanted to bring such a suit had to come to them, which allowed them to pick and choose cases with strong, sympathetic facts. Besides, her favorite argument—that special protections offered a cage and not a pedestal—would not work with facts like these.

To make matters more annoying, when she contacted the Florida lawyer handling the case, Bill Hoppe, she learned he was working for the ACLU in Florida, bringing the case as an ACLU lawyer. One of the hard and fast rules of the ACLU was that before a local affiliate office could initiate a test case, it had to consult first with the national office. Bill Hoppe hadn't done that. During their phone conversation, he agreed to send her a copy of the jurisdictional statement he'd filed with the Supreme Court. Along with the statement, he sent her a request for help. In his cover letter, he explained that he had no idea what to write in the Supreme Court brief, so he was looking for advice. The jurisdictional statement he had presented to the court was so incompetently written that it was a wonder to both Mel and Ruth that the Supreme Court had agreed to hear the case.

Ruth agreed to take over the case to prevent a disaster in the form of a Supreme Court ruling that would set her way back. She hoped to find a way to argue the case without invoking equal protection so she wouldn't sully her strategy. There was just no way to do it, so she asked for a minimal remedy, asking the Supreme Court to declare the Florida statute unconstitutional only insofar as it created an impermissible gender distinction. She deliberately did not ask for a general rule about heightened scrutiny. All she wanted was for the Supreme Court to remand the case back to Florida to allow Floridians to figure out how to bring the statute in line with the equal protection clause. She hoped that Florida would extend the exemption to both widowers and widows. Given that there were so many more widows than widowers due to women living longer, it didn't seem like too much of a burden to enlarge the class of people entitled to the exemption.

Two months before oral argument was scheduled in Melvin Kahn's widower tax exemption case, the federal district court in New Jersey handed Ruth a stunning victory for Stephen Wiesenfeld. The court not only ruled in Stephen's favor, finding that he was entitled to Social Security so he could raise his son Jason, but also went beyond the precedent set by *Frontiero v. Richardson* and found that sex was an inherently suspect category requiring heightened scrutiny.[198] Given the conservative composition of the New Jersey court, Ruth considered the unanimous victory nothing short of miraculous.

Robert Bork, who was then solicitor general, notified the Supreme Court that his office would be challenging the district court's ruling. Because the U.S. government was the defendant, it was entitled to appeal directly to the Supreme Court.

On February 25, 1974, Ruth stood before the justices of the U.S. Supreme Court to argue for Melvin Kahn's widower tax exemption. This time, the justices didn't sit quietly as she spoke. They interrupted her repeatedly, trying to clarify what she was asking for and why. Their main surprise seemed to be that, unlike her last appearance, she was not asking them to regard sex as a suspect classification. Now she made no pleas for the oppressors to remove their feet from the necks of women. Instead, she talked about why the Florida statute, dating from 1885, was rooted in Victorian stereotypes and should be found unconstitutional.

This time the Supreme Court ruled against her, holding that widows deserved their pedestal. There no question, the court said, that widows were more vulnerable financially than widowers.[199] Whether from overt discrimination or the socialization of a male-dominated society, an elderly woman had much less chance of finding employment of any kind.

There was a rational basis, therefore, for the distinction between widows and widowers in the Florida tax code.

There were two bright spots. First, three of the justices dissented. Justice Brennan and Marshall, admittedly two of the more liberal justices, felt it would have been a simple matter for the Florida legislature to bring the statute in line with gender equality, perhaps simply by requiring that the widows show some need before receiving the exception and allowing widowers with need to apply. Justice White also dissented, writing separately to say he found the stereotype that all widows were needier than all widowers to be not based in fact. He therefore found the discrimination was invidious and violated the equal protection clause.

The second bright spot was that there was no mention of suspect classifications anywhere in the majority opinion, which meant that the court had not ruled out the possibility of requiring heightened scrutiny in sex-based discrimination cases. Meanwhile, four of the justices were firmly on her side. She needed only to bring one more around. She had high hopes that Stephen Wiesenfeld's far more sympathetic case would do the trick.

About this time, Ruth switched from the common phrase "sex discrimination" to "gender discrimination." She owed the switch to her secretary at the Columbia Law School, the astute Milicent Tryon. "I'm typing all these briefs and articles for you and the word sex, sex, sex is on every page," Milicent informed her. "Don't you know that those nine men hear that word and their first association is not the way you want them to be thinking?"[200] Millicent suggested that Ruth use the word gender instead, and Ruth thought the idea was a good one.

17

THE DOUBLE-
EDGED SWORD

Initially, many feminists found it hard to take Phyllis Schlafly seriously. Surely, they thought, women didn't really want to go back to the days when the wife was expected to obey her husband. Surely 1970s women didn't want to give up a separate legal identity. Some feminists even collected copies of Schlafly's newsletter for their comic value. Then they realized Phyllis Schlafly's pro-family STOP ERA movement was catching on. Suddenly, states stopped ratifying the amendment. Thirty-five states had already ratified the amendment, but thirty-eight were needed—so they were short three. The fifteen that hadn't approved the amendment were mostly, but not entirely, in the South: Alabama, Arizona, Arkansas, Florida, Georgia, Illinois, Louisiana, Mississippi, Missouri, Nevada, North Carolina, Oklahoma, South Carolina, Utah, and Virginia. When Illinois changed its rules, requiring a three-fifths majority, the chance of Illinois becoming the thirty-sixth state grew dim.

Proponents of the ERA worked to obtain an extension of the initial ratification deadline. Ruth testified before both chambers of Congress in support of the extension, arguing that

Phyllis Schlafly, 1977.

Congress had authority to extend the deadline and explaining the need to do so. Meanwhile, the National Organization of Women coordinated a successful march of one hundred thousand supporters in Washington, DC. Congress agreed to grant an extension until 1982, which gave women's rights groups three years to persuade three more states to join.

Ruth, through speaking engagements and articles, tried to convince skeptics that the Equal Rights Amendment did nothing except prohibit the government from allocating rights, responsibilities, and opportunities solely on the basis of gender. In speeches, she encouraged her audiences to think outside of what she viewed as narrow sex-role stereotypes. "The idea of equality is so basic to democracy that no fair-minded person can reject it," she told an audience in Grand Rapids, Michigan.[201] She talked about how equal rights opened opportunities to women and allowed them to fully participate in all aspects of civil society. The local newspaper, though, summarized her speech under the headline "Equal Rights May Be Painful."[202]

Ruth had always been irked by the Supreme Court's 1961 ruling in *Hoyt v. Florida*, a case that for her perfectly illustrated how being placed on a pedestal prevented women from becoming equal participants in public life.[203] Gwendolyn Hoyt was brought to trial for the murder of her husband. Her defense was that her abusive and philandering husband had beaten and humiliated her to the breaking point. During a fight, described by the court as an "upheaval," she picked up a baseball bat, hit him with it, and caused his death.

She was convicted, and appealed on the grounds that the jurors were all men, and hence she had been denied a jury of her peers who might have been more sympathetic to her state of mind. While she never expected to be acquitted, she believed that a more sympathetic jury might have convicted her of the lesser offense of manslaughter—and she thought women would be more receptive to the battered-woman defense. The law in Florida required that men serve on juries, but made jury service for women optional. Men were automatically listed in the rolls; women had to volunteer. Not surprisingly, not many women volunteered. Hoyt argued that Florida's law resulted in the exclusion of women from jury service because most women, like most men, will avoid jury service unless compelled.

Hoyt's case went all the way to the U.S. Supreme Court, where the justices simply didn't understand how women could complain about Florida's jury laws. It seemed to the court that women had the best of all possible worlds. If they wanted to be on juries they could—nobody was excluding them—but they didn't have to if they didn't want to. The court upheld Florida's jury laws, finding that the distinction between how men and women were treated had a rational basis. According to the court,

> Despite the enlightened emancipation of women from the restrictions and protections of bygone years, and their entry into many parts of community life formerly considered to be reserved to men, woman is still regarded as the center of home and family life.

The Court's rationale—that the primary duty of a woman was to home and family—struck Ruth as the ultimate in romantic paternalism. The fact that the decision was issued in 1961 instead of 1861 was particularly irritating. The result of this ruling was that well into the twentieth century, it was commonplace throughout the country for juries to consist mostly—or even entirely—of men.

Ruth was grateful, therefore, when she had the opportunity to argue a jury case at the U.S. Supreme Court with a view to undoing some of the damage done by *Hoyt v. Florida*. Her case, *Edwards v. Healy*, was a challenge to a Louisiana statute that exempted women from jury duty unless they filed a written declaration of their desire to serve.[204] The result of the Louisiana statute was that very few women served on juries, thereby resulting in most juries consisting only of men.

The challenge to the Louisiana jury composition statute

was brought by a Louisiana citizen, Marsha Healy, and was first heard in a federal district court in the Eastern District of Louisiana. The district court found that given recent advances in the law concerning women, *Hoyt v. Florida* was no longer binding precedent. The court also found that the Louisiana jury composition procedures constituted a denial of due process under the Fourteenth Amendment. The U.S. Court of Appeals for the Fifth Circuit agreed with the lower court and affirmed the decision, ruling that the Supreme Court had been wrong in its 1961 ruling in *Hoyt v. Florida.*

The attorney of the State of Louisiana and the Louisiana governor appealed the decision to the Supreme Court. The task fell to Ruth to defend the lower court's ruling.

On April 20, 1974, after the briefs were filed, but before oral argument could be held, the State of Louisiana adopted a new constitution and new statutory provisions for jury selection. Article V, Section 33(a) of the new constitution of Louisiana required all citizens to serve on juries regardless of gender, leaving exemptions to the Louisiana Supreme Court. The new constitution was scheduled to go into effect on January 1, 1975. At the time of oral argument, Louisiana was able to produce a draft of an order thus calling women to jury duty. The government of Louisiana filed a supplemental brief reflecting the changes and asking for the case to be dismissed as moot.

During oral argument Ruth tried to persuade the justices that the new constitution did not render the issue moot for two reasons. First, the new constitution would not go into effect until January 1, 1975. Second, even after going into effect, the new constitution permitted exemptions for women. There was, she argued, nothing in the wording of the new constitution to prevent Louisiana courts from continuing the policy of not putting women on the lists unless they registered.

Several of the justices, particularly Justice Stewart, were obviously prickly about being told that *Hoyt* had been wrongly decided. After mentioning that *Hoyt* had been decided only thirteen years earlier, Justice Stewart accused Ruth of being cavalier in dismissing the justifications for *Hoyt*. Ruth's response was the soul of tact. She gave two reasons for why she "did not tend to be cavalier."[205] First, she was showing that the Louisiana jury procedures differed from the procedures deemed constitutional in *Hoyt v. Florida*. In *Hoyt*, the court was unable to say that Florida failed to make an effort to have women perform jury duties, whereas it was undisputed that the Louisiana system produces jury lists that rarely include women. With the Louisiana statute now being challenged, there was evidence that women were largely absent from juries as a result of the statute. Also, the thirteen years had shown a remarkable growth in women in the job market so that the rationale that women needed to be excused from jury duty because of responsibilities to their home and children was no longer based in fact.

At the end of her oral argument, Chief Justice Burger gave her a compliment. "I'm not sure you need any defense, Mrs. Ginsburg," he said, "but your brief and argument are much less cavalier toward *Hoyt* than the three judges of the Fifth Circuit."[206]

Three months later, on January 20, 1975, the Supreme Court had still not issued a decision in the Louisiana jury composition statute and the time had come to argue Stephen Wiesenfeld's Social Security childcare benefits case before the Supreme Court.

In oral argument, the government went first, and argued that the Social Security statute giving benefits to widowed mothers but not widower fathers was intended to ameliorate the harsh economic consequences of systemic job discrimination against women, citing *Kahn v. Shevin* as precedent for the notion that widows were more vulnerable and thus entitled to extra protection. The government's position was that the power to allocate welfare funds was squarely within Congress's constitutional power, and that the lower court had erred by applying a strict scrutiny test when rational basis was the proper test. "Sex-based classifications we believe do not merit close judicial scrutiny," Keith Jones told the court.[207]

Then it was time for Ruth to take her place at the lectern and address the court. She wore a red suit, and as always when she appeared before the Supreme Court, she wore her mother's earrings and pin. Directly behind her, at the counsel's table, was Stephen Wiesenfeld. By now the nine justices were familiar with the lawyer they called Mrs. Ginsburg. Observers in the court noticed that when it came time for Ruth to speak, the justices sat up, leaned forward, and listened intently and respectfully. Often during oral arguments they appeared bored and irritated— but never with Ruth. Lynn Hecht Schafran, a lawyer with the National Organization of Women's Legal Defense Fund, thought the respect for her was because "There was no tinge of that dreaded word always laid on women: emotional."[208]

Ruth's argument on behalf of Stephen and his child, Jason, was simple and moving: The Social Security regulation denying Stephen widower benefits was based on outdated gender stereotypes that denied Jason's mother the ability to be able to work to provide for her family. It denied Jason's father the ability to care for his child. Finally it denied a motherless child the opportunity to be cared for by its only surviving parent.

Wendy Williams, a young California lawyer, had come all the way from California to hear the argument, a trip she later said was well worth it. She herself was working on women's rights litigation. The moment Ruth talked about the threefold discrimination, she knew Ruth would win the case. Wendy Williams wasn't the only person impressed. Penny Clark, clerk to Justice Powell, said Ruth's arguments were the best she'd heard during the entire term she clerked in the Supreme Court. Penny described Ruth as "extremely articulate, very self-possessed, not a hint of nervousness or uncertainty, she stated her case very clearly and made persuasive arguments."[209]

Ruth was in her car two months later, on March 19, 1975, listening to the radio on her way to Columbia, when she learned from a news broadcast that she'd won Stephen Wiesenfeld's case. "My first reaction was that I have to get hold of myself or I'll have an accident," she said.[210] She pulled over, found a pay phone, and called Stephen to give him the news. He had heard the news moments before when a neighbor called him after hearing the announcement on the radio. Later he said Ruth sounded so ecstatic she was actually rambling. When Ruth arrived at Columbia, she ran through the halls, kissing the students who had worked with her on the case. At one point, she found herself in tears.

When she read the Court's decision, she learned that her triumph was complete. The Court, in crafting its ruling, settled on an intermediate level of scrutiny for gender-based distinctions without actually calling it that. In fact, the Court made no mention of the standard of review it was using, but for the first time, the Court abandoned a rigid two-tiered approach to the equal protection clause, allowing for heightened scrutiny for gender distinctions. The Court laid down the rule "For a gender-based statute to pass constitutional muster, it had to bear a substantial relationship to an important government objective"—this was definitely heightened scrutiny.[211] No more lowly anything-goes rational basis tests for laws that discriminated on the basis of gender.

The real triumph was that this time, the ruling was unanimous: Six justices joined the majority opinion, and Justice Rehnquist, the lone dissenter in *Reed v. Reed*, wrote a concurring opinion. The question was, how had that happened? What had led Rehnquist to concur instead of dissent? The answer, apparently, was that baby Jason got to him. He'd also been persuaded by some research done by a female law clerk to Justice Brennan, Marsha Berzon, who had followed a clue dropped into one of Ruth's footnotes in the brief and discovered that Congress had written the Social Security widow benefit regulation not to aid wives whose husbands had died but to aid children whose parents had died. It was hard to deny equal protection to babies. Incidentally, Marsha Berzon very nearly didn't get the clerkship because she was a woman. When her mentors at UC Berkeley recommended her to Justice Brennan, he rejected her out of hand, saying, "Send me your best male candidate."[212] But the Berkeley professors persisted, and got their way, and Marsha Berzon—who later became a federal appeals judge on the Ninth Circuit Court of Appeals—was on hand to help sway the justices of the U.S. Supreme Court in favor of Stephen Wiesenfeld.

There was another less tangible element that, for Ruth, explained her victory in the Wiesenfeld case. Supreme Court justices are also citizens who read the newspaper, just like anyone else. They cannot help but be influenced by what they see happening, so they knew that recent years had brought a sea change in the way women were regarded in society, a change brought about by the infiltration of women into the workforce. Ruth understood there was a cycle at work. Once women could control when and whether they had children, they could enter the workforce and demand equal pay. This, in turn, encouraged families to reallocate domestic duties, which could give rise to a father like Stephen, who wanted to raise his own child.

Ruth and Marty had a party in their home to celebrate the victory, inviting Stephen, Jason, and all the students who had worked on the case. Ruth's son, James, greeted Jason with gifts and toys.

Stephen eventually moved to Florida, where he raised Jason and lived on the Social Security benefits Ruth had secured for him. In time, his at-home start-up business venture became so profitable he was no longer eligible for benefits. Ruth and Stephen kept in touch, so she knew when Jason was a college student planning to go to law school. In 1998, Jason graduated from Columbia Law School. Ruth was by then U.S. Supreme Court Justice Ginsburg. Shortly after graduation, Jason asked Ruth to perform his wedding ceremony, which she did. Ruth met Stephen again in 2014 when Stephen was seventy-one years old, and ready once more to be a bridegroom. He married Elaine Harris in front of family and friends—and Ruth performed the ceremony.

18

THE PREGNANCY
PROBLEM

Sally Armendariz was a native of Gilroy, California, a rural farm community in the southernmost corner of Santa Clara County. The daughter of Mexican American farmworkers, she was eager to escape the brutal work of picking in the fields. In 1962, shortly after becoming the first girl in her family to graduate from high school, she took a job as secretary for the Gilroy office of the California Rural Legal Assistance, a program designed to end exploitation of California's farmworkers. Ten years later, she was married with an eight-month-old infant and pregnant with her second child. Her husband had recently become unemployed, so she was the family's sole breadwinner. One afternoon while she was driving along the fields in Gilroy, another driver hit her car in the rear. She felt too sick to work that afternoon after the accident, so her doctor told her to go home. That night, she went into labor. Early the next morning, she lost the child in a miscarriage. She was in such severe pain that she could not stand up. The doctor said it would be weeks before she would be able to return to work.

A small part of her paycheck each week during the ten years

Garlic fields in Gilroy, California.

she'd been working had gone to California's State Disability Insurance program, so she applied for disability benefits to cover the weeks she would be out of work. She was refused benefits on the grounds that pregnancy was not covered as a disability. The insurance company informed her that even though a car accident had triggered her miscarriage, the complications were due entirely to her pregnancy, which meant she was not eligible for benefits. The plan covered all other forms of disability, including elective cosmetic surgery—everything, in fact, except pregnancy.

She found a lawyer, Wendy Williams, the young lawyer who drove from California to listen to Ruth's oral argument in the Wiesenfeld case. Wendy was a recent graduate of the University of California at Berkeley, Berkeley School of Law. She was a fellow in poverty law at the San Mateo Legal Aid, and co-founder of the Equal Rights Advocates in San Francisco. Wendy took Sally's case to the district court. She argued that California's disability insurance program was unconstitutional, denying women equal protection by singling out pregnancy for exclusion.

Wendy lost in the district court. The court said that insurance carriers, even those maintained by the state, had the right to choose which disabilities they would include and which they would not.

In the early 1970s, it was perfectly legal to fire a woman the moment she became pregnant. This meant she lost whatever seniority she had built up and, when she returned to the workforce, often had to start all over, looking for a new job and trying to rebuild her career. While Title VII of the Civil Rights Act of 1964 protected a woman from discrimination at work, employers were still permitted to pay different wages based on seniority and merit, so the fact that women's employment history was so often interrupted allowed employers to pay women less under merit plans. By some calculations, the ability to fire women whenever they became pregnant saved companies $140 billion each year in wages and allowed employers to keep women as a cheap, transient labor force.[213] It seemed obvious to Sally's lawyer that pregnancy discrimination was identical to sex discrimination because of the simple fact that only women became pregnant.

Unfortunately, the U.S. Supreme Court didn't see it that way.

On March 26, 1975, Wendy Williams brought Sally's case to the Supreme Court, consolidated with a similar pregnancy case involving Carolyn Aiello, a woman who was forced out of work by an ectopic pregnancy. Ruth, on behalf of the Women's Rights Project, coauthored an amicus brief on behalf of the women, arguing that laws discriminating on the basis of pregnancy are gender-based distinctions that should be evaluated under heightened scrutiny.

In a 6-3 decision entitled *Geduldig v. Aiello*, the Supreme Court ruled against the women, upholding the right of California to exclude pregnancy complications on the grounds that California could constitutionally choose which disabilities to cover.[214] It made sense to the court that the plan would want to exclude pregnancy benefits on the grounds that covering pregnancy would be too expensive and would threaten the solvency of the fund. The Court also held that discriminating on the basis of pregnancy was not sex discrimination, offering the curious logic that the plan didn't distinguish between men and women—it distinguished between pregnant and non-pregnant people, and while the first group was entirely female, the second group contained both men and women. The Court then reasoned that the second group, which contained both men and women, benefited from the ability of the fund to discriminate against pregnancy on the grounds that costs were kept low.

From the viewpoint of a women's rights advocate, there were so many things wrong with that decision it was hard to know where to begin. If a woman had a husband who was able to work and support her through her pregnancy, being fired the moment she became pregnant would not necessarily consign her to poverty. But a single woman, or a woman who was the sole breadwinner, would find herself suddenly without an income—and an infant on the way.

Three justices—Brennan, Marshall, and Douglas—the three who had been won over by Ruth's arguments in *Reed* and *Frontiero*, dissented on the grounds that complications from pregnancy affected only women, and therefore the regulation discriminating between pregnant and non-pregnant people turned on an invidious gender stereotype and was entitled to a heightened scrutiny.

Meanwhile, another pregnancy case was making its way through the courts—a case with a better chance of succeeding in the

U.S. Supreme Court because it involved employee benefits instead of a state-funded insurance plan. Employee benefits fell under Title VII, which outlawed employment discrimination based on gender, so the lawyers would not have to make a constitutional equal protection argument. Instead, the argument was one of statutory interpretation: Title VII forbids gender discrimination, and pregnancy discrimination was the same as gender discrimination because only women became pregnant; therefore, pregnancy discrimination was unlawful under Title VII.

The case that came to be called *General Electric v. Gilbert* began when women workers at General Electric in Salem, Virginia, wondered why their company disability plan refused to cover workers whose disabilities resulted from childbirth or pregnancy when every other type of disability was covered, including vasectomies and elective plastic surgery.

General Electric not only failed to cover disabilities arising from pregnancy but also forced all pregnant women to take three months unpaid leave from work, even if they felt well enough to continue working. Disability coverage was entirely suspended while women were out on maternity leave, even for issues unrelated to pregnancy. Emma Furch, for example, missed work because of her miscarriage. While she was out of work, she had a pulmonary embolism. Her doctor certified that the embolism had nothing to do with her pregnancy, and General Electric accepted this. But when it came time to pay her disability, General Electric pointed to fine print in the plan that said if the woman was out due to pregnancy, her disability benefits were discontinued until after she returned; therefore, the pulmonary embolism was not covered. General Electric admitted that if a man was away from work for an automobile accident, or even a vacation, he would be covered for any health conditions that arose during his leave from work. Only pregnancy was treated in this manner.

According to the facts alleged on behalf of the women, two-thirds of the women employed by General Electric were working because of financial necessity and had no alternate forms of income, so being denied employment benefits related to pregnancy caused serious financial difficulty. One of the women bringing the suit, Cheryl Steam, had been unable to afford her electric bill once she was out on maternity leave, so she awaited the birth of her child in an unheated, unlighted house with no refrigeration.

The lead attorney in this case was Ruth Weyand, who had earned her law degree from the University of Chicago in 1932 and had devoted her professional life to fighting for women's rights. Ruth Ginsburg, through the Women's Rights Project, coauthored an amicus brief in support of the women of General Electric.

Before *General Electric v. Gilbert* could be argued at the U.S. Supreme Court, the court heard a third pregnancy case, *Mary Ann Turner v. Department of Employment*.[215] Turner challenged a Utah law that made pregnant women ineligible for unemployment benefits for a period of twelve weeks before the expected date of childbirth, lasting until six weeks after childbirth. Ruth submitted an amicus brief for this case, too.

In what many took as a good sign, the Supreme Court ruled in favor of Mary Ann Turner, holding that the Utah statute violated the Fourteenth Amendment because the statute presumed, wrongly, that women were unable to work during this period when in fact, the ability of any particular pregnant woman to work past a fixed time was an individual matter. The Supreme Court did not go so far as to hold that pregnancy discrimination was sex discrimination. The Court merely found that the Utah statute was overly broad, and therefore unconstitutional.

The stage was set for Ruth Weyand to present the case of the women of General Electric to the Supreme Court. The chance of a victory looked particularly good when the Equal Opportunity Commission, a federal agency, took the position that pregnancy discrimination was sex discrimination. Moreover, General Electric's policy, which dated from 1925, appeared to be, on its face, in conflict with Title VII, particularly because the company's reason for excluding pregnant women from coverage was that women who became pregnant "did not understand the responsibilities of life, they just got married and had children."[216]

The Supreme Court ruled in favor of General Electric.[217] The Court held that, while Title VII certainly forbid sex discrimination, Congress never intended to put a stop to the common and widely accepted practice of firing women when they became pregnant. Therefore, companies had the right to fire women on the basis of pregnancy, or simply refuse to offer medical benefits while they were away from their job.

The *New York Times* called the ruling "a major blow," to the women's rights movement, and Ruth Bader Ginsburg agreed.[218] She picked up her pen and coauthored a *New York Times* op-ed piece making clear how she felt about the Supreme Court's ruling:

> A company provides income-replacement benefits to all temporarily disabled employees for all disabilities that both men and women incur, such as lung cancer, alcoholism, and skiing injuries, and all disabilities that only men incur, such as

prostatectomies. There is one exception: Disabilities arising from pregnancy or childbirth.

Is that exclusion sex discrimination? Not at all, ruled the Supreme Court on Dec. 7, 1976, interpreting the Federal law prohibiting job discrimination.[219]

Allowing women to lose their jobs and their benefits any time they became pregnant—for Ruth—simply reinforced the traditional stereotypes that women belonged in the home. The question was how to reconcile the Supreme Court's seemingly contradictory rulings. While the court had ruled in favor of Mary Ann Turner, who wanted to return to work immediately after giving birth but wasn't allowed to return for four months, the court upheld the right of companies to fire women any time they became pregnant. Ruth thought she understood the court's logic. The Court had sympathy for a woman who wanted to return to work immediately after giving birth, but the very notion of pregnancy as a disability stirred up their feelings of romantic paternalism, causing them to wonder: Was she *really* sick, or was she just malingering so she could be home with the baby, where she belonged?

Other prominent women's leaders also denounced the court's decision. Betty Friedan called the ruling the "worst of all the decisions from the Nixon-Ford Court."[220] Karen DeCrow, president of the National Organization for Women, called the decision a "slap in the face to motherhood."[221] Others pointed out the absurdity of paying for vasectomies and nose jobs, but refusing to cover pregnancy.

Women's groups immediately came together to decide how to proceed. One of Ruth's staff attorneys at the Women's Rights Project joined with Ruth Weyand to form a coalition to help draft legislation to protect pregnant women from unemployment. The first meeting was co-sponsored by the ACLU and the Pennsylvania Commission for Women. Two congresswomen and one senator attended the first meeting: Elizabeth Holtzman of Brooklyn, Bella Abzug of Manhattan, and Senator Birch Bayh of Indiana.

The coalition worked quickly. Three months after the Supreme Court handed down its decision in *General Electric v. Gilbert*, Senator Harrison Williams, a Democrat from New Jersey, introduced the Pregnancy Discrimination Act, an amendment to Title VII, which read:

> Employers with 15 or more employees (including part-time and temporary employees) cannot fire, refuse to hire, or deny a promotion to an employee on the basis of pregnancy, childbirth or related medical conditions.

> Employers must treat pregnant workers the same way they treat workers with other temporary illnesses, disabilities and medical conditions. This applies to all employment policies, including benefit programs.

With bipartisan support, Carter signed the amendment into law on October 31, 1978.

The term "barefoot and pregnant" has long been associated with the idea that women should remain in the home caring for children during their childbearing years. In the 1970s, the National Organization for Women began offering annual Barefoot and Pregnant awards to "persons in the community

Carter signs the Pregnancy Discrimination Act into law.

who have done the most to perpetuate outmoded images of women and who have refused to recognize that women are, in fact, human beings."[222] Among the award recipients were the Veterans of Foreign Wars for its repeated refusal to admit qualified women on the grounds that they wanted to "keep this a fighting man's outfit,"[223] and Republican state senator Henry Sayler for reneging on campaign promises to back the Equal Rights Amendment.

19

DISCRIMINATING
AGAINST MEN

On the theory that young women were more responsible than young men, the state of Oklahoma passed a law allowing women over the age of eighteen to buy 3.2 percent beer—a light, low-alcohol content beer—but not allowing young men to buy the beer until they were twenty-one. In support of the law, the Oklahoma legislature provided statistics showing that 427 young men had been arrested for driving drunk in 1974, as opposed to 24 women.

Mark Walker and Curtis Craig, fraternity men under the age of twenty-one, didn't like the law. Neither did Carolyn Whitener, a liquor store owner in Stillwater, Oklahoma, who wanted to be able to sell them beer. So all three challenged the law, claiming that it violated the equal protection clause of the Fourteenth Amendment by discriminating against young men.

The store owner and young male plaintiffs lost in the Tenth Circuit Court of Appeals when a three-judge panel ruled unanimously that the state had made a rational legislative judgment in determining that young men were more likely to get into trouble from drinking than young women.

When the Supreme Court accepted the case on review, the

lower court lawyer, Frederick Gilbert, invited Ruth to write a supporting ACLU brief. She agreed to write an amicus brief, but tried hard to persuade Gilbert to let her write his opening brief as well. She even tried to get him to allow her to argue the case for him. He resisted, but he took so many of her suggestions that she got everything she wanted into his brief. She was particularly interested in the fact that the lower court had upheld the statute after applying the rational basis test, so she wanted him to specifically ask the Supreme Court to clarify that the test should have been heightened scrutiny.

At the same time, she had another case ready to go to the Supreme Court, a follow-up to her victory in Stephen Wiesenfeld's Social Security challenge. This client, Leon Goldfarb, was a childless widower challenging a Social Security regulation that required a widower to prove he had been dependent on his wife's income to qualify for benefits, whereas a widow was automatically entitled to benefits upon the death of her husband. As Ruth put it, the case was basically "Wiesenfeld minus the baby."[224]

Ruth won Leon Goldfarb's case in the district court, where a three-judge panel held that treating widows and widowers differently constituted an invidious discrimination against female wage earners by denying them the ability to provide benefits for their spouses. The government brought the case to the Supreme Court, with argument to be held on October 5, 1976—the same day oral argument was scheduled for the beer-buying case. Ruth arranged for Frederick Gilbert to argue his case in the morning, while she argued hers in the afternoon.

During oral arguments for the beer case, the justices spent some time questioning whether 3.2 percent beer could actually intoxicate someone. They agreed that it was difficult but not impossible to actually get drunk on 3.2 percent beer. They also talked about the fact that the young men had by now turned twenty-one, which perhaps mooted the case. Gilbert pointed out that given the length of time that cases drag out, rendering this case moot would make it difficult for anyone to challenge the law. The substantive part of Gilbert's argument was that the law was based on stereotypes that didn't always hold. There were reckless young women and responsible young men.

After a break for lunch, it was time for Ruth's Social Security benefits case. The government went first, and argued that Goldfarb was just another greedy widower looking for a windfall when everyone knew widows, in general, were needier. He pointed to *Kahn v. Slevin* as controlling precedent—the case of the widower from Florida who claimed that he was entitled to the widow property tax benefit.

When it was Ruth's turn and she stood at the lectern, facing the justices, Justice Stewart seemed genuinely confused about the fact that both of that day's equal rights cases featured male plaintiffs. He'd read her amicus brief in the beer case and he just didn't get it. The tone of his questioning hinted at what he was wondering: Wasn't she supposed to be a champion of *women's* rights? What was up with all these male plaintiffs? She was spinning the Goldfarb case as discrimination against the female wage earner who was unable to provide Social Security benefits to her family despite paying into the system, but the case just as easily could be seen as a greedy widower trying to cut into funds for needy widows. He asked Ruth whether the constitutional argument would be different if the wage earner was a male and the beneficiary was female. He addressed her as "Mrs. Bader." She quickly corrected him with "Ginsburg." She then responded to his question by telling him that *every* gender discrimination was a two-edged sword and hence harmful to both men and women.

Justice Stewart explained that he was asking because the tendency of courts was to try to compensate for past discrimination. If Leon Goldfarb's case was actually an anti-male discrimination case—a widower looking for a windfall—wouldn't he be rather undeserving in light of the fact that men have never faced anti-male discrimination?

She said no, her argument would be the same if the wage earner was a man because she didn't know of any purely anti-male discrimination. "In the end," she said, "the women are the ones who end up hurting."[225]

Justice Stevens jumped in to clarify the question:

> Can I interrupt you just to be sure to understand your position in response to Justice Stewart. Is it your view that there is no discrimination against males?[226]

"There *is* discrimination against males," she responded.[227]

Justice Stevens then wanted to know if discrimination against males was to be tested by a different standard than discrimination against females. Again she said that every discrimination against males operated against women as well, so the standards should be the same. Her view, quite simply, was that gender discrimination hurt everyone. Justice Stevens then brought up the beer-buying case from that morning, saying,

> But we heard a case this morning involving a law that would not permit males to make certain purchases that females could make. It was attacked as a discrimination against males. My question is whether we should examine that law under the same or different standard than if it were a discrimination

against the other sex?[228]

To which Ruth replied no, because even the beer-buying law had an invidious impact on women because it was based on gender stereotypes—in this case the stereotype that young women were more responsible than men—and stereotypes always ended up hurting women.

Justice Stevens came right out and asked Ruth if she thought the Supreme Court had decided *Kahn v. Shevin* wrongly—an interesting question given that the court had ruled against her. The question was asked respectfully, though—he honestly wanted to know what she thought. Tactfully, she said that allowing for a small property tax break for widows wasn't likely to significantly perpetuate gender stereotypes in the way favoring the male wage earner in Social Security benefits would. She explained that the law Goldfarb was challenging could harm women. By making it easier for a widow to draw Social Security against a spouse's earnings than for a widower encouraged men to remain the primary breadwinners, thus perpetuating the traditional roles by discouraging couples from breaking out of gender pigeonholing.

Justice Stevens probed a little farther. "Mrs. Ginsburg," he said, "really it was not too clear whether you thought we decided that case wrongly, or what your view is." Again, she sidestepped the question. Instead of answering directly, she again distinguished the cases, telling the justices that the critical difference was that the ruling in *Kahn v. Shevin* didn't do much harm, whereas upholding the statute requiring men to prove that they were dependent on their wives would do a considerable amount of harm by perpetuating invidious stereotypes.

Later a colleague asked her why she had twice avoided answering Justice Stevens's question. She said, "Because if I had answered him, my answer might have lost Justice Powell's vote, and if I didn't answer Stevens, I was going to get his vote anyway."[229]

The Supreme Court handed Ruth a victory in Leon Goldfarb's widower benefits case and the young men a victory in Oklahoma's beer-buying case.

In the widower benefits case, styled *Califano v. Goldfarb*,[230] the Supreme Court found that Leon Goldfarb's situation was indistinguishable from *Weinberger v. Wiesenfeld*, in which the court had invalidated a similar statute. The Court rejected the government's stereotyped generalization that the husband was more likely to be the breadwinner, holding that old-fashioned notions of gender roles were insufficient to justify different treatment of widows and widowers—exactly the ruling Ruth had been after. She won by a mere 5-4, but she still won. Rehnquist and three other justices dissented—Blackmun, Stewart, and Burger. The dissenters wanted to follow the precedent in *Kahn v. Slevin* and uphold the statute. Apparently *Wiesenfeld* without the baby just didn't do it for them.

The real victory came in the beer-drinking fraternity brothers case, when for the first time, the Supreme Court acknowledged that it was using an intermediate-level test, or a heightened scrutiny, to evaluate laws that distinguished based on gender.[231] The term "intermediate scrutiny," was slipped in, ironically enough, in Justice Rehnquist's dissent when he criticized the Court for applying a stricter intermediate standard. Later Ruth quipped that the Supreme Court might have selected a less frothy case for announcing its new standard.

Ruth followed up these Supreme Court wins by having her staff at the Women's Rights Project compile a list of all state statutes with gender classifications rendered unconstitutional by these two decisions. She sent the list with instructions on follow-up litigation and legislative lobbying suggestions to ACLU affiliates nationwide. Kathleen Willert Peratis, with the Women's Rights Project, wrote to James Cardwell, an administrator at the Social Security Administration, demanding that the Social Security benefits due to husbands on their wives' accounts under *Goldfarb* be paid retroactively.

About this time, Marty decided he'd had enough of the high-stakes, high-pressure world of Wall Street tax lawyering. He was, by then, hailed as one of New York's top tax lawyers, counting among his clients such influential business figures as Ross Perot. Marty had no trouble getting teaching offers. During the spring semester in 1977, when Ruth was invited to be a resident fellow for a term at Stanford's Center for Advanced Study, he took a visiting position teaching in the Stanford Law School so the family could be together in California. He found teaching to his liking, and after they returned to New York, he was named to the newly created Charles Keller Beekman professorship at Columbia, making husband and wife law faculty colleagues.

That year, their daughter Jane graduated Phi Beta Kappa from the University of Chicago. She remained at the university for one more school year to complete a master's degree. The following fall, she enrolled at Harvard Law School. There were one hundred women in her class, making up about 30 percent of all law students. During the spring semester of Jane's first year at Harvard, Ruth was invited to give the keynote speech at a law school celebration. After observing how many women were enrolled, Ruth rather impishly told her audience, "I understand some of the men came to the Harvard Law School these days because—what better place to find a suitable woman?"[232]

20

TOKENS
WON'T DO

On a clear winter day in 1978, Carol Meyer, Columbia professor of social work, was surprised to receive an invitation from Ruth Bader Ginsburg for tea at the home of Madame Wu, a renowned chemistry professor and Nobel laureate. She arrived at Professor Wu's stunning apartment overlooking the Hudson River to find that all eleven senior female Columbia professors had been invited. She felt shy and awkward. "Women meeting together," she wondered. "Was this to be a cell meeting of some kind?"[233] Her impression of Ruth was that she was petite, gracious, and witty as she greeted the guests.

Carol soon learned why they had been called together. They were there to discuss the fact that female professors at Columbia were paid less through the university pension system than male professors. Ruth also suspected that many of the female professors were paid less than male professors, particularly those who had been with the university since before the enactment of the Equal Pay Act. Ruth wanted to bring a class action lawsuit demanding that women receive equal pay and pension benefits.

Carol Meyer had been through the turmoil of the 1960s and 1970s, and even though her "head was awhirl with the changes that had taken place," she never understood what it meant to be a feminist until she sat in that meeting, listening as Ruth spoke "so quietly, so competently, and so radically about fairness and action."[234] Carol silently speculated that the other professors who attended the tea were in various stages of awareness of their own oppressed status. For Carol, the meeting was an epiphany. Ruth taught her how simple it would be to fight for justice: Recognize the problem, learn about it, make a plan, and help others become engaged.

So the women organized. They contacted all the retired female professors and others with a vested interest in the lawsuit. They met several times in cafeterias on the Columbia campus. "Whenever Ginsburg appeared," Carol said, "the room suddenly grew quiet, for despite her slight figure and the quaint, almost demure look she affected in wearing her hair bow, she was the kind of person who stilled a room when she entered it."[235]

When eventually the women learned what their male counterparts were earning, their suspicions were proven right. Ruth was paid as well as her male peers because she made sure of it when hired, but the inequities had never been addressed for the women who started work at Columbia before the Equal Pay Act. The Women's Rights Project at the ACLU challenged the unequal pay and the retirement programs that were used not only by Columbia but also by most other colleges. The class action against the university had one hundred named plaintiffs. The basis of their claim was that the policies used separate mortality tables for men and women, which resulted in women receiving less when they retired than a man who had worked the same number of years.

The university justified the separate tables on the ground that women lived longer, so fairness required that they should receive smaller pensions. Ruth's attitude was, "Yes, that's certainly true on average, but there are some men who live long and some women who die early."[236] The women suggested that the universities merge the mortality tables. Ruth summarized the university's reaction in this way: "Horrors! We just couldn't do that! Then all the men would desert the plan and get private insurance."[237]

While bringing a lawsuit against her own place of employment could have caused a backlash—and indeed, most of her male colleagues disagreed with the position the women were taking—the Columbia Law School faculty and dean shielded Ruth from accusations of disloyalty. Later she explained that many of her male colleagues recognized the value of having the question aired and discussed, even if they didn't agree.

As the lawsuit against Columbia was progressing, the U.S. Supreme Court heard a similar complaint from California and ruled in favor of the women. Columbia, therefore, settled the case, giving the women equal benefits and pay, including back pay. Under the terms of the settlement, women would receive pensions equal to the men. The retirement plans were such good deals that when the insurance companies did merge the tables as the women requested, none of the men left.

When Ruth agreed to take on a case challenging Missouri's jury composition law, she didn't know her career as a litigator and professor would soon come to an end and this would be the last case she would argue before the Supreme Court. She was eager to try again to go after the odious ruling in *Hoyt v. Florida*.

The petitioner, Billy Duren, was tried in Jackson County,

Missouri, for first-degree murder and assault with intent to kill. The jury was all-male. Prior to trial, Duren filed a timely motion objecting to the composition of the jury on the grounds that women were systematically eliminated, rendering a jury that was not a fair cross section of the community. According to the jury selection procedures in Missouri, women were permitted to serve on juries but any woman was allowed to opt out. Men were not given this option. Not surprisingly, relatively few women served on Missouri juries. The Missouri Supreme Court upheld the procedure as fully consistent with Fourteenth Amendment rights to equal protection and Sixth Amendment rights to a fair jury.

When the Supreme Court granted review in the case, the lawyer, a twenty-five-year-old public defender named Lee Nation, asked Ruth to be his co-counsel. He thought of her because he read about her work in Sharron Frontiero's case while he was in law school. Before the oral argument, he traveled to New York to prepare the case for presentation to the Supreme Court. He stayed in the Ginsburgs' Upper East Side apartment, sleeping in Jane's now-empty bedroom.

He recalled sitting with Ruth and Marty in the evenings, drinking wine and talking. "She was real curious about what it was like to be a big-city public defender, with murder and drugs,"[238] Lee said.

Ruth often suggested that he go to the library and study, which he did, but he was also a young man in the Big Apple eager to enjoy himself, so he also spent time exploring the city.

The Supreme Court oral argument was held on November 1, 1978. Lee and Ruth divided their tasks at the oral argument. He talked about the particulars of the Missouri jury selection procedure while she made the equal protection argument. At the conclusion of Ruth's oral argument, Justice Rehnquist asked her, "You won't settle for putting Susan B. Anthony on the new dollar, right?"[239] At which point Chief Justice Burger interjected with, "I think you have no jurisdiction to make that concession, Mrs. Ginsburg." On the drive home, Ruth thought of a good comeback to Justice Rehnquist's quip: "No, Mr. Justice Rehnquist," she wished she had said, "tokens won't do."[240]

The Supreme Court handed down its decision on January 9, 1979.[241] The vote was 8-1 in her favor, with only Justice Rehnquist dissenting. The majority held that systematic exclusion of women from jury pools resulted in jury pools that were not representative of the general population, and thus violated a defendant's Sixth Amendment right to a fair jury. The decision—finally—took all the teeth out of the ruling in *Hoyt*.

As the 1970s drew to a close, Ruth was able to say she had succeeded. Most of the overt gender distinctions had been removed from the statutes, and the Supreme Court had settled on what has been called the intermediate level of scrutiny for gender-based statutes.

It is impossible to overstate the extent to which Ruth personally orchestrated the gender equality legal strategy of the 1970s. She contributed in one way or another to almost every gender discrimination case decided by the Supreme Court, beginning with *Reed v. Reed* in 1971. In the words of one scholar, what was remarkable about Ruth's strategy was how well it succeeded:

> Quite literally it was her voice, raised in oral arguments and reflected in the drafting of briefs, that shattered old stereotypes and opened new opportunities for both sexes. She built and persuaded the Court to adopt a new constitutional framework for analyzing

the achievement of equality for men and women. In doing so, Ginsburg in large part created the intellectual foundations of the present law of sex discrimination.[242]

21

JUDGE
GINSBURG

One of Jimmy Carter's campaign promises was to appoint women as judges. In fact, both the Democratic and Republican party platforms during the 1976 election included a commitment to appoint more women to the federal bench. Prior to Carter taking office in 1977, women on the federal bench—or any bench at all—were few and far between. Franklin Roosevelt had appointed Florence Allen to the Sixth Circuit Court of Appeals in 1934. Truman appointed Burnita Matthews to the District of Columbia district court in 1949. When Florence Allen died in 1966, there were no female federal appellate judges until 1968, when President Johnson appointed Shirley Mount Hufstedler to the Ninth Circuit Court of Appeals. To make good on his campaign promise, Jimmy Carter created a citizens' nominating committee to compile lists of possible nominees to the federal bench. Women's groups set to work making sure women were included in the lists.

Florence Allen, the first female federal appellate judge.

Almost immediately, Ruth's name began appearing on the lists of possible nominees. Marty helped out with a letter-writing campaign. He had plenty of people to call on, between the Ginsburgs' wide circle of friends, lots of cousins, current colleagues, former colleagues, and influential people who knew Ruth and respected her work. One of Marty's early mentors, Ted Tannenwald, was a judge on the U.S. Tax Court. The White House and senators began receiving phone calls and letters in support of Ruth Bader Ginsburg for judge.

Ruth was interviewed for a federal district court judgeship, but the screening committee told her that she was not qualified because she'd never handled any major securities litigation. Later she was at a legal conference and ran into reporter Nina

Totenberg. They'd become phone friends during the years Nina had covered the Supreme Court. Both were bored by the conference, so they ducked out for some shopping. In the cab, Ruth—still stung over the screening committee telling her she wasn't qualified because she'd never handled securities litigation—muttered to Nina, "And I wonder how many gender-discrimination cases they have handled."[243]

When the first round of appointments was filled, and only men were appointed, women's groups were furious, and Ruth was disappointed.

Jane graduated from Harvard Law School and clerked for Judge John J. Gibbons of the Court of Appeals for the Third Circuit in New Jersey. While at Harvard, she met her future husband, George T. Spera, who had grown up in Mays Landing, New Jersey. George's father was a certified public accountant, and his mother was a tax collector for Hamilton Township in New Jersey. George had graduated magna cum laude and Phi Beta Kappa from Princeton University. Upon graduating from Harvard Law, George took a clerkship with Judge Arlin M. Adams of the Court of Appeals for the Third Circuit in Philadelphia. James, meanwhile, now a teenager, was an avid collector of classical music records.

In 1979, when more federal judgeships became available, Marty himself paid a visit to Marilyn Haft, counsel to Vice President Walter Mondale, to lobby for Ruth. Marilyn Haft, a former ACLU lawyer, knew Ruth well, and was enthusiastic about pressing Ruth's candidacy. Marty also called Ross Perot, along with a few other influential friends in his academic, political, and corporate circles.

In March of 1979, Ruth's name was one of nine submitted by the District of Columbia's judicial nominating commission.

Among the others recommended were Abraham Goldstein, provost of Yale University, formerly dean of its law school, and Charles F. Luce, chairman and chief executive officer of the Consolidated Edison Company. Charles Luce was an honors graduate of the University of Wisconsin Law School and had been a clerk to Supreme Court Justice Black. From the list of nine, two finalists would be chosen, their names forwarded to the president later that month.

The painfully slow process was complicated by the reluctance of the Republicans to confirm another Carter appointment to the bench in an election year, particularly when there was a good chance Carter would lose his bid for reelection. So Marty made more phone calls. One of Marty's former partners, Ira Millstein, knew Senator Orrin Hatch personally. Ira's opinion was that the Republican senator was open-minded. Ira believed if the senator met Ruth he'd see that there was much more to her intellect and temperament than a one-issue lawyer.

Ira was an effective spokesperson on Ruth's behalf. His wife Diane, Ruth, and Marty had long been personal friends. Diane, too, was a professional woman, so Ira had seen firsthand how hard it was for women of their generation to achieve positions of prominence. In his view, Ruth had become a powerful advocate for women's rights because she essentially had no choice. Had she been a man with her intellect and credentials, she would have started her career as a Supreme Court clerk, and would have been in demand by the top law firms and the most prestigious law school faculties. Instead she rose to the task of making sure the women who came after her would be judged on their merits instead of their gender.

Ira called Senator Hatch and asked if he would meet him and Ruth for lunch so that he could reach his own conclusions about her instead of relying on gossip and rumor. Senator

Hatch agreed. By the end of lunch, the senator was completely won over. He concluded that while Ruth had some strong ideas about gender equality, she was a balanced legal scholar with the temperament and makings of a fine judge.

On December 16, 1979, legal sources inside the Carter administration revealed to reporters that Ruth's name had been sent for background checks to the American Bar Association and the Federal Bureau of Investigation. Soon after, President Carter decided to appoint Ruth to replace Harold Leventhal on the U.S. Court of Appeals for the District of Columbia, known as the DC Circuit. This was a particularly prestigious judicial appointment. Due to its location, the DC Circuit had the special task of reviewing legal challenges to the conduct of the national government. The disputes were often complex, dealing with environmental regulation and national security. Appointees to the DC Circuit were generally drawn from outside the District of Columbia and had national reputations. Because the court was considered a national instead of regional bench, Supreme Court justices were often selected from the DC Circuit.

The day of Ruth's nomination hearing, the *New York Daily News* ran the headline "A Judge Grows in Brooklyn." In a statement to the press, evidently intended to dispel rumors that she was a one-issue lawyer, Ruth emphasized her civil procedure expertise and said she was looking forward to hearing a broad range of cases.

When the vote was taken, only one senator opposed her appointment—Republican senator Strom Thurmond of South Carolina. Immediately after her appointment, Marty and Ruth sold all their securities so that she would not have to be recused from any cases due to financial conflicts. The family relocated to Washington, DC, and moved into a luxury apartment in the Watergate Complex—an apartment, incidentally, that had once belonged to Senator Abraham Ribicoff. Marty explained the move by deadpanning, "My wife got a good job."

After taking her judgeship in Washington, DC, Ruth never cooked another meal. Marty, whose schedule was now far more flexible, did all the cooking. Even though Marty was a tax lawyer, he had more cookbooks in the house than tax books—three entire sets of shelves in the living room from floor to ceiling. Ruth told people that he read cookbooks with the same interest he read mystery novels. He accepted a faculty position at Georgetown University, and maintained a connection with the DC law firm of Fried Frank. After the time Ruth drove her car into a gate, he also took on the task of driving her to and from the court each day.

Ruth asked her former professor, Gerald Gunther, to deliver the address to the court at her investiture ceremony. With characteristic modesty, she asked him to talk about the traits of a good judge instead of talking about her personally. So mostly he talked admiringly about the great Learned Hand, "the modest but creative judge, a judge who is genuinely open-minded and detached, the judge who is heedful of limitations stemming from the judge's own competence and, above all, from the presuppositions of our constitutional scheme."[244] When he added that in his view, Ruth Bader Ginsburg had "the character and temperament, the persistence, the open-mindedness, the sense of responsibility, the modesty as well as the courage and strength reflected in Learned Hand's words and deeds," many in the audience were skeptical.[245] Her new colleagues, many of whom were very conservative, knew of her work on behalf of the women's movement, and expected her to become what they thought of disparagingly as a liberal activist.

During the ceremony that followed Gunther's remarks, several judges from the DC Circuit approached him. They indicated their skepticism that Ruth might be another Learned Hand. Gunther, supremely confident in his former student, wagered five dollars that within a few years, she would be widely seen as the most independent, thoughtful, and modest judge on the bench.

It has often been said that Ruth Bader Ginsburg had two distinct careers, first as a leading equal rights lawyer who—had she never become a judge—would nonetheless have earned a place in history as the lawyer whose litigation strategy helped change the equal protection law. At the age of forty-seven, she was about to embark on her second career, as Judge Ginsburg.

After the Ginsburgs settled into their new Watergate home, they were often seen, elegantly dressed, at the opera, theater, and symphony. James, the music lover, became a supernumerary at the Washington National Opera. While attending social gatherings in Washington, DC, the Ginsburgs were amused when someone would introduce Judge Ginsburg and the person would reach to shake Marty's hand. Several people asked the newly appointed judge how she was managing the commute from New York to Washington, DC. For many people in 1980 it was simply unthinkable that a man would give up a lucrative career and move to a new city, putting his wife's career first.

The DC Circuit judges were housed in the same building as the trial judges of the district court. As Chief Justice John Roberts, who himself had been a judge on the DC Circuit, explained, this allowed the appellate judges the unique opportunity of sitting down to lunch next to a trial judge who, moments before, they had found guilty of abuse of discretion or clear error—which could make for a very short lunch. One benefit of the close proximity to the district court judges for Ginsburg was that she had the opportunity to meet with someone she'd always admired, the iconic Burnita Shelton Matthews, the first woman to have been appointed to the federal bench. When Ginsburg joined the DC Circuit, Matthews was eighty-five years old. Instead of retiring, she had taken senior status and reduced her workload, but she continued hearing occasional cases until 1983.

Burnita Matthews, appointed to the D.C. District Court in 1949.

One of Ginsburg's new colleagues, Judge Edward Tamm, gave Ginsburg advice about judging. He told her to work hard on each case, do her best, but don't look back. Once a case has been decided, it is not productive to worry about whether the decision was right. Later, when she was the more experienced person on the bench, she gave the same advice to new judges.

Shortly after her appointment to the court, a male lawyer asked for an oral argument to be postponed because the argument was set for the week his baby was due. The argument he wanted postponed was a reargument before the full court. Postponements for rearguments were rarely granted, and Ginsburg's colleagues were prepared to deny the request. She sent a note to the other ten justices asking them how they would react if the lawyer was a woman. Her note persuaded her colleagues to grant the postponement.

Ginsburg told a story that, for her, exemplified how unusual female judges were at that time. She was assigned to a panel with Judge Patricia Wald and Judge Roger Robb. A lawyer persisted in addressing both women as "Judge Wald." At last, Ginsburg said, "Here's the sign in front of me that says 'Ginsburg,' and here's the sign in front of Judge Wald that says 'Wald.'"[246] The lawyer made an effort, but continued to confuse them.

In 1981, the year after Ginsburg took her place on the DC Court of Appeals, President Reagan—not to be outdone by President Carter, who had appointed so many women to the federal bench—nominated Arizona judge Sandra Day O'Connor to replace Justice Potter Stewart on the Supreme Court.

O'Connor's story was similar to other women who tried to enter the legal profession in the 1950s. After earning a BA in economics at Stanford, she enrolled in Stanford Law School. In 1952—while Ginsburg was an undergraduate at Cornell—

O'Connor graduated ranked third in a class of 102. William Rehnquist, her classmate—whom she dated for a while—was ranked first. Rehnquist immediately secured a Supreme Court clerkship with Justice Jackson. O'Connor was unable to find employment as a lawyer. The only job offer she received was as a legal secretary. She landed a job in the San Mateo, California, District Attorney's Office by offering to work free with the promise that if, after a few months, her employers were happy with her work, they would hire her and pay her a salary.

Her work—no surprise—was exemplary and she received the promised paid position. Eventually she and her husband, a Stanford classmate, settled in Phoenix, Arizona, where she became an assistant attorney general of Arizona. The following year she was appointed to the Arizona State Senate to fill a vacated seat. In 1970, she was elected to a full term. She became a trial judge in 1974, and was elevated to the Arizona Court of Appeals in 1979.

She was unanimously approved by the Senate and was confirmed as the first female Supreme Court justice.

Sandra Day O'Connor at her Confirmation Hearing, 1981.

Four years earlier, Kathleen Peratis Frank, who worked with Ginsburg at the Women's Rights Project and later became director, named her daughter Ruth. When Ruth Peratis was old enough to understand, Kathleen told her she was named after the woman who was going to be the first woman appointed to the U.S. Supreme Court. After Sandra Day O'Connor was appointed, Ruth Peratis, who was then four years old, said to her mother, "Mom . . . you told me Ruth would be first!"

"Just wait," Kathleen told her.[247]

The new justice—a Republican from the West—may have been quite different from Ginsburg on the surface, but Ginsburg knew right away from an early case O'Connor decided that they were kindred spirits in their approach to women and law. The case involved a man who wanted to attend a nursing school, but the only school available to him—a school run by the state—was closed to men. The state did not offer any comparable education for men. Those hoping to keep the school all-women spun the school as essentially offering affirmative action to women by giving them special opportunities. O'Connor understood right away that the best thing for female nurses was for men to enter the school because any profession that was all-women tended to be paid lower and carried less prestige. O'Connor wrote the opinion for the court. She applied a heightened level of scrutiny to the gender distinction—the law that Ginsburg had led the court to adopt—and found that a state-run school that excludes men from enrolling when no comparable program is offered to them violated the equal protection clause of the Fourteenth Amendment.[248]

22

DIFFERENT
VOICES

In the 1980s there arose a new wave of feminists who offered a sharp critique of Ginsburg's litigation strategy on behalf of equal rights. This attack came not from the conservatives, but from the left.

Susan Brownmiller's 1975 book on rape, *Against Our Will*, was one of the precursors to this new wave of feminism. *Against Our Will* outlined the history of rape laws and cultural attitudes toward rape. Brownmiller argued that rape was not the inevitable result of human nature, as many at the time assumed, but a means of exerting patriarchal power. She offered the unsettling conclusion that rape was the way *all* men kept *all* women in fear. This was not to say all men rape—but in her view, all men benefited from the fact that some men do rape because this allowed them to assume the role of protector, which in turn relegated women to spheres where they would be safe. As Mae West quipped decades earlier, "Every man I meet wants to protect me. I just can't figure out from what." Mae West poked gentle fun at the irony. Susan Brownmiller was angry—and she stirred anger in others.

Under English common law—and the law in early America—rape was a violation of a man's property and not a crime against the woman. The idea was that an unmarried girl was her father's property, and his financial interests required that she be marriageable and thus a virgin. Forcing sex on an unmarried woman who was not a virgin often wasn't seen as a crime based on the theory the property was already ruined. A married woman was the property of her husband, which meant a man could not be convicted of raping his own wife. Rape of a slave woman was not a crime because, among other reasons, the slave owner benefited financially if she had more babies. Early rape laws were thus designed to protect the economic interest of men. They were also designed to protect men against being falsely accused of rape. To support a charge of rape, a woman had to promptly complain to law enforcement and provide corroborating evidence. A man accused of rape could defend himself by introducing evidence about the victim's past sexual history and about her character on the theory that a promiscuous woman had most likely been willing. If a woman was wearing provocative clothing, a man could argue that she had provoked him. Women were thus discouraged from bringing charges of rape because the trial was likely to turn into a trial of *her* character, not her attacker's.

Women, empowered by the uprisings of the 1960s, rejected the idea that they were the property of men and insisted on reform of the rape laws. Rape became a crime against the women, and rape shield laws were passed, limiting a defendant's ability to introduce evidence about the victim's past sexual history, and prohibiting the publication of a rape victim's name.

Catharine MacKinnon's 1979 book, *Sexual Harassment of Working Women*, pioneered the legal claim of sexual harassment. MacKinnon, who earned a law degree and PhD in political science from Yale, argued that sexual harassment, which had never before been discussed or defined, was so pervasive in

American society as to be completely invisible. Later she claimed that pornography was a violation of civil and human rights.

While Ginsburg was still teaching at Columbia, she and a colleague went to hear MacKinnon speak. Ginsburg was not impressed. "That woman has bad karma," she said afterward.[249]

MacKinnon criticized Ginsburg's legal strategy of the 1970s, saying lawyers should have been looking for ways women have been systematically disadvantaged and then finding ways to correct the disadvantage instead of just seeking to have women treated the same as men. In Sally Reed's case, for example, the remedy Ginsburg had sought—rewording the statute so that men were not automatically favored and the selection of executors became merit-based—was not enough. The fact that the law preferred men as executors demonstrated that society had systematically created a culture whereby men were by and large better educated and more qualified to be executors. Simply changing to a merit-based statute would not correct the problem: Men tended to have more education, so women would be chosen less often than men.

MacKinnon—and others who embraced her theories—called what Ginsburg was after "formal equality," which they saw as essentially assimilationist. Because the legal system had been created by men in their own best interests, they called Ginsburg phallocentric for accepting the male world order and trying to fit herself into it. And because of the intrinsic differences between men and women, they believed that encouraging women to act like men and assimilate themselves into a social order consisting of male values would hurt women more than help them.

Moreover, in MacKinnon's view, the whole approach of treating sexism like racism was wrongheaded. While there were not intrinsic differences between the races, sex *was* a distinction, particularly in the areas of reproduction and sexual harassment.

Before the litigation of the 1970s, for example, the law assumed it was better for children to remain with their mothers, and tended to give mothers custody. As a result of Ginsburg's work, laws were changed to favor joint custody, but divorced women with children wanted custody more often than men, so they often made financial concessions to their former husbands in exchange for custody, thereby suffering an economic harm they were previously protected from. All Ginsburg had done—according to MacKinnon—was narrowly open the doors to those women willing and able to act like men, instead of carving a safe place for what was distinctly feminine.

In the words of one scholar, Ginsburg's work and reputation were "consigned to the dustbin of formal equality."[250]

Ginsburg called such criticism unfair. She felt her critics were not giving her credit for all she had accomplished in "helping to unsettle previously accepted conceptions of men and women's separate spheres."[251] At the time she brought her cases, the idea that women and men were similar and could perform the same work was radical, and given her audience—older, white, well-heeled men—an appeal to courts couldn't have been expected to do more. As she put it,

> A teacher from outside the club, or the home crowd, seeking to open minds . . . knows she must keep it comprehensible and digestible, not too complete or intimidating, or risk losing her audience.[252]

She also pointed out the limited capacity of the courts. Once the law books had been cleared of regulations that automatically favored men and discouraged or prevented women from fully participating in the political process, women could move into positions of power, became legislators, and pass the kinds of laws they thought best. Asking courts to do more than clear away the obstacles was, in Ginsburg's view, asking courts to overstep their limits.

The next theorist to shake things up was Harvard professor Carol Gilligan, who, in 1980, published *In a Different Voice*, in which she claimed there were significant differences in the way men and women respond to moral dilemmas, with boys tending to adopt individualistic, rights-based analysis, and girls more likely to approach problems emphasizing connections between individuals. Under this theory, men defined themselves through separation, while women defined themselves through connections. Gilligan saw the same problem MacKinnon saw: Society itself was set up to reward male inclinations and traits while devaluing female ones.

Gilligan's idea—that men and women spoke in different voices and experienced the world differently—gave rise to decades of popular psychology about the inherent differences between men and women. Deborah Tannen's *You Just Don't Understand: Women and Men in Conversation* spent four years on the *New York Times* bestseller list. Tannen analyzed the difference between male and female modes of communicating to illuminate why the sexes so often simply failed to understand each other. Two years after the publication of Tannen's book came John Gray's *Men Are from Mars, Women Are from Venus*, a relationship self-help book designed to help men and women understand each other by acknowledging the differences between their needs and desires.

Ginsburg resisted these ideas. After all, she'd spent a lifetime trying to get rid of gender stereotypes so women wouldn't be pigeonholed, and now people were recreating the pigeonholes. After being told all through the 1950s that "men think, and women feel," she was afraid these ideas were a road back to the days when girls were sugar and spice and needed to be protected from the real world. Ginsburg also believed the psychological differences between men and women were the result of cultural conditioning. "People say that women care more about individuals and are more humane," she said. "I think women occupy that caring role because society expects it of them."[253] She insisted that during the entire seventeen years she taught law school, she was unable to see any difference in the quality of thinking exhibited by the men and the women. She didn't even see any difference in their penmanship.

Her answer to the theory that women and men responded to the world differently was to point to the exceptions. What about the mannish women? What about the feminine men? The problem with pigeonholing was that there were always people who did not fit the stereotypes. Moreover, the issue for her was deeply personal. By now, she realized that her own mother would have made a wonderful lawyer—had she lived in a time when a girl's achievements were prized as highly as a boy's. She also understood that Celia would have had a richer, fuller life had she been allowed a career of her own.

While Ginsburg didn't agree that her work for gender equality had hurt women more than it helped, she did appreciate that her task had been fairly straightforward because there was nothing subtle about the legal gender distinctions she'd found in the statute books. She also acknowledged that her victories did nothing to get rid of the subtler forms of discrimination, what she called unconscious bias.

She enjoyed telling the story of how symphonies went from being almost entirely male, with perhaps the exception of the harp player, to having an equal mix of men and women. People used to believe there were differences in the quality of performances of musicians based on gender. New York Times critic Howard Taubman, for example, said you could blindfold him and he would be able to tell whether the piano player was a man or woman. Then someone got the idea to drop a curtain between the musician auditioning and the judges so the judges would not know whether the musician was male or female. Suddenly judges were giving higher marks to female musicians, and more women were admitted to the major symphonies. Another step forward occurred when someone got the idea to have the musicians walk onto the stage behind the curtain without shoes so the judges would not be able to guess from the sound of the clicking of heels whether the musician was a man or a woman. Soon the numbers of men and women performing in symphonies were evened up. Ginsburg also talked about the studies in which an African American man, a white woman, and an African American woman would attempt to buy a car. The person quoted the highest price was always the African American woman, proving the existence of either overt or unconscious bias.

Ginsburg gave various answers when asked how she felt about the fact that she subscribed to a now-outdated form of feminism. She denied that her form of feminism was outdated. Instead she said the feminist movement had become "a house of many gables with rooms enough to accommodate all who have the imagination and determination to think and work"[254] toward the empowerment of women. She said there was a danger in each strand of feminism believing theirs was the only one that was right and true. Finally, she said that formal equality had been a good place to start.

On the other end of the political spectrum, Phyllis Schlafly and her Anti-Equal Rights campaign succeeded in killing the Equal Rights Amendment. By the 1980s, the political pendulum was swinging to the right as the Republican Party became more conservative. In 1980 the Republican Party removed the ERA from its platform. In 1982, the ERA deadline was reached. Despite marches, picketing of the White House, fundraisers, and walkathons, the proponents of the amendment never succeeded in getting the last three states to approve the amendment. The Equal Rights Amendment has been reintroduced in Congress each year since 1982, this time without deadlines, but has languished ever since.

In a recent interview on National Public Radio, Phyllis Schlafly said the entire feminist movement was wrongheaded and bad for women. In her own words:

> A lot of people don't understand what feminism is. They think it is about advance and success for women, but it's not that at all. It's about power for the female left. And they have this, I think, ridiculous idea that American women are oppressed by the patriarchy and we need laws and government to solve our problems for us.[255]

She repeated her belief that women should be perfectly happy with separate spheres, with women in the home and men in the work world. In her view, American women were the "most fortunate people who ever lived on the face of the earth," because

> When I got married, all I wanted in the world was a dryer so I didn't have to hang up my diapers. And now women have paper diapers and all sorts of conveniences in the home. And it is the men and the technology that has [sic] made the home such a

pleasant place for women to be. So I hope they will use that pleasant place to raise their children.[256]

There was irony in the fact that Phyllis Schlafly had a law degree from Washington University and a master's in political science from Harvard—something that wouldn't have been possible in earlier centuries without the feminists of previous generations, who made her education possible. She stated, however, that as a good wife and mother, her political work and lobbying efforts were just a hobby.

23

HITTING DOWN
THE MIDDLE

As a professor and litigator, Ginsburg had a reputation for being focused on details. She was known to correct her colleagues' typos and small errors. It was no surprise, therefore, that her approach to judging and drafting decisions was also detail-oriented. She summed up good judging and opinion writing as "get it right, keep it tight."[257] Lawyers who appeared before her sometimes saw her as a nitpicker. She wasn't afraid to put lawyers on the spot. Marcia Greenberger of the National Women's Law Center said that any litigants arguing before her had to "take very seriously their obligation to understand the case."[258] She was cautious, "more likely to refine an existing legal doctrine than chart a new one."[259]

Because judges on the DC Circuit sat on panels of three, the task was to get at least one other judge on your panel to agree with you. Whenever possible, Ginsburg preferred all three judges to speak with a single voice. This required compromise, something Ginsburg was comfortable with. After all, years earlier, she'd learned the lesson that the spirit of liberty was the spirit that wasn't too sure of itself. She was aware of her own human fallibility and of the heady responsibility that she was writing not just for herself but also for the court. When she circulated drafts of her opinions for comments from the other judges, she made the changes others asked for whenever possible. If a colleague said, "Please take that footnote out," or even "add a citation to one of my own cases," she thought, why not? If a colleague wanted to put something in, in it went— even if it was a little out of place. She joked that the law schools could devise theories about why this or that note was there.

The court's calendar was arranged so that in each of the year's several sitting periods, each judge sat with a different set of colleagues. Each member of the court would sit with every other member for at least one week during the year, which required working with each of the other judges on the court. The DC Circuit judges all had their chambers in the same building, but they rarely conferred about a case before argument, or even exchanged written statements of their positions. However, directly after arguments—without even stopping for lunch— they met to reach tentative decisions. The judges would offer their opinions to the others in reverse order of seniority. The immediacy of the conference encouraged each judge to be thoroughly prepared before going into the argument.

Appellate judging has a lot in common with teaching law because the chief task of an appellate court is an academic one: to make sure the lower court correctly applied the law. In cases of constitutional matters, the appellate court makes sure that the lower court correctly interpreted the Constitution. On appeal, there was no new trial on the facts. As Ginsburg put it, an appellate court does not question why the lower court believed Mr. Badegg instead of Ms. Goodkind. The facts found by the trial court are taken as true by the appellate court, except in the case of clear error.

Ginsburg won the respect of her colleagues by her

impressive work habits. In the words of one of her clerks, "She works through the night, she's there during the day. And it's just this bottomless energy."[260] She also got along—and often got her way—because of her calm, reasonable demeanor, entirely lacking anger. To take an example, the American Law Institute held a luncheon in the Century Club in Manhattan, a place long closed to women. A month before the group's meeting there in January 1980, Ginsburg drafted a six-page memorandum, complete with nine footnotes, urging that functions be moved until the club changed its policies. As a result, the luncheons were moved. It was quintessential Ginsburg. A fellow member of the American Law Institute, Charles Alan Wright, described her low-key but effective advocacy. "You never hesitated in making your own position known with force and candor. What I have marveled at, however, is the complete serenity with which you take part in these debates. No lock of hair is ever askew. No hint of anger or elation ever appears on your face or in your voice. Yours is always the position of calm reason and confidence."[261]

Always reasonable and controlled, she was quietly driven by a desire for moral justice and order.

One of Ronald Reagan's campaign promises for the 1980 presidential election had been to appoint judges who would behave with judicial restraint. He came to office partly on a backlash to the Warren court of the 1960s, which gave the country *Miranda* warnings, *Brown v. Board of Education*, and many other liberal decisions. Reagan's election coincided with the founding of the Federalist Society in law schools, which was formed as a reaction to the majority of law school professors, who generally applauded the way the Warren court had transformed America. The Federalist Society believed in states' rights and a limited federal government, which meant limiting the reach of the Constitution into local and state governments.

Two of Reagan's appointments to the DC Circuit were selected from the member roster of the Federalist Society: Robert Bork, appointed in 1982, and Antonin Scalia, appointed in 1983. Kenneth Starr, another conservative appointed to the DC Circuit in 1983, would become best known as the special prosecutor in the Clinton–Monica Lewinsky scandals of the late 1990s. Ginsburg knew Scalia from the time she was teaching at Columbia and he was on the faculty of the University of Chicago. She'd heard him lecture once, and while she'd disagreed with almost everything he said, she'd enjoyed his brash humor. She couldn't have known that her response to his lecture would set the pattern for a friendship and professional relationship that would last many decades, until his death. Scalia explained their friendship by saying, "If you can't disagree ardently with your colleagues about some issues of law and yet personally still be friends, get another job, for Pete's sake."[262]

Scalia and Bork were both originalists, which Scalia described this way:

> The Constitution that I interpret and apply is not living but dead, or as I prefer to call it, enduring. It means today not what current society, much less the court, thinks it ought to mean, but what it meant when adopted.[263]

Robert Bork was also a staunch originalist. The originalism of Bork and Scalia was a reaction to—and repudiation of—the theory of contemporary ratification that had dominated the Warren court of the 1950s and 1960s. Under the theory of contemporary ratification, the drafters of the Constitution never intended to enshrine a status quo and require that future generations remain entrenched in the specific beliefs of the drafters. Their intent was to put in place general principles of liberty, fairness, and balance to guide the government.

Bork opposed the civil rights movement and the women's movement on the principle of individual liberty. He believed if a white restaurant owner wanted to prevent a black person from eating in his public restaurant, he should be allowed to. Blacks could find another place to eat. If a company wanted to fire women when they became pregnant, they should be allowed to do that, too. Women who didn't like the policy could work elsewhere. Bork's critics painted him as a racist and segregationist. In fact, he said segregation was wrong, but he compared laws outlawing segregation to Prohibition, in which—in his words—"the morals of the majority were self-righteously imposed on the minority."[264] Not everything that is immoral can be criminalized or regulated, and in his view, outlawing segregation was a misguided attempt to regulate morality.

Critics of Scalia and Bork pointed out that the Constitution was a result of compromise, which meant that different drafters had different intentions. Whose intention do you follow? Besides, why follow the intent of the drafters of the Constitution and not the "people" in "We the People?" Moreover, how do you really know the intention of someone who died generations earlier? And what about all the places where the Constitution was sketchy and vague? There were also those who claimed that language is not precise enough for there to be one and only one meaning.

Scalia, who believed there was only one correct way to read the Constitution, minced no words in telling his colleagues when he thought they were wrong. He dismissed an opinion written by one colleague by calling the reasoning "irrational," saying that the opinion, "cannot be taken seriously."[265] About another opinion, he said, "the account of the clear-statement rule reads like a really good lawyer's brief for the wrong side" and that the law was "entirely made up."[266] The natural result of believing there was only one way to read the Constitution was that Scalia rarely compromised, preferring to write a biting dissent.

Despite their differences, Scalia and Ginsburg bounced ideas off each other, sharpening their own views by challenging each other. Scalia described their relationship this way: "When you write a piece for law review, or a book in academia, you always circulate it to your colleagues before it's in final form, and if they are good colleagues, they read it and make suggestions. Ruth and I used to do that with each other's opinions and welcomed—*welcomed*—the assistance."[267] About their friendship, he said, "Call us the odd couple. She likes opera, and she's a very nice person. What's not to like? Except her views on the law."[268]

Antonin Scalia, 2013.

Because of Ginsburg's penchant for narrow, procedure-focused opinions, the result was just as Gerald Gunther predicted: Ginsburg soon had the reputation for being a moderate judge who just as often sided with the conservatives as the liberals. In fact, she sided most often with the extremely conservative Kenneth Starr. In 1984, for example, she voted to dismiss a case brought by a gay sailor discharged by the Navy. The sailor had challenged the military's ban on homosexuals. The argument made on behalf of the sailor was familiar to Ginsburg because she had made it herself as a lawyer advocating for women. The sailor's lawyer argued that the military's policy violated the sailor's constitutional right to privacy and denied him equal protection of the laws. The case sparked a bitter split among the ten judges on the court. Conservatives on the court thought the idea that an enlisted officer had a right to privacy was absurd. The liberals were enraged by the conservatives' cavalier dismissal of the legal claims.

Ginsburg—in the middle—rejected the sailor's claim based on a one-line Supreme Court order from 1976. The Supreme Court, in a case called *Doe v. Commonwealth*, rejected the claim that homosexuals were guaranteed a right to privacy.[269] "I am of the view that the Supreme Court's dispositive disposition in *Doe* controls our judgment in this case," she said.[270] While she later insisted that she deplored all forms of discrimination, including discrimination against gays, in that moment she did not think she had the authority, as a Circuit Court judge, to do anything other than follow the law set down by the Supreme Court.

Gay rights activists were incensed. "She missed an opportunity to stand up on behalf of a vulnerable minority being deprived of its rights by a discriminatory government policy," said Evan Wolfson of the Lambda Legal Defense Fund, who filed an amicus brief on Dronenburg's behalf.[271]

Later President Clinton lifted the ban on gays in the military. Yes, Ginsburg's decision had been narrow and cautious, but the result was that another branch of government stepped in and created policy.

In criminal matters, she never tried to expand or enlarge protections for defendants; instead, she worked to preserve the protections already in place. In this way, she was nothing like the liberal icons such as Thurgood Marshall and William Brennan, who enlarged protections for defendants at every opportunity. At the same time, she wanted to make sure that she and her clerks understood firsthand that ordinary people were affected by their decisions. Most years, if her clerks were so inclined, they visited the local jail and Lorton Penitentiary.

Ginsburg on the DC Circuit.

She'd also taken her clerks to visit St. Elizabeth's, a facility for the criminally insane.

One of her former clerks, Peter Huber, explained that it was her almost Talmudic reverence for procedure that enabled her to forge close friendships with even the most conservative members of the court. "You can't feel very politically antagonistic toward someone who is centered on the process rather than the politics," he explained.[272]

A family friend who played golf with the Ginsburgs remarked that she played golf the way she decided cases: She aimed left, swung right, and hit down the middle.

Five years after she took her place on the court, Gerald Gunther won his bet. One day he received an envelope in the mail containing five dollars and a clipping from the *Washington Post* depicting her as the moderate centrist on the DC Circuit.

Columbia Law School held its fifth annual Myra Bradwell Day on April 13, 1984, the day named in honor of the 1873 Supreme Court decision that held Bradwell unfit to practice law because she was a woman. As of 1984, women made up almost one-third of Columbia Law's student body. Ten faculty members were women. Geraldine Ferraro of Queens, looking around at the audience, observed wryly that it was clear *Bradwell v. Illinois* was no longer good law. Part of the festivities was the unveiling of a new portrait of Ruth Bader Ginsburg. The portrait, to hang with former chief justices Charles Evans Hughes and Harlan F. Stone, was the thirty-seventh portrait to hang at the law school.

Meanwhile, Ginsburg's son, James, followed in his sister's footsteps and enrolled at the University of Chicago. He graduated in 1987, and then, to use his phrase, went into the "family business" of law.[273] During his first year at the University of Chicago Law School, though, he realized that law just wasn't his thing. At the end of his first year, instead of taking the usual law firm summer job, he spent his summer producing albums. He then took a leave of absence from law school to produce a few more. He never returned to law school, dedicating himself instead to founding a classical music label.

In the late 1980s, Ross Perot wanted Marty's legal help with the sale of his company, Electronic Data Systems, to General Motors. Marty didn't feel comfortable because the firm he was associated with represented competitors of Electronic Data Systems. Although there was no actual conflict of interest, helping with the acquisition would have been unseemly. But Marty wanted to do the work, which he knew would be particularly interesting and challenging. To avoid the appearance of impropriety, Marty offered to do the work without pay.

The acquisition proved difficult. Marty resolved a number of difficult issues that ended up saving Perot a lot of money. Perot, in gratitude, wanted to do something to repay him, but Marty balked. So Perot said he planned to create the Martin D. Ginsburg chair. He asked Marty to pick a law school. Marty said, "Well, Ross, you know, in our religion you don't name things after people until they die."

Perot insisted, but Marty and Ruth were uneasy about accepting such a gift so they never named a school. Eventually Perot said, "You're taking so much time to make up your mind. So I'm going to set up the Martin D. Ginsburg chair at Oral Roberts University." This prompted Marty to burst out with, "Georgetown! Georgetown is where I would like the Martin D. Ginsburg chair!"[274]

But still, Marty dragged his feet about filling the chair, insisting that endowed chairs were only for dead people. So the chair remained empty, with the money from the endowment being used to pay for books at the law school library. A few of

Ginsburg's clerks gave her a gift, which she placed on a shelf in her Watergate apartment: a six-inch chair with a small plaque identifying it as the Martin D. Ginsburg chair.

When Chief Justice Burger announced his retirement, President Reagan nominated Justice Rehnquist to succeed him as chief. The Senate debate was long and rancorous, but at last, by a divided vote, Rehnquist became America's sixteenth chief justice. President Reagan then nominated Antonin Scalia to fill Rehnquist's seat. Scalia was confirmed without opposition, perhaps because everyone was so worn out from the Rehnquist battle.

The year after Scalia's appointment to the Supreme Court brought major changes to Reagan's presidency. The Iran-Contra scandal lowered his favorability ratings, and the midterm elections brought in a Democratic Senate. Many people credited the election of Democratic senators to the results finally reaped from the Voting Rights Act of 1965, which assured blacks in the South of the vote by ending the tactics that had kept them from the voting booths. More blacks voting meant more Democrats sent to Washington.

When Reagan nominated Robert Bork to replace Justice Powell, civil rights activists sounded the alarm. For years, the outspoken Bork had pilloried the liberal Supreme Court justices in speeches and in print, calling them unprincipled and worse. Now he got a taste of being pilloried in the press. Civil rights activist circulated the article Bork had written arguing that segregation was constitutional. Far more people read the article now than had read it upon publication. Benjamin Hooks of the NAACP said of Bork's nomination, "We will fight it all the way—until hell freezes over, and then we'll skate across the ice."[275] After a bruising nomination hearing in which Bork admitted that he opposed civil rights, the Judiciary Committee voted against him 9-5. Bork, however, didn't want to quit. He wanted the Senate to vote. He lost in the Senate 58-42, the largest margin of defeat for a Supreme Court nomination since the founding of the Supreme Court.

Reagan next nominated Anthony Kennedy from the Court of Appeals for the Ninth Circuit, a Republican described as a moderate conservative who had no trouble getting through the nomination process. The next Supreme Court justice was appointed in 1991, when George H. W. Bush nominated Clarence Thomas, a judge generally considered even more conservative than Antonin Scalia. After another bruising nomination hearing in which attorney Anita Hill accused Thomas, her former boss, of sexual harassment, the Senate approved Thomas's appointment 52-48. The balance on the court was now tipped in favor of conservatives for the first time in a generation.

After eleven years of Republican control of the White House, *Roe v. Wade* was in trouble. Local governments had been whittling away at *Roe v. Wade*, passing laws that made it harder for women to obtain abortions, and local judges had been upholding the new laws. One Pennsylvania statute created several requirements before a woman could obtain an abortion: Her consent needed to be informed; a twenty-four-hour waiting period was required before the procedure; minors seeking an abortion required the consent of one parent, although the law allowed for judicial bypass; and a married woman who wanted an abortion had to notify her husband of her intention. The ACLU lawyer handling the case, Kathleen Kolbert, then devised what one commentator called "one of the most audacious litigation tactics in Supreme Court history."[276] She presented her case to the Supreme Court in 1991 with a simple question: Has *Roe v.*

Wade been overturned? She was going for broke, all or nothing. Either strike down the Pennsylvania law, or come right out and say, "We are overturning *Roe v. Wade.*" What made this audacious was that it was 1992, an election year, and she wanted to force the Supreme Court to answer the question in time for the vote.

Rehnquist, aware of what she was doing, tried to stall her case, but she persisted and got onto the calendar. After oral arguments, Rehnquist, Thomas, Scalia, and Kennedy were prepared to overturn *Roe v. Wade*. The problem was they could not get a fifth vote. O'Connor was rankled by the spousal notification requirement, which struck her as both paternalistic and sexist. Souter was worried about undoing precedent, afraid that overturning a major decision that had become part of the American fabric and that so many depended upon would come across as a whimsical, political move that would undermine the legitimacy of the court. Kennedy similarly felt that overturning *Roe v. Wade* would undermine the credibility of the court by putting the court in the middle of the political fray.

The result was a scattered decision, with three justices in the plurality, the others either dissenting, or concurring in part and dissenting in part. In a narrow 5-4 decision, the court struck down the spousal notification requirement, upheld the 24-hour waiting period and parental consent for minors—and made clear it was upholding the basic right to an abortion protected by *Roe v. Wade*. It was a victory for pro-choice advocates. The conservatives were deeply enraged. It wasn't the first time conservatives learned that you couldn't rely on appointees to vote the conservative agenda after they were safely on the bench with lifetime tenure.

Roe v. Wade was still the law of the land—but it was hanging by a thread.

24

I'M RUTH,
NOT SANDRA

When Ross Perot ran for president in 1992, Marty Ginsburg served as his economic advisor—but later Marty said he supported Clinton. At the start of the election season, incumbent George H. W. Bush's favorability ratings were high and he was widely expected to win reelection. When Bill Clinton won by a plurality, disgruntled conservatives blamed Perot for splitting the conservative vote.

One of Clinton's first acts as president was to sign into law the Family and Medical Leave Act, which allowed up to twelve weeks of unpaid, job-protected leave to workers who needed the time for such things as childbirth, child care, recovering from a serious medical illness, or caring for an ill family member. The new law was motivated by the changes that had taken place in American families over the past few decades, with more than half the women either the primary breadwinner or equally sharing the responsibility. While the act was gender-neutral, allowing both men and women to take advantage of the benefit, the intention was to help women, who were most often the caretakers and more often ran into trouble with their jobs when they had to take time away from work.

The new president's first opportunity to appoint a Supreme Court justice came a little more than a year after he took office, when Justice Byron White, who was then seventy-five years old, announced that he would retire at the end of the 1992–1993 term. "It has been an interesting experience," Justice White wrote in his public statement. "But after 31 years, Marion [his wife] and I think someone else should be permitted to have a like experience."[277] For the first time since 1967, when President Johnson appointed Thurgood Marshall to the court, a Democratic president would nominate a Supreme Court justice. Clinton wanted to nominate Mario Cuomo, the former three-term governor of New York, his one-time political rival who had given a rousing speech at the 1991 convention nominating Clinton. Cuomo, who had practiced law but had never been a judge, took two weeks to think about the offer before declining, becoming one of the few people in history to turn down a position as a Supreme Court justice. White House staff began compiling lists of possible nominees, prompting furious lobbying on all sides.

Marty was already busy with his own letter-writing campaign. Once again, he contacted his influential friends and asked them to write letters and make phone calls on his wife's behalf. Ruth's cousin Beth—the niece of her mother, Celia Bader—was married to Stephen Hess, a good friend of Senator Daniel Patrick Moynihan of New York. Stephen Hess and the senator served together in the Nixon White House. Brooklyn-born Moynihan had never personally met Ginsburg, but he knew about her from her writings and advocacy. He became one of her sponsors in the Senate. One of Ginsburg's clerks also wanted her to take action. "If you do nothing at all," he said, "maybe you'll be number 25 on the president's list. So we have to do something to put you forward."[278]

White House favorites were Interior Secretary Bruce Babbitt and federal appeals court judge Stephen Breyer, but Clinton wasn't crazy about either. He wanted a big, bold choice. Clinton met with Breyer for a few hours on June 11. Afterward, Dee Dee Meyers, a White House spokesperson, said that while the meeting went well, the president still had not made a decision. Then the word was out that Judge Breyer had failed to pay Social Security taxes for household staff, so his name was removed from the list. This prompted even more furious lobbying.

After discarding several possibilities, Clinton got the idea to ask Janet Reno, the newly appointed attorney general, for her suggestions. The first thing she said when she came to the phone was, "Why aren't you people looking at Ruth Bader Ginsburg?"[279]

Senator Moynihan gave Clinton a copy of Dean Griswold's 1985 address to the Supreme Court in which he praised "the work done by lawyers representing groups interested in the rights of women, of whom Ruth Bader Ginsburg is an outstanding example."[280] Griswold also compared what Ginsburg had done for the women's movement to what Thurgood Marshall did for civil rights. Clinton perked up and took interest. Who could be bigger and bolder than another Thurgood Marshall?

Once the word leaked out that the Clinton was considering Ginsburg, abortion rights groups, still stung by Ginsburg's criticism of *Roe v. Wade*, opposed her appointment. As a result, Clinton initially told his advisors that he couldn't appoint Ginsburg because women's groups would object. Next letters poured in from women's groups praising her. Clinton himself read the articles Ginsburg had written about *Roe v. Wade* and understood that she had criticized the court's reasoning, not the result. Meanwhile, White House counsel Bernard Nussbaum told Marty that given his wife's background as an academic, if the White House didn't receive at least seven letters from academics on her behalf, the president would get very nervous.

So Marty started contacting professors, including Stanford Law professor Barbara Babock. Marty told her she was one of a handful of feminist law professors who could reassure the White House that Ruth Bader Ginsburg was well respected among academics. Professor Babock, in turn, called her former student Cheryl Mills, who was now deputy White House counsel. The presidents of both Stanford and Columbia wrote letters to the White House, praising Ginsburg.

To reassure conservatives that she was indeed a moderate— on all issues except equal protection—Bruce Ennis, a one-time ACLU legal director and now partner with a major corporate law firm in Washington, DC, told reporters that Ginsburg "harbors no animosity toward Corporate America."[281] Not everyone, though, was happy with Ginsburg's inclination to compromise with conservatives. Mel Wulf with the ACLU thought she should be more confrontational instead of placing such a high premium on collegiality. He believed if she wanted to be a truly great judge, she had to take the chance of offending her colleagues.

Moynihan took to calling Clinton every single day, telling him he should nominate Ginsburg. Texas governor Ann Richards, a Democrat, also pressed for Ginsburg's nomination, as did former secretary of transportation William Coleman. About this time, Nussbaum received a phone call from one of his friends at New York University Law School, asking if Nussbaum and his wife would like to join him for dinner at nice little inn in nearby Virginia. The other couple would be Marty and Ruth Ginsburg. Nussbaum knew what they were up to, but he went along—and he was impressed by Judge Ginsburg.

On the morning of June 11, 1993, Ginsburg was attending

a conference at the Tides Inn, in Irvington, Virginia, when she received a telephone message from Nussbaum, asking where she would be over the weekend. She called back and told him that she and Marty would be attending a wedding in Vermont. They planned to return home on Sunday. She gave Nussbaum the phone number of the Vermont hotel where she could be reached. On Saturday, Nussbaum called her in Vermont and asked if she could take the first available flight back to Washington, DC, the following morning.

The next morning, shortly after she and Marty returned home, Nussbaum arranged for himself and several members of the White House staff to interview her. They came to her home. While several White House staff members spoke to her in one room, others were in another room with Marty, going over all their tax records, Social Security returns, and personal financial reports. Not surprisingly, all their records were meticulous, and all appropriate Social Security taxes had been paid for anyone they'd hired.

At about 11:00 a.m., Nussbaum escorted Ginsburg to the White House to meet President Clinton. She and the president talked for an hour and fifteen minutes. In Ginsburg's view, they hadn't talked about anything serious, mostly children and other personal things. He did ask her why he should appoint her to the Supreme Court. At first she didn't answer. Then she said, "I never thought I'd be here, sitting in front of the president of the United States talking about whether I should be on the Supreme Court."[282] After one of her characteristic pauses, she told him she thought she'd be good at healing divisions. Clinton's view of the conversation was that he'd seen something all of his advisors had missed: Underneath her reserved exterior was a big heart, a woman who fought for the underdog. He was also impressed by her humility. After their brief talk, she returned home. Later Marty joked that if the president had invited her to lunch, they'd still be eating.

By the time Nussbaum met with Clinton toward the evening, the president had made up his mind that Ginsburg was his choice. He said he'd call her after watching a basketball game. Nussbaum knew Ginsburg would be on pins and needles, so he called her himself and told her not to go to sleep—the president wanted to talk to her, and may be calling fairly late. It was close to midnight when the president called and offered her the nomination. She was "overwhelmed with joy."[283] Clinton told her that they'd have a little ceremony in the morning in the Rose Garden, and he'd like her to give a few remarks. So she had to pull herself down from cloud nine, sit down at her writing table, and come up with a short speech.

The next morning, Ginsburg entered the Rose Garden with Clinton, smiling shyly and shaking hands with well-wishers as they walked to the podium. Clinton gave a brief speech and introduced her. Then she stepped to the microphone. The highlight of her remarks was her moving thank-you to her mother, Celia Amster Bader. "I pray that I may be all that she would have been, had she lived in an age when women could aspire and achieve and daughters are cherished as much as sons."[284]

When Ginsburg first stepped into the national public spotlight as a Supreme Court nominee, people did not know what to make of this tiny, reserved woman with a measured and precise way of speaking. As one journalist asked, "How do you square the staid, quiet, achingly precise legal scholar with the cutting-edge crusader of the 1970s campaign for gender-blind justice?"[285] Was she a gray-toned moderate judge, a dull proceduralist, as her judging history and fascination with civil procedure suggested? Her shy and aloof personality suggested that she was in fact a dry proceduralist—even though there was no doubt she had once stood at the podium in front of the justices of the Supreme Court asking that men "take their feet from our necks."

Marty enjoyed playing a supporting role. "As a general rule," he told reporters, "my wife does not give me any advice about cooking, and I do not give her advice about the law. This seems to work quite well on both sides."[286]

The day Ginsburg was led around the Hill to meet with senators and others, she spoke cordially with everyone, and was friendly with the tourists pressing to see her. Republican senator Charles Grassley asked her if she would like to attend an ice cream social in the Capitol sponsored by his Iowa constituents. She said she'd be happy to. At the ice cream social, it was clear the women and girls were delighted by her nomination. Her cool reserve momentarily fell away when she saw one of her former clerks, and spontaneously kissed her on the cheek.

To prepare Ginsburg for the nomination hearings, White House staff staged a mock questioning session—but it was clear to everyone in the room that Ginsburg knew more than anyone questioning her. Republican senator Hatch told reporters that everyone expected her nomination hearing to go smoothly with minimal opposition. Nonetheless, she prepared as if she had to convince every person in the room. She told those briefing her that she would not disparage the ACLU in any way, or distance herself from the organization. This was significant as six years earlier, during the 1988 presidential race between George H. W. Bush and Governor Dukakis, much was made of Dukakis's ACLU membership. Bush had attempted to disparage Dukakis as "a card-carrying member of the ACLU,"[287] so they expected her ACLU affiliation to be an issue.

Ahead of the nomination hearing, she was required to submit biographical and financial information. The information showed that during her thirteen years on the DC Circuit Court, she had a hand in judging over seven hundred cases. She had also received honorary degrees from American University, Vermont Law School, Georgetown University Law Center, Brooklyn Law School, Hebrew Union College, Rutgers University, and Lewis and Clark College. The financial record showed that as of 1993, the Ginsburgs' assets came to over $6 million, including their Watergate apartment, valued at $1.3 million.

The nomination hearing was held in room 216 of the Senate Hart Office Building. Ginsburg arrived early. She was calm and ready, with Marty right behind her. The room was packed with senators, White House staff, reporters, and her family and friends. For three full days of questioning, she spoke in careful measured tones, demonstrating the breadth of her knowledge. To her surprise—and to the surprise of the White House— nobody asked a single question about her ACLU affiliation.

Ginsburg at her confirmation hearing, July 21, 1993.

On August 3, 1993, when Ginsburg was sixty years old, her nomination to the Supreme Court was confirmed by a Senate vote of 96-3. At an American Bar Association meeting shortly after her appointment, a much younger woman asked Ginsburg if she'd always wanted to be a judge. She smiled and explained what things were like for female law graduates in 1959 and why the idea would have never occurred to her.

Shortly after Ginsburg's appointment, the National Association of Women Judges held a reception for both Ginsburg and O'Connor at the court. Anticipating the sort of confusion that would occur—and, in fact, *did* occur—the Association presented Justice O'Connor and Justice Ginsburg with T-shirts. O'Connor's read, "I'm Sandra, not Ruth." Ginsburg's read, "I'm Ruth, not Sandra." Ginsburg even received a gift from Strom Thurmond, the former segregationist from South Carolina who had voted against her appointment to the DC Circuit: a keychain with the words, "With Best Wishes, Strom Thurmond."[288]

People asked Ginsburg if her life changed after she was confirmed as a U.S. Supreme Court justice and the second woman to sit on the court. Her answer was an emphatic yes. The hardest part was getting used to the loss of privacy and intense media attention. Suddenly people recognized her in shops and theaters. When a reporter asked her about her habit of reading by flashlight in movie theaters, she explained that she didn't like commercials or previews, so before the feature started, she read her mail. Why waste valuable minutes when she could be productive? As a result, well-wishers sent her small pen lights.

Another thing had definitely changed: When she and Marty were at social gatherings and someone introduced "Justice Ginsburg," nobody reached for Marty's hand.

25

JUSTICE, SHALL
YOU PURSUE

After her swearing in ceremony at the Supreme Court, Ginsburg returned to her chambers to find her secretaries in a panic. They had just received a phone call from a woman who said, "Tell Mrs. Ginsburg she will not live to sit on that Court."[289] Feeling uneasy, Ginsburg went about her weekend, as planned—guarded by the U.S. Marshals Service. It was a full weekend. The next day, a Saturday, she attended a celebration at Harvard Law School with her daughter, Jane. On Sunday she celebrated her granddaughter's third birthday at the court—a rare occasion in which peanut butter and jelly sandwiches were served at the U.S. Supreme Court. Monday rolled around, and she showed up for her first day without incident.

O'Connor remarked once that she didn't mind being the first woman on the Supreme Court—she just didn't want to be the last. "If you think I'm happy there is another woman on this Court," O'Connor said when Ginsburg arrived, "you can't imagine how happy John is."[290] A tradition among the Supreme Court spouses was quarterly lunches, and John O'Connor was a little tired of being the only male spouse. When John met Marty, he proposed that they form the Denis Thatcher Club.

The requirement for admission was that your wife has the job that, in your heart of hearts, you wish you had. O'Connor's view of the situation was that if she and Ruth Ginsburg had not encountered so many barriers when they'd tried to enter the legal profession, they would have been happy to accept a prestigious clerkship, followed by a job in a major law firm, where they would have worked their way up to partner. At that stage in their lives, they would have been retired law partners.

Ginsburg liked to tell the story of Sara Grimke, a nineteenth-century feminist lawyer and anti-slavery activist from South Carolina who once had the opportunity to visit the Supreme Court. The court, during her visit, was not in session. The justices invited her to sit in the chief justice's seat. She sat down and said, "Who knows but this chair may one day be occupied by a woman." While the justices laughed heartily, she thought perhaps she had uttered a prophecy.[291]

It was expected that Ginsburg would take the newly vacated chambers on the first floor, where all the other justices had their offices, but she was put off by the lingering smell of cigar smoke—so she opted instead for larger, airier chambers on the second floor. Supreme Court justices were allowed to select art from the National Gallery to hang in their chambers. Ginsburg, who preferred modern art, chose paintings by mid-century Americans, like Ben Cunningham and Max Weber. Her favorite was Josef Albers's "Homage to the Square."

She hung a large silver mezuzah on the doorpost of her office, a gift from the Shulamith School for Girls in Brooklyn. On her wall, in beautifully drawn Hebrew letters, was the command from Deuteronomy, "*Zedek, zedek, tirdof,*" which translated as "Justice, Justice, shall you pursue." She kept a baton from her high school days in her chambers and was known on occasion to twirl it for visitors. Sometimes she also showed visitors her favorite photograph: her son-in-law gazing at her grandson when the baby was about two months old. She loved the photograph because it captured the deep love between father and son, and her dream that men would participate equally in the spheres that had once been designated for women only.

When Ginsburg arrived, there was one bathroom in the justices' robing room, and it was labeled "Men." Anytime O'Connor had to use the restroom, she had to go back to her chambers. Now, with two women on the court, a second bathroom was added in the robing room. Ginsburg took it as an optimistic sign when the newly created women's bathroom was as large as the men's.

The Supreme Court operates as nine distinct and separate law offices, with each justice hiring his or her own staff, including law clerks and messengers. Like most justices, Ginsburg did not review applications from the hundreds of new lawyers who applied to work with her each year. Instead, she left the screening to others, most notably Columbia's law school dean, who didn't bother her with even five or six applications. Instead, he would recommend a single applicant. He understood what she wanted in a clerk: She didn't just want a top graduate; she also wanted someone who had already clerked for a year. She had another requirement: Her clerks had to be respectful and humble. She had a clerk once who was rude to one of the secretaries. After that, she made sure not to hire anyone she thought was haughty enough to behave arrogantly with the secretaries. She said, "I tell my clerks, if push came to shove, I could do your work— but I can't do without my secretaries."[292]

She also relied on judges on the Court of Appeals to recommend their best clerks. Marty helped with the screening of these applicants, looking over the writing samples, eliminating those with elaborate writing styles who would be harder for Ginsburg to work with. Ginsburg preferred legal writing to be direct and simple. While she didn't look for applicants with a particular ideology, it often happened that like-minded clerks gravitated toward her. She did once have a clerk, though, who was a Federalist Society member.

Her first excursion each year with her new clerks was a visit to the Washington National Opera on the evening when the young artists take over the lead roles. She celebrated their birthdays and anniversaries, usually with Marty's homemade cakes. She gave "grand clerk" baby T-shirts as gifts if clerks became parents.

To get started, Ginsburg asked one of her former clerks, David Post, to come back and work with her. When she had first hired him, he'd been attending night school at Georgetown Law. His wife, an economist, had a demanding job, and he needed a night program because he had to take care of the children in the morning and early afternoon. It was a story after her own heart. She hired him and allowed him the flexible schedule he needed. It was no surprise to her that his work was exemplary.

The task of a Supreme Court justice differed in important ways from the task of a federal appellate judge. The Supreme Court had the responsibility of keeping the law more or less uniform. If all the lower courts were in agreement on how to interpret a particular statute, there was little reason for the Supreme Court to grant review of a challenge to that statute. But often lower courts differed, partly because so many statutes were vague. Sometimes the vagueness resulted from the inability of the legislature to anticipate all particulars that might arise in the application of the statute. Other times, statutes were vague on purpose, as when the issue was such a political hot potato that the legislature simply couldn't be too specific without angering one group or another, so they used fuzzy language to get the law passed, essentially punting the task of teasing out the meaning of individual words and phrases to the courts. The daily work of a Supreme Court justice consisted mostly of selecting the seventy-five or so cases the court would hear in a given term, reading the briefs, preparing to hear oral arguments, and drafting decisions. While they were largely assisted by clerks at each step, Ginsburg did much of the work herself.

Ginsburg revered the institution of the Supreme Court, and immediately took to the customs, particularly those based on a tradition of collegiality. For their routine gatherings, when they entered the robing room and before conferences, the justices began with handshakes—thirty-six of them. They ate lunch together in the Justices' Dining Room, by choice, not rule. The dining room was elegant, but the food came from the same public cafeteria everyone else used. Sometimes they discussed a lawyer's performance in oral arguments, but mostly they made small talk.

Supreme Court, 1993-1994. From the top left: Thomas, Kennedy, Souter, Ginsburg, O'Connor, Blackmun, Rehnquist, Stevens, Scalia.

239

The first opinion Ginsburg was assigned to write was a divided decision on a complicated case brought under an extremely complex piece of legislation, the Employee Retirement Income Security Act, known as ERISA. Generally, a newly appointed Supreme Court justice would be issued a unanimous opinion to write. In other words, the chief justice usually started the newbie off with an easy one. A little rattled by the assignment, Ginsburg went to speak to O'Connor, who knew Chief Justice Rehnquist well. "How could he do this to me?" she asked. O'Connor encouraged her, and said, "Just do it"—which was her answer to any difficulties she faced.

The case that would become Ginsburg's signature decision, *United States v. Virginia,*[293] came to the Supreme Court a few years after she took her place on the bench.

The case against the Virginia Military Institute—VMI—started when a female student who wanted to apply to VMI complained to the Justice Department that the Institute refused to admit women. VMI, established in 1839, was a state-funded institution with a reputation for rigorous academics, particularly in math and science. Students learned in an "adversative"[294] environment that included ritualized hazing intended to create strong character and solidarity. While the Institute initially started as a training for military cadets, by the 1990s only about 15 percent of VMI graduates entered the military. Others entered fields as diverse as law, medicine, engineering, and public service.

The United States brought a suit against VMI on behalf of women capable of succeeding in the program, and thus began the decade's most controversial, highly publicized gender equality case. Litigation at the trial level was about the physiological differences between men and women and the question of whether women could endure the rigors of a VMI education. Those arguing in favor of keeping women out claimed that accepting women would undermine the very value of the program because the ritualized hazing would play out differently with women involved. Supporters of the school also claimed that if women could make it through the program, success would no longer be evidence of manhood, and would thus destroy what made VMI unique and great. VMI based its case partly on Carol Gilligan's theory that the feminine and masculine modes of thinking were distinct. Gilligan herself was called to the stand to testify. Gilligan was not supportive of VMI's exclusion of women, and tried to explain that in her theory, the distinct voices were not intended to be ironclad rules about gender differences.

At trial, VMI won. The trial court found that the weight of expert witnesses fell on the side of excluding women on the grounds that the innate differences between men and women would undermine the methods of instruction at VMI. On appeal, the Fourth Circuit reversed, finding that the exclusion of women violated the equal protection clause of the Fourteenth Amendment.[295]

In response to its loss in the appellate court, Virginia established the Women's Institute for Leadership, or the VWIL, which they housed at a private women's college, Mary Baldwin College. Whereas VMI was based on an adversarial method of teaching with the purpose of building character, the VWIL was based on a cooperative theory of teaching, purporting to be following the experts on how the genders differed. There were other differences between the schools as well. The average SAT scores of admitted women at VWIL were about one hundred points lower than the scores for VMI freshmen. Fewer of the faculty at the women's institution held PhDs and they were paid considerably less. The women's institution offered only bachelor of arts degrees, while VMI offered degrees in science and engineering as well.

The case went back to the trial court to determine whether the twin schools satisfied the equal protection clause. The trial court found that the new women's institution did satisfy the requirements of equal protection by allowing women a comparable education. When the case went up on appeal once more, the Fourth Circuit upheld the trial court's ruling, agreeing that the educational opportunities were substantially similar even though the women's institution lacked the prestige of a VMI degree.

The government appealed to the U.S. Supreme Court. Organizations such as the National Organization of Women and the ACLU submitted amicus briefs supporting the government's position. One woman quipped that if men could not acquire the same training alongside women, well, maybe they weren't as tough as they thought. Another amicus brief was submitted by eighteen active and retired female military officers, including a woman who had been shot down and held prisoner during Desert Storm. The female officers were strongly in favor of admitting women to VMI, and held up their own experiences as examples of how tough women could be. One misconception in certain media outlets was that single-sex schools were at issue. They weren't. The issue had nothing to do with private all-women schools, but rather whether the state could make a particular kind of education available to men, but not women.

The case then came before the Supreme Court with oral argument scheduled on January 17, 1996. Ginsburg sat on the bench wearing black robes, listening as the attorney for the government made the same arguments she had made at that same podium so many years earlier. The government made her signature argument that the exclusion of women from the Institute perpetuated and reinforced invidious gender stereotyping. This was the sort of case she would have never dared bring in the 1970s because it would have been too radical for the era.

Immediately after the oral argument, the justices, as was their custom, sat down to a conference. Once discussion started, it was clear that there would be enough votes to rule in favor of the government and force VMI to admit women. Only Rehnquist and Scalia wanted women kept out of VMI because they saw no constitutional grounds for the government's position. There was nothing in the Constitution at all about women, much less women's education, so for Scalia, reading the Fourteenth Amendment as applying to VMI's admission policy was a simple matter of making things up. Clarence Thomas had recused himself because his son had attended VMI, so it looked like the decision would be 6-2. Because Rehnquist was in the minority, the task of assigning the opinion fell to Stevens, the most senior justice in the majority. Initially he planned to assign it to O'Connor, the most senior woman in the majority, but she said no, it should go to Ginsburg. Rehnquist changed his mind after the writing of the opinions had begun, announcing to the others that he was switching his vote, leaving Scalia as the lone dissenter.

The last time the Supreme Court had issued a ruling on gender equality had been in *Craig v. Boren*, the beer-drinking fraternity men case for which Ginsburg had written an amicus brief. So the law stood just where the Supreme Court had left it, with a vague sort of heightened scrutiny with the term "intermediate" dropped into Rehnquist's dissent. Ginsburg—who had once argued for the same level of scrutiny afforded in race-based distinctions—now drafted an opinion that unequivocally made a heightened, intermediate scrutiny the law. It was like her not to stray from the established precedent. However, while defining "intermediate," she upped the standard slightly to a level of scrutiny that she called "skeptical scrutiny," requiring that a gender-based statute, to survive, must have an exceedingly persuasive justification. She concluded that VMI did not.

Late on a Friday, when she'd been hard at work with her clerks, drafting the opinion and preparing it for circulation to the other justices, Scalia walked in and handed her his dissent—a lengthy, passionately argued defense of the men-only policy at VMI. She was a little dismayed. Later she said it ruined her weekend, but his dissent allowed her to focus and sharpen her own argument. She spent the next few days rewriting.

The opinion issued by the Supreme Court on June 26, 1996, held that Virginia violated the Fourteenth Amendment by offering the unique opportunities afforded by a VMI education only to men.[296] The Institute was left with a choice: It could admit women, or it could sever its ties with Virginia and become a private institution. *The United States v. Virginia* became the final case in the line of gender equality cases that began with *Reed v. Reed* in 1971. The law was settled. Ginsburg had finished what she started in the late 1960s.

For three months, VMI did nothing. Then, on September 22, 1996, the board voted 9 to 8 to admit women. In what was characterized by the *New York Times* as an act of defiance because school officials had previously made clear that they were "galled" by the idea of admitting women, a spokesperson for the school said that they would require women to "get crew cuts and meet the same fitness requirements as men."[297] On August 18, 1997, VMI announced that it had admitted thirty-

Virginia Military Institute.

one female freshmen cadets. One of the first women admitted said she felt special—but added that she'd "feel more special when she walked across the stage with that diploma."[298]

To use Ginsburg's phrase, the VMI decision played to mixed reviews.[299] She received a letter from a 1967 graduate of VMI who told her that he personally knew a few young women as physically, intellectually, and emotionally tough as he was thirty years ago when he completed his education. With the letter, he enclosed a gift—the pin given to mothers of the graduating class. His own mother was no longer living, so he wanted Ginsburg to have her pin. "This pin makes you an adjunct member of the VMI family. I'm sure it would have made my mother proud to know it is in your possession."[300]

Not all responses were so kind. Phyllis Schlafly, in an open letter from her conservative interest group, Eagle Forum, accused Ginsburg of an activist determination to write her own radical feminist goals into the Constitution. Schlafly said every senator who voted for Ginsburg's confirmation shared the shame of the decision. To the VMI students and alumni, she said, "Your VMI training not only taught you to be tough, courageous and honorable, but also to survive humiliation and harassment. You are now facing your greatest challenge. . . . If you allow Ginsburg et al. to do to VMI what Pat Schroeder et al. have done to the United States Navy, you are not the exemplars of manhood we thought you were."[301]

Some called for Ginsburg's resignation from the Supreme Court. VMI's superintendent sent her a video with poetry entries, including

> We could not win this last campaign,
> Or the Institute protect
> From the army of self-righteousness—
> The politically correct.

Often people—horrified at the ruling—asked Ginsburg if she'd want her own daughter to attend such a school. For Ginsburg, that was entirely beside the point. She herself would not want to enroll, nor would Jane. The ruling—as she saw it—was a victory for individualism, for the woman who doesn't fit the stereotypes, the woman who desperately wanted to attend VMI. Nobody, least of all Ginsburg, expected large numbers of women to want to enroll. But the women who did—if Ginsburg's experiences were any guide—would probably work harder than anyone else so that a failure would not reflect badly on women who might come later.

People often assume that *United States v. Virginia* was Ginsburg's favorite case. In fact, her favorite case was one in which a county government terminated a woman's parental rights on the grounds that she was an unfit parent, and the woman wanted to appeal.

Parental rights termination cases occupy a strange hybrid in the law—a charge that a parent is unfit and should lose parental rights is brought under a civil code, but has much in common with criminal cases because the state brings the action against the individual. The initial findings against parents are made on the lowly preponderance of the evidence burden of proof used in civil cases instead of the heightened criminal burden of proof of beyond a reasonable doubt because, in theory, the law was not intended to punish the parent but to act in the best interest of the child. Ginsburg, though, understood that the pain of losing a child forever was much greater than, say, paying a fine or serving a light sentence as a result of a criminal infraction.

The issue in the case that came before the Supreme Court was straightforward: A local court in Mississippi terminated a mother's parental rights to her two children. The mother wanted to appeal but could not afford the transcripts, which came to more than $2,300. The issue was whether the state was obligated to provide her with free transcripts so she could appeal.

Ginsburg, writing for the majority, said the state may not "bolt the door to equal justice," by setting up a system where only those with money could appeal.[302] Rehnquist, Scalia, and Thomas dissented because they didn't think parents accused of unfitness should have the same protections offered to criminal defendants.

Ginsburg's response to the woman's plea was motivated by her belief that the "law is the protector of the oppressed, the poor, the minority, the loner."[303]

The Ginsburg family gathered each year in New Mexico in the foothills of the Sangre de Cristo Mountains before the Supreme Court began its new term. James was now married to Lisa Brauston, an art historian, and he was the head of a successful classical music label. Jane was a professor of law at Columbia, with an expertise in copyright law. Between them they'd given their parents four grandchildren. New Mexico was their meeting place because Ginsburg considered the Santa Fe Opera to be the finest summer opera company in the world.

The Ginsburgs, 1998.

They took tours of the countryside and hikes in the hills. They were given VIP access to the works of Georgia O'Keefe, and of course, enjoyed delicious dinners prepared by Marty and Jane, who Ruth said was almost as good a cook as her father.

Ruth Bader Ginsburg was sixty-six years old during the summer of 1999 when she became ill while teaching a law school program on the Greek island of Crete. Initially doctors thought she had a disorder of the large intestine. Upon closer examination she was found to have both an intestinal disorder and colon cancer. A small tumor measuring about two centimeters by three centimeters had invaded her colon. Further testing showed no evidence that the cancer had spread.

O'Connor, who'd had extensive surgery for breast cancer, offered her some advice. "You're going to get a lot of cards. Don't even try to answer them. Just concentrate on what you have to do."[304] It was O'Connor's usual *just do it* advice. O'Connor, who had returned to the bench immediately after chemotherapy and nine days after major surgery, had other, even more practical advice: She should schedule her chemotherapy for Friday, so she could be able to be back in court on Monday."

Ginsburg's law clerks were aghast when she insisted on doing court business from her hospital bed. They sent her novels to read so she would relax and rest—but she wasn't about to spend her time reading fiction when there was court work to be done. Treatment was aggressive, including massive surgery, daily radiation, and chemotherapy. Despite all this, Ginsburg never missed a day of oral arguments. She showed her spirit when she said, "There is nothing like a cancer bout to make one relish the joys of being alive."[305] Her surgery was successful and her prognosis was excellent.

Afterward, though, Marty said she looked like a concentration camp survivor. He wanted her to hire a personal trainer to regain her strength, so she did. She had always exercised regularly. Clerks from her days as a DC Circuit judge recall running into her in the elevator while she was wearing her gym clothes. But now she began a regime designed to help with her recovery.

Her colleagues rallied around her, offering whatever help she might need. Chief Justice Rehnquist spoke to her privately, and said he thought they should keep her workload light. He then asked her what case she would like. This was something he had never before offered. She told him she didn't want a lighter load because she didn't think she'd need it. She wanted to save such favors for the day she might need them. Meanwhile, she mentioned that there were two cases she'd love to be assigned. She told him which cases she wanted. He said he was thinking of keeping those two for himself—but he gave her one of them.

For Ginsburg, the reaction of her colleagues to her illness illustrated that the court worked as a family. In speeches she praised her colleagues, saying that above all else she valued the collegial spirit of the court. They had their differences and yet they were personal friends. The Ginsburgs and Scalias had a tradition of sharing New Year's Eve together. Maureen Scalia and Marty Ginsburg did the cooking.

Ginsburg and Scalia also shared a love of opera. She had a photograph of the time she and Scalia—in a moment of sheer levity—appeared on the opera stage as supernumeraries wearing full eighteenth-century costume. She also kept in her office a photograph of the time she and Scalia rode an elephant together while they were in India as judicial delegates. Her feminist friends responded to the photograph by asking why Ginsburg was riding in the *back*. She assured her friends that the seating arrangement was entirely due to the distribution of weight.

26

THE EYE OF
THE BEHOLDER

The collegial spirit of the Supreme Court was shattered in November of 2000. Florida ran into trouble counting its ballots in the presidential contest between Republican George W. Bush and Democrat Albert Gore—and the Supreme Court decided to get involved.

On the eve of the election, all the states had reported, and the outcome hinged on the results in Florida. The networks predicted that Gore would win the state and thus the election. At 3:00 a.m., the votes were still being counted, and Bush had taken the lead by a tiny fraction of a percentage point. As daylight approached, the networks backed off their predictions and declared Florida too close to call. Gore was ahead in the nationwide vote, but in Florida, Bush led by a few hundred votes—or .00000056 percent. There were complaints of ballot irregularities. Because of an odd way some of the ballots were printed, the holes were not lined up with the names, so in one county, Buchanan got votes which he admitted had been intended for Gore. Upwards of a thousand votes could have been miscounted and attributed to Bush—a number that in most elections would not matter, but in this election would change the outcome.

Florida law allowed for Gore to demand a recount, which he did. The Florida secretary of state, Katharine Harris, a Republican and Bush supporter, refused to order the recount, saying that it would take too long for her to meet her deadline to certify the results. Gore took the case to court. The Florida legislature was Republican, as was Governor Jeb Bush, brother to the presidential candidate. But the Florida Supreme Court leaned liberal. The Florida Supreme Court heard the case, and held for Gore, finding that the Florida election statute required that all legitimate votes be counted. The court ordered Miami-Dade County to count the nine thousand questionable ballots by hand. The court also required manual recounts of all Florida counties with irregular ballots.

George Bush filed an emergency application in the U.S. Supreme Court, asking the court to stop the recount on the grounds that the Florida Supreme Court was changing the rules in allowing a recount to continue. The Gore team responded by pointing out that the Florida Supreme Court's reading of the rules was perfectly legitimate, and besides, this was up to the Florida Supreme Court under well-established principles of federalism.

The conservative majority, Rehnquist, O'Connor, Scalia, Kennedy, and Thomas, voted to grant review. But then, almost as if regretting the decision to step into the fray, the court took the easy way out, essentially sending the decision back to the Florida Supreme Court to explain its position more clearly.

So Gore and Bush returned to the Florida Supreme Court. Four days later, on Friday, December 4, the Florida Supreme Court handed Gore a stunning victory by ordering the recount of all sixty thousand under votes in the remaining counties. The Florida Supreme Court's interpretation of Florida's election statute was that the overriding concern when the legislature had passed the statute was to make sure every legitimate vote was counted. The Florida court, therefore, concluded that the state had the duty to count *all* the votes.

By now, after some of the recounting that had occurred, Gore had narrowed the gap to approximately 193 votes—a stunning number given that millions of votes had been cast in Florida. That weekend, the recounting was to begin. Bush worked quickly. By that Friday afternoon, his legal team was already drafting a brief to ask the U.S. Supreme Court to intervene and overturn the Florida Supreme Court decision. The brief was submitted to the Supreme Court at 9:18 p.m. on the evening of December 8.

Linda Greenhouse, a *New York Times* reporter who covered the Supreme Court, told her superiors not to worry—in her opinion, the conservative majority would not accept review of the case. The conservatives believed too deeply in the principles of federalism to entertain a challenge as to how Florida should count its votes.

In fact, Chief Justice Rehnquist wanted to order Florida to stop counting ballots without offering a reason. Thomas, Scalia, Kennedy, and O'Connor agreed. Ginsburg and the other moderate to liberal justices were stunned. The conservatives were the justices who railed against judicial activism, and preached judicial restraint. If interfering in Florida's election process and basically handing the election to one party wasn't judicial activism, what was?

The conservative majority announced the decision to hear the Bush appeal just before the 3:00 p.m. deadline for the Sunday *New York Times*. For the first—and only time—in a forty-year career in journalism, reporter Linda Greenhouse actually heard an editor shout, "Hold the presses!"[306] The conservative majority set a breakneck schedule. Briefs were due Sunday. They would hear oral argument on Monday. They would issue an opinion on Tuesday. It was unheard of for the Supreme Court to move so quickly.

On Sunday, one of Ginsburg's clerks whose brother worked for the *Wall Street Journal* learned that the media would be releasing a political bombshell in the Monday papers about O'Connor. Apparently, on the eve of the election, O'Connor had attended a party. When the networks called the election for Gore, she said, "This is terrible!" Her husband John explained to the others at the party that she was disappointed because she hoped to retire. She wanted Bush to win because she wanted a Republican president to select her replacement. Upon hearing that her statement would appear in the Monday papers, the clerks assumed that O'Connor would recuse herself instead of face accusations that she was acting from personal motives, but she insisted on remaining on the case. At one point during the weekend, tempers so flared that the clerks of one of the conservative justices had a screaming fight with the clerks of one of the liberal justices. Ginsburg attributed the tension to exhaustion. The breakneck pace meant none of them got much sleep over the four days.

At oral argument, Gore argued that the Supreme Court lacked jurisdiction over what was essentially a state matter. Bush argued that his constitutional rights were being denied because different counties were using different standards for counting, and that the entire process was a mess.

The justices met immediately after the arguments, as was their custom. Rehnquist, Scalia, Thomas, O'Connor, and Kennedy—the conservatives—wanted to reverse the Florida Supreme Court decision and halt the recount. The others dissented. They had twenty-four hours to draft their opinions.

Protesters outside the Supreme Court, December 11, 2000.

The majority opinion held that equal protection was violated because different counties in Florida were using different standards. The majority gave a second reason for halting the recount: They said there wasn't time to do an adequate job of recounting the votes. Oddly, the majority also stated that "Our consideration is limited to the present circumstances"[307]—a declaration essentially saying the case would not become precedent for the future, making it appear that the ruling was deliberately intended to help one individual in one case, discarding the obligation of the court to set and follow precedent.

Because time was so short, there was not time for the four dissenters to join a single statement, so Ginsburg drafted her own dissent. Scalia flew into a rage when he saw one of her drafts. In a footnote, she accused the majority of engaging in Al Sharpton tactics. Seeing how angry—and hurt—Scalia was over the accusation, she removed the footnote. What she left in was the implication that the majority was overturning the Florida Supreme Court ruling not on legal grounds but simply because they didn't personally like the result. She relied on theories of federalism and the Constitution's mandate that federal power be limited and that states govern their own affairs—the very principles that Scalia and Rehnquist held so dear—to conclude that the U.S. Supreme Court had no business interfering with what was a matter of Florida state law. Finally, she concluded there was no reason to believe that Florida could not count all its votes in a timely and organized manner.

The majority and dissenting opinions issued to the public were so confusing that journalists covering the Supreme Court were unable to understand exactly what the court was saying. What law were they following? What did this mean for the future? There was a plurality, a concurrence, and four separate dissents. The only thing that was immediately clear to the public was that the Supreme Court was ordering Florida to stop counting its votes, essentially declaring Bush the winner of the 2000 election. To this day there remain conflicting opinions on who would have won the election in Florida had all the votes been counted.

After the decision was released on Tuesday, Ginsburg sent her clerks to Justice Kennedy's office to watch what was being said of the decision on the news. Late that evening, she was still in her chambers when Scalia called her and said, "Ruth, what are you doing still at the court? You should go home and take a hot bath."[308] A few weeks later, Scalia and Ginsburg kept to their usual New Year's Eve plans—but it would be a long time before relations on the court would return to normal.

Each of the justices was affected by the backlash against the court. It was one thing to be called an extremist, or wrong, or worse. Judges were used to that. It was quite another to be accused—by large segments of the population—of participating in a partisan sham, a political fix, and a coup. There were those accusing the Supreme Court of stealing the election from the voters. They accused the court of violating the Constitution and handing the election to their own political party. Defenders of the majority decision said the Florida Supreme Court had engaged in partisan politics, and because a national election was at stake, the Supreme Court was right to intervene. Others defended the decision on the grounds that the Supreme Court saved the country from a debacle of endless recounts and uncertainty. Anger ran high among Democrats because there was no doubt that Gore won the popular vote nationally.

Justice Souter was so devastated by the decision and the public reaction that he nearly resigned from the court. Scalia, who generally welcomed a fight, got so tired of people questioning the decision and suggesting that it had been politically motivated that in an interview eight years later, he burst out and said, "I really don't wanna get into—I mean this is—get over it. It's so old by now."[309]

Justice O'Connor was not the type to feel or express regret—she was a practical, don't-look-back type of person— but later, Ginsburg told journalist Terry Gross that O'Connor regretted the decision that handed the presidency to George Bush:

> Did she regret the Bush presidency? You bet she
> did, and you bet she does. The war in Iraq. The war
> on terror. John Ashcroft as attorney general. The
> Terri Schiavo case. All these things filled Justice
> O'Connor with revulsion, and you can be sure that
> her vote in *Bush v. Gore* weighs on her mind. Now,

regret it? Saying she regretted it? Did she regret it? You bet.[310]

Not long after Ginsburg made this statement, O'Connor publicly expressed misgivings about *Bush v. Gore* because it gave the court a "less than perfect reputation."[311] She said, "Maybe the Court should have said, 'We're not going to take it, goodbye.'" She also said Florida had been making a mess of its recount, but at the end of the day, the Supreme Court probably made things worse by getting involved. Jeffrey Toobin, who wrote extensively about the Rehnquist court, agreed that O'Connor's change of mind came from the direction of the Republican Party under Bush. O'Connor had been a more moderate Republican. George H. W. Bush was her ideal president. She thought his son's presidency would be similar, but under the second George Bush, the Republican Party swung so far to the right she didn't recognize it as the party she'd been loyal to for so long.

For Ginsburg, the *Bush v. Gore* decision demonstrated that judicial activism was in the eye of the beholder. When people asked her to define judicial activism, she said the meaning depended on "whose ox is being gored."[312]

In December of 2000, shortly after the Supreme Court decided *Bush v. Gore*, Marty and Ruth went to New York City to see the play *Proof*. After the first act intermission, they walked down the aisle toward their seats. Suddenly the entire audience rose to its feet and applauded Justice Ginsburg. She stood, shyly smiling. Marty—the serial wisecracker—could not resist. "I'll bet you didn't know," he said, "there's a convention of tax lawyers here!"[313]

27

THE POWER
OF DISSENT

One day Ginsburg brought home a newly drafted Supreme
Court decision concerning the Family Medical and Leave Act.
Marty read the decision—which held that an individual may sue
a state for damages in federal court under the Family Medical
and Leave Act—and assumed his wife was the author because
of the bold declaration of the law regarding gender distinctions:

> We have held that statutory classifications that
> distinguish between males and females are subject
> to heightened scrutiny . . . The State's justification
> for such a classification must not rely on overbroad
> generalizations about the different talents, capacities,
> or preferences of males and females.[314]

Another passage looked as if it had been lifted from one of her
ACLU briefs:

> The history of the many state laws limiting women's
> employment opportunities is chronicled in—and,
> until relatively recently, was sanctioned by—this

Court's own opinions. For example, in *Bradwell v. State*, and *Goesaert v. Cleary* the Court upheld state laws prohibiting women from practicing law and tending bar, respectively. State laws frequently subjected women to distinctive restrictions, terms, conditions, and benefits for those jobs they could take. In *Muller v. Oregon*, for example, this Court approved a state law limiting the hours that women could work for wages, and observed that 19 States had such laws at the time. Such laws were based on the related beliefs that (1) woman is, and should remain, "the center of home and family life."[315]

Marty was thus amazed when she told him that she wasn't the author—Rehnquist was—Chief Justice Rehnquist, who had often been the sole dissenter in the cases she presented to the court in the 1970s. Rehnquist had evidently had a change of heart, and a major one.

Many thought this was Ginsburg's ultimate triumph—that she'd finally brought around the one justice she had been unable to persuade from the Burger court years. Ginsburg insisted that Rehnquist's change of heart had little to do with her, and more to do with his own life experiences. She said there was a side of him that people rarely saw: the loving, tender grandfather who adored his granddaughters, and understood the struggles his daughter faced as a single, divorced mother. Ginsburg believed it was his experience caring for his granddaughters—often leaving court early to pick them up—that helped him understand what she had been trying to do on behalf of women.

The fact was she'd probably done more to influence him than she realized—or admitted. She still saw herself as a teacher. She always carried a copy of the Constitution with her. When school children visited the court, she read portions to them. She varied which sections she read aloud, but she always read the preamble, showing how "We the people" was linked to "a more perfect union." For her, this meant that as the "people" expanded to include more people—blacks, women, Native Americans—the union became more perfect.

O'Connor did not resign during Bush's first four-year term, perhaps not wanting to add fuel to the accusations that her vote in *Bush v. Gore* had been self-serving. In July of 2005, she announced she was retiring before the start of the new term beginning in October, or whenever the Senate confirmed her successor. For eleven years—since Clinton appointed Breyer in 1994—there had been no new appointments. It had therefore been one of the longest uninterrupted stretches in history. Immediately after O'Connor announced her resignation, the lobbying began for the next appointment, with both liberal and conservative groups setting up phone banks and building support for their choices among senators.

Bush nominated John Roberts, a graduate of Harvard Law School and former editor of the law review. Roberts had once clerked for Chief Justice Rehnquist. He'd served as the first President Bush's principal deputy solicitor general. In 2003, George W. Bush appointed him to the DC Circuit. On September 3, 2005, before the Supreme Court nomination hearings could begin, Chief Justice Rehnquist died of cancer. A memorial was held in the Upper Great Hall of the U.S. Supreme Court to praise his years of service to the court.

Now the president had two seats to fill. He withdrew his nomination of Roberts for O'Connor's seat, and instead nominated Roberts to fill the office of chief justice. For O'Connor's seat, he nominated Samuel Anthony Alito, Jr., from the U.S. Court of Appeals for the Third Circuit.

Both Roberts and Alito were easily confirmed, Alito by a comfortable margin and Roberts by a large margin. O'Connor, while a Republican, had been relatively moderate on most issues, and was usually the swing vote. Rehnquist had grown somewhat more moderate in his later years. There was nothing moderate about either Roberts or Alito. When Roberts and Alito replaced Rehnquist and O'Connor, the court took a decisive and sharp turn to the right.

Whereas once Ginsburg had been seen as a moderate and incrementalist, she was now one of the most liberal voices on the court, not because she changed but because the court changed around her.

Two years after O'Connor's departure came the Lilly Ledbetter case. If *United States v. Virginia* was Ginsburg's signature decision, *Lilly Ledbetter v. Goodyear Tire and Rubber Company* was her signature dissent.

Lilly Ledbetter was born in a small town in Alabama, in a house without running water or electricity. In 1979, with two young children at home—and over the objections of her husband—she applied for a job at the Goodyear tire factory. She was one of the first women hired as a manager. In 1985 she was promoted to area manager. For much of the nineteen years she worked at Goodyear, her fellow managers were all men. Her view of her years at Goodyear Tire was that she experienced constant gender prejudice and frequent sexual harassment. If she and a male colleague made the same error, she was disciplined but he was not.

She was close to retirement when she received an anonymous note in her mailbox confirming her suspicions: She was paid less than her male colleagues. The note consisted of her salary, along with the salaries of three other managers. Her salary was correct down to the dollar. The note told her that even the most junior of her male colleagues, a man whom she herself had trained, was earning more than she was.

She sued Goodyear under both the Equal Pay Act and Title VII of the Civil Rights Act. Goodyear records showed that over time, her pay slipped in comparison to her male colleagues who had equal or less seniority. At the end of 1997, she was the only woman working as an area manager. The pay discrepancy between her and her fifteen male colleagues was stark. At the trial, her supervisor acknowledged that one year, her pay fell below the minimum threshold for the position. Goodyear's defense was that her lower pay was because of poor performance, but the supervisor testified that just before her pay dropped, she received a Top Performance Award.

A jury found for Ledbetter and awarded her $3.5 million, which the district judge reduced to $360,000.

On appeal, Goodyear argued that the decision was wrong as a matter of law because Title VII requires that discrimination complaints be made within 180 days of the employer's discriminatory conduct. The decisions to pay her less had occurred more than 180 days before she brought her complaint. Therefore, it was too late. The U.S. Court of Appeals agreed with Goodyear. The court reversed the lower court's decision, finding that the 180 days was long past.

Ledbetter petitioned the U.S. Supreme Court to hear her case. After both sides presented their arguments, the Supreme Court justices split 5-4, with the conservative majority—Roberts, Alito, Scalia, Thomas, and Kennedy—upholding the appellate court's decision that Ledbetter's complaint was untimely because she should have brought her action within 180 days of her first unequal paycheck.[316] They believed their decision was necessary to protect employers from the burden of defending claims arising from employment decisions that were long past.

Ginsburg dissented, joined by Stevens, Souter, and Breyer, pointing out that often a worker has no way of knowing if her pay is lower than her colleagues. She may have little reason to suspect discrimination until a pattern emerges. It takes time for evidence to emerge that pay differences were gender-related instead of merit-based. It might take years for an employee to know that her pay is not equal to her male colleagues, and years to gather the evidence that her work is as good. In Ginsburg's view, each paycheck created increasing harm, so the 180 days should start from the time of the most recent paycheck.

When the Supreme Court announced its decision on May 29, 2007, Ginsburg did something dissenting justices rarely do. She spoke from the bench to the public about the case and the reasons for her dissent. She concluded with her plea to Congress to correct the Supreme Court's "parsimonious" reading of Title VII.[317] In her words,

> In 1991, Congress passed a Civil Rights Act that effectively overruled several of this Court's similarly restrictive decisions including one on which the court relies today.

> Today, the ball again lies in Congress' court. As in 1991, the Legislature has cause to note and to correct this court's parsimonious reading of Title VII.[318]

Congress listened—and drafted the Lilly Ledbetter Fair Pay Act, which specifically overturned the Supreme Court's interpretation of Title VII. Under the Lilly Ledbetter Act, each paycheck becomes a separate violation that can be challenged in

President Obama signs the Lilly Ledbetter act. Ms. Ledbetter stands behind, watching.

court. One of President Obama's first acts after taking office in January of 2009 was to sign the Lilly Ledbetter Act into law. For Ginsburg, her dissent and the reaction of Congress illustrated the kind of dialogue that should happen between the branches of government. It also showed the power of dissent.

28

THE CONTOURS
OF LIBERTY

With the court having moved so far to the right, Ginsburg found herself writing dissents more often. In her dissent in *Gonzales v. Carhart*, the challenge to the Partial-Birth Abortion Ban Act, she made clear that she was irked that her male colleagues felt they had to rule the way they did to prevent a woman from making a choice she might regret, which Ginsburg found patronizing and insulting.[319] For her, it was the same old "Big Brother must protect the woman against her own weakness and immature misjudgment."[320] She thought the court could at least have admitted that an adult woman—even a pregnant one—was as capable as a man of making a choice that was best for her.

She dissented in *Shelby County v. Holder*, a challenge to the Voting Rights Act of 1965, a major piece of civil rights legislation designed to make sure that African Americans would not be disenfranchised. The conservative majority found that certain sections were no longer needed because there was no longer blatant discrimination in the South against blacks, and thus put an undue burden on the states.[321] In Ginsburg's view, the conservative majority had now gutted the very act that made sure African Americans were given the right to vote.

She dissented in *Citizens United v. FEC*, the case in which the Supreme Court struck down federal legislation limiting campaign contributions.[322] In an interview, she said she thought *Citizens United* v. *FEC* was one of the Supreme Court's worst rulings and that one day the court would see the error of its decision to interfere with what should be the province of the legislature.

George W. Bush, while campaigning, promised to appoint conservative judges who would follow the law and not legislate from the bench, but here were his newly appointed justices striking down, one after another, laws passed by Congress—an elected body that represented the will of the people. She said, "This Court has the reputation of being conservative, but if you take activism to mean readiness to strike down laws passed by Congress, I think the current Court will go down in history as one of the most active Courts in that regard."[323] With the court so often striking down laws, it was becoming—to Ginsburg—nothing more than a "higher chamber where a legislator who has failed to persuade his [or her] colleagues . . . can always renew the battle."[324]

Despite the biting dissents and differences of opinion, the collegiality on the court remained a high priority for everyone—particularly Ginsburg. The handshakes continued, all thirty-six of them, which Ginsburg took to mean, "Even though you circulated that nasty dissent, we're in this together, and we'd better get along with each other."[325] She was proud to point out that the court still managed to reach unanimous decisions in about 40 percent of the cases, and given the political composition of the court and the fact that the Supreme Court hears only the most difficult cases, 40 percent was impressive.

In 2009 and 2010, President Obama appointed two more women to the Supreme Court. Sonia Sotomayor, a native of the Bronx and a graduate of Yale Law School who George H. W. Bush had nominated to the U.S. Court of Appeals for the Second Circuit, joined the Supreme Court in 2009. The following year, Obama appointed Elena Kagan, dean of Harvard Law School. Ginsburg was happy to see her years as the only woman on the court come to an end. She felt it was important for school children visiting the court to see women scattered across the bench. Because she'd been on the court so long, she sat to the center. Kagan and Sotomayor, newer appointees, sat to the sides.

Kagan and Sotomayor replaced Souter and Stevens. Although both Souter and Stevens were Republican appointees, their leanings were liberal to moderate in comparison to Alito and Roberts, who were positioned far to the right. The new replacements, therefore, didn't do much to shift the composition of the court, which remained firmly conservative, and therefore receptive to the 2012 challenge to a woman's access to contraceptives in the name of religious liberty.

O'Connor, Sotomayor, Ginsburg, and Kagan.

Hobby Lobby was a national arts and crafts chain with over five hundred stores and thirteen thousand employees. The corporation was owned by the Green family, who organized their business around the principles of their Christian faith. Under the Patient Protection and Affordable Care Act—colloquially known as Obamacare—employee health care plans must provide certain types of preventive care, which included FDA-approved contraceptive methods. While there were exemptions in Obamacare for religious employers and non-profit institutions, there were no exceptions available for corporations run for profit, such as Hobby Lobby.

Among the contraceptives approved by the FDA were those that operated by preventing an already fertilized egg from attaching to the uterus, thereby putting an end to its growth. The Green family said that any attempt to prevent a fertilized egg from attaching to the uterus amounted to killing an embryo, and thus violated their religion. They further said that forcing them to provide such methods to employees violated their sincerely held religious beliefs. So on September 12, 2012, the Green family sued the secretary of the Department of Health and Human Services, arguing that the requirements of Obamacare violated their freedom of religion, guaranteed by the First Amendment and the Religious Freedom Restoration Act of 1993.

Instead of evoking the store owners' constitutional right to freedom of religion, the majority, in a narrow 5-4 split, decided the case under the Religious Freedom Restoration Act. The majority held that corporations were "people" under the Religious Freedom Restoration Act, and as such, a corporation could have a religion. So requiring Hobby Lobby to engage in conduct that went against its religion violated the religious freedom guaranteed by the Religious Freedom Restoration Act.

Ginsburg issued a lengthy dissent, stating that the majority "falters at each step of its analysis" and has a "blind spot" on issues affecting women. For her, the issue was one of female autonomy. In an interview, she said, "Contraceptive protection is something every woman must have access to, to control her own destiny. I certainly respect the belief of the Hobby Lobby owners. On the other hand, they have no constitutional right to foist that belief on the hundreds and hundreds of women who work for them who don't share that belief." [326] Her position in effect was that "Your right to swing your own fists stops at my nose."

As a result of these dissents, Ginsburg became an icon of the left. When asked how she felt to be so often on the losing side, she quoted Yogi Berra, "It ain't over till it's over."[327] She pointed out that beauty of our government is that the laws are constantly evolving. In the early twentieth century, Supreme Court Justices Holmes and Brandeis had written powerful dissents on the subject of free speech. Today their dissents are the law of the land. Similarly, Justice Curtis wrote a dissent in the now infamous *Dred Scott v. Standford*, the 1857 case that declared slavery constitutional.[328] There came a time when Justice Curtis's dissent was widely hailed as moral and brave. Other examples abound, including *Plessy v. Fergusson*, the case legalizing segregation and eventually overturned in *Brown v. Board of Education*, and the Supreme Court approval of the internment of Japanese during World War II, a wrong that was corrected not by the judiciary but by the president and Congress.

There were those who, at one time, thought judicial dissents were a bad idea, weakening the voice of law by showing a divided opinion. Ginsburg, though, believed dissents strengthened America by enshrining alternate viewpoints, and by paving the way later for change.

Her dissents were intended to persuade. She could not persuade her colleagues, so she hoped to convince others. A dissent is written for the readers of tomorrow—and it will be up to future generations to evaluate and define the legacy of Ruth Bader Ginsburg.

In January of 2009, when Ginsburg was seventy-five years old—the same month the Lilly Ledbetter Act became law—she was undergoing a medical examination at the Memorial Sloan Kettering Hospital in New York when a CT scan revealed a tumor in her pancreas one centimeter in length. On February 5, 2009, she underwent surgery, and remained hospitalized for ten days. The doctors removed the tumor—which proved to be benign—but while searching her pancreas, discovered a previously undetected tumor, too small to have been detected in the CT scan. This tumor was malignant. Doctors removed her spleen and a portion of her pancreas. Her lymph nodes were negative for cancer, and no metastasis was found. Because the cancer was stage one, her prospects for full recovery were excellent.

Ginsburg returned to Washington, DC, to recuperate, and was back on the bench when the court heard oral arguments in late February.

Within the year, Marty was also diagnosed with cancer. Toward the end of his illness, when he knew he was losing the battle, he wrote her a letter on a yellow legal pad, beginning,

> 6/17/10
> My dearest Ruth—
>   You are the only person I have loved in my life, setting aside, a bit, parents and kids and their kids, and I have admired and loved you almost since the

day we first met at Cornell some 56 years ago.

What a treat it has been to watch you progress to the very top of the legal world!! [329]

She found the letter when he was at the hospital. On a Sunday in June of 2010, four days after their fifty-sixth wedding anniversary, Marty died in their Washington, DC, home of complications due to metastatic cancer. The following day, Ginsburg startled her colleagues by showing up for work wearing a black velvet bow in hair. Her children urged her to go, and she said it was what Marty would want her to do. At the opening of the session, Chief Justice Roberts read a statement about Marty, mentioning his sharp wit and gourmet cooking. As he spoke, Scalia wiped away a tear.

Marty was buried in a private ceremony at Arlington National Cemetery.

Ginsburg's daughter Jane was afraid that without her father around, her mother wouldn't eat properly, so once monthly she visited her mother and spent a few days cooking and packaging individual meals for the freezer.

Marty said once that he believed the most important thing he did in his life was help Ruth Bader Ginsburg to achieve her potential. He'd also helped her balance her life. Without Marty, she worked even longer hours. He had always been the one to say it was time to put away the books and the brief and go to sleep. Now she didn't have anyone to tell her when to stop.

She finally accepted an honorary degree from Harvard. She joked that her hesitation came from the fact that she'd gotten so much mileage over the years from not having one. On May 26, 2011, she accepted an honorary degree along with Placido Domingo, a Spanish tenor, conductor, and arts administrator. The planners of the program had written lyrics for him to sing to the tune of "Celeste Aida." When it was his turn to step to the podium, he took the microphone, turned, and serenaded her. She later said it was one of the great moments of her life.

She took special delight when an opera written was about her. Law student Derrick Wang was struck by what he saw as the dueling dissents between Ginsburg and Scalia, and it occurred to him that their rivalry of ideas would make a great opera. The result was called *Scalia/Ginsburg: A (Gentle) Parody of Operatic Proportions.*[330] The score opens with the Scalia character having a rage aria about how the changeable justices are forever reading into the Constitution things that are not there:

> The Justices are blind!
> How can they possibly spout this—?
> The Constitution says absolutely nothing about this. . .
>
> Oh, Ruth, can you read? You're aware of the text,
> Yet so proudly you've failed to derive its true meaning
> And never were so few
> Rights made so numerous—
> It's almost humorous
> What you construe![331]

Then the floor bursts open and the Ginsburg character appears. Scalia cannot figure out how she got in because the doors were all sealed. She says,

> Then you have no idea with whom you are dealing.
> It's not the first time I've had to break through a ceiling.[332]

In the final duet, the Scalia and Ginsburg characters sing about how they are different, but they are one in their reverence for the institution they serve.

After Ginsburg turned eighty, people began asking when she planned to retire. In response, she recited from Article III of the Constitution, which states that federal judges shall hold their offices during good behavior. She also said a Supreme Court justice should work as long as she was able—and Ginsburg said she would know when her mind ceased to be as sharp. She proudly pointed out that she was still the fastest justice on the Supreme Court with handing down opinions. She hadn't slowed down yet.

She'd been working with her personal trainer since 1999, and was still doing vigorous workouts. She weighed about a hundred pounds and could do twenty pushups—the old-fashioned knees-off-the-ground kind. Her personal trainer, Bryant Johnson, counted her pushups and cheered her on. "Way to go, Justice!"[333]

While admittedly impressed with her exercise regime, people nonetheless watched for clues that Ginsburg was becoming frail. Once, after oral arguments, it took her a long time to get up from the bench. Reporters were instantly asking if she felt ill. Not at all, she said. Later in an interview she revealed that she had kicked off her shoes, and she couldn't find her right shoe. She smiled when telling the story because it reminded her of a time many decades earlier when she'd been told that women were not wanted in the workplace because men wanted to feel comfortable enough to be able to just kick off their shoes.

In speeches, she enjoyed contrasting the world of today with the world she knew growing up. She told a story of her oldest granddaughter, Clara—a University of Chicago alum

Justice Ginsburg, 2010.

who was then a second-year law student at Harvard. When Clara was eight years old and asked what she wanted to be when she grew up, she said, "The president of the United States of the World"[334]—something that would never have occurred to a girl growing up in the 1940s.

When asked how many women on the Supreme Court will be enough, Ginsburg startled some people—and upset others—by saying, "When there are nine."[335] Her reason? When there were nine men on the Supreme Court, nobody thought anything of that. Why not nine women, if those are the most qualified?

Ginsburg is often asked whether the Equal Rights Amendment is still necessary now that we have Title VII, Title IX, the Family and Medical Leave Act, the Lilly Ledbetter

Act, and the line of Supreme Court cases from *Reed v. Reed* to *United States v. Virginia*. Yes, she says. There is always value in constitutional protection because statutes are much more easily revoked. Equally important, she insists that we still need the amendment for the symbolic value—and for the reminder that "We the People" includes *all* the people.

Her hope is that one day her granddaughters will be able to read the U.S. Constitution and find themselves in it.

SUMMARY OF APPLICABLE LAW
AND GLOSSARY OF LEGAL TERMS

Under the doctrine of judicial review, courts have the authority to review laws and statutes to determine whether they are compatible with the Constitution. Courts then strike down laws that are unconstitutional, or modify them to bring them in line with the Constitution.

When laws discriminate between groups of people, thus potentially violating the equal protection clause of the Fourteenth Amendment, courts balance the government's need for the law against the liberty interests of the citizens. For most laws that discriminate—for example, laws that discriminate based on the size of town populations—the court applies the rational basis test, upholding the law if it is rationally related to a legitimate government purpose. Most, but not all laws, pass this test.

When laws discriminate based on suspect classifications, like race, the courts apply a stricter level of scrutiny. Under the strict scrutiny test, the law must further a compelling government interest and must be narrowly tailored to achieve that interest. Most laws fail this test.

Amicus brief, or amicus curiae: Literally a friend of the court, someone not a party who has an interest in what is being litigated and has information or an opinion to offer the court.

Certiorari, or writ of certiorari: A written document asking a higher court to review the decision of a lower court.

Concurring opinion: A decision written by one or more judges who agree with the decision, but wish to offer different or additional reasons for the decision.

Due process: A clause in the Fourteenth Amendment, guaranteeing fundamental fairness and legal protection to all people. A person's rights cannot be infringed without due process of law.

Dissenting opinion: Written by one or more judges who disagree with the majority opinion.

Equal protection: A clause in the Fourteenth Amendment guaranteeing all people equal protection of the laws.

Intermediate scrutiny: Sometimes called heightened scrutiny, a test used by courts to determine whether a law is constitutional. Intermediate scrutiny is more rigorous than the rational basis test, but not as rigorous as strict scrutiny. Under the heightened scrutiny test, a law that discriminates on the basis of gender is constitutional only if it furthers an important government interest.

Judicial review: The doctrine under which courts have the power to review laws and invalidate those that are not compatible with the Constitution.

Jurisdictional statement: The statement that explains why the court has the authority to hear the case and (when appealing to the Supreme Court) why the court should hear the case.

Majority opinion: A judicial opinion agreed to by more than half of the judges. A majority opinion becomes precedent for future cases.

Moot: There is no longer a controversy, so there is nothing for the court to decide. Cases that become moot during the course of litigation are usually dismissed by the court.

Plurality opinion: When the majority of justices do not agree. A plurality opinion decides the case, but does not become precedent and is not binding precedent on future cases.

Precedent: The doctrine by which earlier cases become law that subsequent courts must follow. Precedent—which binds courts to follow previous decisions—creates stability and ensures that decisions are uniform and fair and that citizens can predict what courts will do.

Rational basis test: When evaluating whether a law that discriminates between categories of people violates the Constitution, the court considers whether there is a rational basis for the law. For a law to pass this test, it must serve a legitimate government purpose.

Strict scrutiny: The most stringent standard of review used by courts to evaluate whether a law that discriminates violates the Constitution. To pass strict scrutiny, a law must further a compelling government interest.

Summary judgment: The court can decide the matter without a full trial because there is no factual dispute.

Suspect classification: Certain kinds of classifications are inherently suspect, such as discrimination on the basis of race. When a law discriminates on the basis of a suspect classification, courts apply strict scrutiny in determining whether the law is constitutional.

1. ONE LAWYER'S
BEGINNINGS

[1] Christopher Mele, *Selling the Lower East Side: Culture, Real Estate, and Resistance in New York City* (Minneapolis: University of Minnesota Press, 2000), 110.

[2] A focal point of the traditional Passover Seder is the telling of the Biblical story of the Exodus from Egypt. The story begins when the youngest person at the table asks the Four Questions, beginning with "How is this night different from all other nights?"

[3] David von Drehle, "Conventional Roles Hid a Revolutionary Intellect," *Washington Post*, July 18, 1993, www.washingtonpost.com/archive/politics/1993/07/18/conventional-roles-hid-a-revolutionary-intellect/38a8055a-d575-4eee-b59a-44c2d58771f5.

[4] David Margolick, "Trial by Adversity Shapes Jurist's Outlook," *New York Times*, June 25, 1993, www.nytimes.com/1993/06/25/us/trial-by-adversity-shapes-jurist-s-outlook.html?pagewanted=all.

[5] *Shiva*, in Judaism, is a period of seven days of formal mourning for the dead beginning immediately after the funeral.

2. A TOP STUDENT
AND A TOP GOLFER

[6] Ruth Bader Ginsburg, "Justice Ginsburg Addresses the Women's Law and Public Policy Fellowship Program," C-Span video, 1:01:01, Sept. 25, 2003.

[7] Beth Saulnier, "Justice Prevails: A Conversation with Ruth Bader Ginsburg, '59," *Cornell Alumni Magazine*, Nov./Dec. 2013, 2, www.cornellalumnimagazine.com/index.

php?option=com_content&task=view&id=1765.

8   Claudia MacLaughlin, "Mr. Ginsburg's Campaign for Nominee," *National Law J.*, June 27, 1993.

9   Jeffrey Toobin, "Heavyweight: How Ruth Bader Ginsburg Has Moved the Supreme Court," *New Yorker*, Mar. 11, 2013, para. 7, www.newyorker.com/magazine/2013/03/11/heavyweight-ruth-bader-ginsburg.

10   Margolick, "Trial by Adversity," para. 26.

11   Von Drehle, "Conventional Roles," para. 29.

12   Jay Mathews, "The Spouse of Ruth," *Washington Post*, June 19, 1993, www.washingtonpost.com/archive/lifestyle/1993/06/19/the-spouse-of-ruth/a57e6536-3e1b-4c30-8bab-1f2c629cf172.

13   Neil Lewis, "Woman in the News; Rejected as a Clerk, Chosen as a Justice: Ruth Joan Bader Ginsburg," *New York Times*, June 15, 1993.

14   Ginsburg repeated this story in numerous interviews. See, for example, Ginsburg, "Justice Ginsburg Addresses."

3. AXIOMATIC TRUTHS
ABOUT WOMEN

15   From A. Kraditor, *Up from the Pedestal: Selected Writings in the History of American Feminism* (Harper Collins, 1968), as quoted by Ruth Bader Ginsburg in the Appellant's Brief for *Reed v. Reed*, 404 U.S. 71(1971), 27.

16   *Bradwell v. The State*, 83 US 130, 132 (1873).

17   Ibid., 133.

18   Ibid., 142.

19   *Minor v. Happersett*, 88 US 162 (1875).

20   C. Epstein, *Women and Professional Careers: The Case of the Woman Lawyer* 140 (1968), as quoted by Ruth Bader Ginsburg in "Women at the Bar—A Generation of Change," 2 U. *Puget Sound L. Rev.* 1 (1978).

21   Cynthia Grant Bowman, "Women in the Legal Profession

from the 1920s to the 1970s," *Cornell University Law School Faculty Publications*, 2009, 10.

22   Richard Kluger, *Simple Justice* (Vintage Books, 1977), 476.

23   Lynn Gilbert and Gaylen Moore, "Ruth Bader Ginsburg," in *Particular Passions* (New York: Clarkson Potter, 1981), 156.

4. RUTHLESS
RUTHIE

24   Mathews, "Spouse of Ruth."

25   Ibid.

26   Ibid.

27   Ibid.

28   Stephanie Ward, "Family Ties," *A.B.A. J.*, Oct. 1, 2010, www.abajournal.com/magazine/article/family_ties1.

29   The phrasing is borrowed from how their second child, James, later described his family.

30   Fred Strebeigh, *Equal: Women Who Reshape American Law* (New York: W.W. Norton, 2009), 36.

31   Philip Galanes, "Table for Three: Ruth Bader Ginsburg and Gloria Steinem Speak with Philip Galenes," *New York Times*, Nov. 14, 2015, www.nytimes.com/column/table-for-three.

32   Strebeigh, *Equal*, 36.

33   Ruth Bader Ginsburg, "Legally Speaking: Ruth Bader Ginsburg," UCTV video, 1:25:47, from an interview by Joan Williams at Hastings College of the Law, Nov. 3, 2011.

34   Ruth Bader Ginsburg, "Interview with Ruth Bader Ginsburg," Academy of Achievement, Aug. 17, 2010.

35   Jeffrey Rosen, "The New Look of Liberalism on the Court," *New York Times Magazine*, Oct. 5, 1997, www.nytimes.com/library/politics/scotus/articles/100597nytmag-ginsburg-profile.html.

36   Nina Totenberg, "Notes on a Life," in *The Legacy of Ruth Bader Ginsburg*, ed. Scott Dodson (New York: Cambridge University Press, 2015), 4.

[37] Ruth Bader Ginsburg, "Women at the Bar—A Generation of Change," *U. Puget Sound L. Rev.* 2, no. 1 (1978): 1.

[38] Gilbert and Moore, "Ruth Bader Ginsburg," 156.

[39] Ward, "Family Ties."

[40] Margolick, "Trial by Adversity," para. 42.

[41] Jeffrey Rosen, "The Book of Ruth," *New Republic*, Aug. 2, 1993, www.newrepublic.com/article/61837/the-book-ruth.

[42] bid.

[43] Ruth Bader Ginsburg, "The Changing Complexion of Harvard Law School," speech, Harvard Law School, Nov. 14, 2004, *Harvard Women's Law Journal* 27 (2014): 303–308.

[44] Gerald Gunther, "Ruth Bader Ginsburg: A Personal, Very Fond Tribute," *U. of Hawai'i L. Rev* 20, no. 583 (1998).

[45] "Changing Complexion," 305.

5. THE SPIRIT
OF LIBERTY

[46] Tracy Schroth, "At Rutgers, Ginsburg Changed," *New Jersey Law J.*, June 21, 1993.

[47] Ibid.

[48] Stephanie Goldberg, "The Second Woman Justice," *A.B.A J.*, Oct. 1993, 42.

[49] Malvina Halberstam, "Ruth Bader Ginsburg: The First Jewish Woman on the United States Supreme Court," *Cardozo L. Rev.* 19, no. 4 (1998): 1441, 1446.

[50] Ruth Bader Ginsburg, "A Conversation with Associate Justice Ruth Bader Ginsburg," YouTube video, 1:17:45, from the Annual Stevens Lecture, University of Colorado Law School, Sept. 19, 2012.

[51] "Nomination of Ruth Bader Ginsburg to Be Associate Justice of the Supreme Court of the United States," 1993, 399.

[52] Ruth Bader Ginsburg, "A Conversation with Justice Ruth Bader Ginsburg: Her Life as a Woman, a Jew, and a Judge," PRX recording, 53:48, from an interview recorded by *Only in*

America, Sept. 2, 2004.

[53] Learned Hand, "The Spirit of Liberty," 1944, www.providenceforum.org/spiritoflibertyspeech.

[54] Margolick, "Trial by Adversity," para. 17.

6. AN AMERICAN
LAWYER IN SWEDEN

[55] "Memorial Tribute to Hans Smit," Columbia Law School, Feb. 9, 2012, www.law.columbia.edu/media_inquiries/news_events/2012/january2012/Justice-Ginsburg-on-Hans-Smit.

[56] Ibid.

[57] Galanes, "Table for Three," www.nytimes.com/column/table-for-three.

[58] Von Drehle, "Conventional Roles," para. 65.

[59] Ginsburg, "Interview," Academy of Achievement.

[60] Ruth Bader Ginsburg, "Justice Ruth Bader Ginsburg Remarks," C-Span video, 1:02:30, Feb. 4, 2015.

[61] Ibid.

[62] Schroth, "At Rutgers."

[63] Adam Liptak, "Kagan Says Her Path to Supreme Court Was Made Smoother by Ginsburg's," *New York Times*, Feb. 10, 2014.

7. A STEEL
BUTTERFLY

[64] Schroth, "At Rutgers."

[65] Ibid.

[66] Ward, "Family Ties."

[67] Ibid.

[68] Rosen, "New Look," para. 37.

[69] Ginsburg, "Interview," Academy of Achievement.

[70] Leslie Oelsner, "Columbia Law Snares a Prize in the Quest for Women Professors," *New York Times*, Jan. 26, 1972.

[71] As quoted by Ruth Bader Ginsburg and Barbara Flagg in

"Some Reflections on the Feminist Legal Thought of the 1970s," *U. Chi. Legal Forum* 1 (1989): 9.

[72] Strebeigh, *Equal*, 14.

[73] .S. section 2494, codified at Idaho Code Ann. section 32-903 (repealed in 1974), quoted by Ginsburg in "Remarks on Women's Progress in the Legal Profession in the United States," *Tulsa L. Rev* 33, no. 13 (1997): 15.

[74] Margolick, "Trial by Adversity," para. 52.

8. SPECIAL
TREATMENT

[75] *Muller v. Oregon*, 208 U.S. 412, 422 (1908).

[76] *In re Kayaloff*, 9 F. Supp. 176 (S.D.N.Y. 1934), as quoted by Ruth Bader Ginsburg in *Reed v. Reed*, 404 U.S. 71(1971), Appellant's Brief.

[77] A. P. Herbert, "The Myth of the Reasonable Man: The Case of *Fardell v. Potts*," in *Uncommon Law* (New York: Methuen, 1935).

[78] *Goesaert v. Cleary*, 335 U.S. 464, 467 (1948).

[79] Ibid.

[80] Jo Freeman, "How 'Sex' Got into Title VII," *Law & Ineq.* 9, no. 163 (1991).

[81] Ruth Bader Ginsburg, "Treatment of Women by the Law: Awakening Consciousness in the Law Schools," *Valparaiso University Law Review* 5, no. 2 (1970–1971): 480–488.

[82] *Reed v. Reed*, 404 U.S. 71(1971), Appellant's Brief.

[83] Ginsburg, "Treatment of Women," 481.

9. CATCHING
FIRE

[84] Army Reg. 601-280, as quoted by Ginsburg, "Treatment of Women," 487.

[85] Gilbert and Moore, "Ruth Bader Ginsburg," 1.

86 Strebeigh, *Equal*, 22.

87 "Nomination of Ruth Bader Ginsburg," 136.

88 Ruth Bader Ginsburg, "Ruth Bader Ginsburg: Interview with Professor Deborah Jones Merritt and Professor Wendy Webster Williams," *Ohio State Law Journal* 70 (2009): 806.

89 Ruth Bader Ginsburg, "A Conversation with Justice Ruth Bader Ginsburg and Gillian Metzger, Dean and Columbia Law School," Columbia Law School video, 60:00, Feb. 10, 2012.

90 Strebeigh, *Equal*, 25.

91 Ruth Bader Ginsburg, "A Conversation with Justice Ruth Bader Ginsburg," by Abbe R. Gluck, *Faculty Scholarship Series*, Paper 4905, Mar. 1, 2013. The same exchange, given with slightly different wording, is reported by Strebeigh in *Equal*, 22.

92 Ibid.

93 Strebeigh, *Equal*, 26.

94 Ibid.

95 Ginsburg, "Legally Speaking."

96 Schroth, "At Rutgers."

10. THE TIMES THEY
ARE A-CHANGING

97 *Plessy v. Ferguson*, 163 U.S. 537 (1986).

98 Richard Kluger, *Simple Justice* (New York: Vintage Books, 1977), 476.

99 *Brown v. Board of Education*, 347 U.S. 483 (1954).

100 From A. Montaga, *Man's Most Dangerous Myth* (1964), as quoted by Ruth Bader Ginsburg in *Reed v. Reed*, 404 U.S. 71(Walnut Creek: AltaMira Press, 1971), Appellant's Brief.

101 "The Woman's Rights Convention—The Last Act of the Drama," *N.Y. Herald*, Sept. 12, 1852, as quoted by Ruth Bader Ginsburg, "Gender and the Constitution," *U. Cin. L. Rev.* 44 (1975): 1, 3.

102 "Tribute: The Legacy of Ruth Bader Ginsburg and the WRP

Staff," ACLU website, www.aclu.org/tribute-legacy-ruth-bader-ginsburg-and-wrp-staff.

103 Ibid.

104 *White v. Crook*, 251 F. Supp. 401 (M.D. Ala. 1966).

105 Ginsburg, "Justice Ruth Bader Ginsburg Remarks."

106 Ruth Bader Ginsburg, "Advocating the Elimination of Gender-Based Discrimination: The 1970s New Look at the Equality Principle," U. of Cape Town, South Africa, Feb. 10, 2006.

11. A DRY PROCEDURALIST
OR A RABBLE ROUSER?

107 Ruth Bader Ginsburg, "Reflections of Justice Ginsburg," C-Span video, 1:28:36, Aug. 20, 1995.

108 *Reed v. Reed*, 404 U.S. 71(1971), Appellant's Brief.

109 Strebeigh, *Equal*, 27.

110 *Reed v. Reed*, 404 U.S. 71 (1971).

111 *Reed v. Reed*, 404 U.S. 71(1971), Appellant's Brief, 5.

112 Ibid., 6.

113 Ibid.

114 Ibid., 21. Ginsburg borrowed the phrase "The pedestal . . . a cage" from a recent case from *California, Sail'er Inn, Inc. v. Kirby*, 5 Cal. 3d 1, 20 (1971).

115 *Goesaert v. Cleary*, 335 U.S. 464, 466 (1948).

116 Ibid.

117 *Reed v. Reed*, 404 U.S. 71(1971), Appellant's Brief, 47.

118 Ibid., 60.

119 Ruth Bader Ginsburg, "Transcript of Panel Discussion with Ruth Bader Ginsburg," Journal of Gender, *Social Policy & the Law 20*, no. 2, article 1 (2001): 316.

120 Ibid.

121 *Reed v. Reed*, 404 U.S. 71 (1971), Oral Arguments before the Supreme Court.

12. WOMEN
WORKING

[122] Gilbert and Moore, "Ruth Bader Ginsburg," 4.

[123] Ruth Bader Ginsburg, "A Conversation with Justice Ruth Bader Ginsburg," *Kansas Law Review* 53 (2005): 957.

[124] Ruth Bader Ginsburg, "Transcript: Interview with Supreme Court Justice Ruth Bader Ginsburg," WNYC Public Radio, in collaboration with the *New York Times* and WGBH Boston, Sept. 16, 2013.

[125] "Conversation," *Only in America.*

[126] Herma Hill Kay, "Ruth Bader Extraordinaire," in *The Legacy of Ruth Bader Ginsburg*, 12.

[127] "Tribute," para. 22.

[128] Ibid., para. 23.

[129] Von Drehle, "Redefining Fair," para. 27.

[130] Ginsburg, "Legally Speaking."

[131] Elizabeth Kolbert, "Firebrand," *New Yorker*, Nov. 7, 2005, www.newyorker.com/magazine/2005/11/07/firebrand.

[132] Ruth Ginsburg, "The Need for the Equal Rights Amendment," *A.B.A. J.* (1973): 1013, 1017.

[133] Free to Be . . . You and Me." YouTube video, from a TV special aired Mar. 11, 1974, posted by "ftbfoundation," May 17, 2010, www.youtube.com/watch?v=_26FOHoaC78. Recording of the opening sequence of Marlo Thomas's project for the Ms. Foundation for Women, a record album and illustrated book first released in Nov. 1972.

13. FREE TO BE
YOU AND ME

[134] "The Real Story behind the Passage of Title IX 35 Years Ago," *Women in Higher Education*, Jossey Bass, wihe.com/the-real-story-behind-the-passage-of-title-ix-35-years-ago.

[135] Oelsner, "Columbia Law."

136 Ibid.

137 Ibid.

138 Kay, "Ruth Bader Extraordinaire," 19.

139 Emily Bazelon, "The Place of Women on the Court," *New York Times Magazine*, July 7, 2009, para. 28, www.nytimes.com/2009/07/12/magazine/12ginsburg-t.html.

140 Ibid.

141 Ruth Bader Ginsburg, "Introduction," *Colum. J. Gender and Law* 1 (1991): 1.

142 Oelsner, "Columbia Law."

143 Margolick, "Trial by Adversity," para. 9.

144 *Moritz v. Commissioner of Internal Revenue*, 469 F.2d. 466 (10th Cir. 1972).

145 Ginsburg, "Advocating."

146 Ginsburg, "Ruth Bader Ginsburg: Interview with Professor Deborah Jones Merritt," 816.

147 Ginsburg, "Interview," Academy of Achievement.

148 "Justice Ginsburg Addresses."

149 Ibid.

150 Saulnier, "Justice Prevails," 3.

151 Abigail Pogrebin, *Stars of David: Prominent Jews Talk About Being Jewish* (New York: Broadway Books, 2007), 20.

152 Ruth Bader Ginsburg, "'Notorious RBG': Conversation with United States Supreme Court Justice Ginsburg," European University Institute, YouTube video, 1:55:05, Feb. 4, 2016.

153 Ruth Bader Ginsburg, "Conversation between Ruth Bader Ginsburg and Professor Robert A. Stein," *Minnesota Law Review* 99 (Sept. 16, 2014): 1.

154 Ward, "Family Ties."

155 Bill Hewitt, "Feeling Supreme," *People*, June 28, 1993, 50.

156 Ward, "Family Ties.

14. THE ABORTION
QUESTION

[157] Jessica Weisberg, "Susan's Choice: Ruth Bader Ginsburg's Defining Case," *Elle Magazine*, Oct. 21, 2014.

[158] Ibid.

[159] Ibid.

[160] *Struck v. Secretary of Defense*, 409 U.S. 409 U.S. 1071 (1972), Petitioner's Brief.

[161] Alan Gutmacher, *Margaret Sanger: An Autobiography* (New York: Pergamon Books, 1938), 89.

[162] Ibid., 91.

[163] *Griswold v. Connecticut*, 381 U.S. 479 (1965).

[164] *Eisenstadt v. Baird*, 405 U.S. 438 (1972).

[165] *Buck v. Bell*, 274 U.S. 200 (1927).

[166] As quoted by Susan K. Cahn, *Sexual Reckonings: Southern Girls in a Troubling Age* (Cambridge, MA: Harvard University Press, 2012), 163.

[167] Dorothy E. Roberts, *Killing the Black Body: Race, Reproduction, and the Meaning of Liberty* (New York: Vintage, 1998), 23.

[168] Goldberg, "Second Woman Justice," 43.

[169] Weisberg, "Susan's Choice."

[170] Allen Pusey, "Ginsburg: Court Should Have Avoided Broad-Based Decision in *Roe v. Wade*," A.B.A. J., May 13, 2013.

[171] *Roe v. Wade*, 410 U.S. 113 (1973).

[172] Ruth Bader Ginsburg, "Some Thoughts on Autonomy and Equality in Relation to *Roe v. Wade*," N.C. L. Rev 63 (1985): 373.

15. PLEASE TAKE YOUR
FEET FROM OUR NECKS

[173] Von Drehle, "Redefining Fair." 3.

[174] Opinion of the District Court for the Middle District of Alabama, Civil Action No. 3232-N, *Frontiero v. Secretary of*

Defense as quoted in *Frontiero v. Richardson*, 411 U.S. 766 (1973), Jurisdictional Statement.

[175] Ibid.

[176] *Frontiero v. Richardson*, 411 U.S. 766 (1973), Appellant's Brief, 29.

[177] "Nomination of Ruth Bader Ginsburg to Be Associate Justice of the Supreme Court of the United States," 1994, 51.

[178] Erwin Chemerinsky, *Constitutional Law: Principles and Policies* (New York: Aspen Law and Business, 1997), 26.

[179] *Marbury v. Madison*, 5 US 135, 137 (1803).

[180] Ginsburg, "Transcript of Panel Discussion," 337.

[181] Supreme Court of the United States website: www.supremecourtpress.com/chance_of_success.html.

[182] *Frontiero v. Richardson*, 411 U.S. 677 (1973).

[183] "Tribute," para. 28.

[184] Oral Arguments before the Supreme Court, Jan. 17, 1973, *Frontiero v. Richardson*, 411 U.S. 766, 1973.

[185] As quoted by Strebeigh, *Equal*, 54.

[186] Von Drehle, "Redefining Fair," 5.

[187] *Frontiero v. Richardson*, 411 U.S. 677, 682 (1973).

[188] *Sail'er Inn, Inc. v. Kirby*, 5 Cal.3d 1 (1971).

[189] *Bradwell v. The State*, 83 US 130 (1873).

[190] *Frontiero v. Richardson*, 411 U.S. 677, 682 (1973).

[191] Ruth Bader Ginsburg, "Ginsburg Supreme Court Nomination Speech in the White House Rose Garden," C-Span video, 23:42, June 14, 1993.

16. YOU CAN'T GET
BETTER THAN THAT

[192] Ginsburg, "Interview," Academy of Achievement.

[193] The letter is printed in full in Irmin Carmon and Shana Kniznik Shana's *Notorious RBG: The Life and Times of Ruth Bader Ginsburg* (New York: Dey Street Books, 2015), 70.

[194] Ruth B. Cowan, "Women's Rights through Litigation," *Colum.*

Human Rights L. Rev. 8 (1979): 373, 385.

195 Robert Barnes, "Ginsburg Performs Wedding," *Washington Post*, May 25, 2014.

196 Rosen, "New Look," para. 24.

197 Strebeigh, *Equal*, 67.

198 *Wiesenfeld v. Secretary of Health, Education, and Welfare*, 367 F. Supp. 981 (D.N.J. 1973).

199 *Kahn v. Shevin*, 416 U.S. 351 (1974).

200 Catherine Crocker, "Ginsburg Explains Origins of Sex, Gender," *Los Angeles Times*, Nov. 21, 1993.

17. THE DOUBLE-EDGED SWORD

201 Gail Cooper, "Equal Rights May Be Painful," *Grand Rapids Gazette*, May 10, 1974.

202 Ibid.

203 *Hoyt v. Florida*, 368 U.S. 57 (1961).

204 *Edwards v. Healy*, 421 U.S. 772 (1975).

205 Oral Arguments before the Supreme Court in *Edwards v. Healy*, 421 U.S. 772 (1975), www.oyez.org/cases/1974/73-759, Oct. 16, 1974.

206 Ibid.

207 Oral arguments before the Supreme Court in *Weinberger v. Wiesenfeld*, 420 U.S. 636 (1975), www.oyez.org/cases/1974/73-1892, Jan. 20, 1975.

208 Margolick, "Trial by Adversity," para. 26.

209 Linda R Hirshman, *Sisters in Law* (New York: HarperCollins, 2015), 102.

210 As quoted in Carmon and Knizhnik, *Notorious RBG*, 71.

211 *Weinberger v. Wiesenfeld*, 420 U.S. 636 (1975).

212 Strebeigh, *Equal*, 75

18. THE PREGNANCY
PROBLEM

[213] These statistics were presented to the Supreme Court by Ruth Weyand during oral arguments in *General Electric v. Gilbert*, 429 U.S. 125 (1975).

[214] *Geduldig v. Aiello*, 417 U.S. 484 (1974).

[215] *Mary Ann Turner v. Department of Employment*, 423 U.S. 44 (1975).

[216] Ibid.

[217] *General Electric v. Gilbert*, 429 U.S. 125 (1975).

[218] Leslie Oelsner, "Supreme Court Rules Employers May Refuse Pregnancy Sick Pay," *New York Times*, Dec. 8, 1976.

[219] Ruth Bader Ginsburg and Susan Deller Ross, "Pregnancy and Discrimination," *New York Times*, Jan. 25, 1977.

[220] "Feminist Leaders Plan Coalition for Law Aiding Pregnant Women," *New York Times*, Dec. 15, 1976.

[221] Ibid.

[222] National Organization for Women, Philadelphia Chapter Records, 1968–1977, www2.hsp.org/collections/manuscripts/n/now2054.xml.

[223] Patrick McMahon, "The Barefoot and Pregnant Awards," *St. Petersburg Times*, Apr. 1, 1978.

19. DISCRIMINATING
AGAINST MEN

[224] Amy Leigh Campbell, "Raising the Bar: Ruth Bader Ginsburg and the ACLU Women's Rights Project," *Texas J. of Women and the Law* 11, no. 157 (2002): 227.

[225] Oral Argument before the Supreme Court, *Califano v. Goldfarb*, 430 U.S. 199 (1977), www.oyez.org/cases/1976/75-699, Oct. 5, 1976.

[226] Ibid.

[227] Ibid.

[228] Ibid.

[229] Totenberg, "Notes on a Life," 7.

[230] *Califano v. Goldfarb*, 430 U.S. 199 (1977).[231] *Craig v. Boren*, 429 U.S. 190 (1976).

[232] Ruth Bader Ginsburg, Keynote Speech at Harvard Law School Celebration 25, Apr. 15, 1978, on file with the Library of Congress manuscript division, as quoted in Carmon and Knizhnik, *Notorious RBG*, 73.

20. TOKENS
WON'T DO

[233] Carol Meyer, "On Feminism in Action: The First Activist Feminist I Ever Met," *AFFILIA* 9 (1994): 1984.

[234] Ibid.

[235] Ibid.

[236] Ginsburg, "Interview," Academy of Achievement.

[237] Ibid.

[238] Ward, "Family Ties."

[239] *Duren v. Missouri*, 439 U.S. 357 (1979), www.oyez.org/cases/1978/77-6067.

[240] "Without Precedent: Ruth Bader Ginsburg Honored at Law School," *Columbia Magazine*, Spring 2012.

[241] *Duren v. Missouri*, 439 U.S. 357 (1979).

[242] Herma Hill Kay, "Ruth Bader Ginsburg, Professor of Law," *Columbia L. Rev* 104 (2004): 2.

21. JUDGE
GINSBURG

[243] Totenberg, "Notes on a Life," 3.

[244] Gunther, "Ruth Bader Ginsburg," 586.

[245] Ibid.

[246] Goldberg, "Second Woman Justice," 43.

[247] Catherine Crocker, "Ginsburg Explains Origins of Sex,

Gender," *Los Angeles Times*, Nov. 21, 1993.

[248] *Mississippi U. for Women v. Hogan*, 458 U.S. 718 (1982).

22. DIFFERENT
VOICES

[249] Rosen, "Book of Ruth," www.newrepublic.com/article/61837/the-book-ruth.

[250] Joan Williams, "Beyond the Tough Guise: Justice Ginsburg's Reconstructive Feminism," in *The Legacy of Ruth Bader Ginsburg*, ed. Scott Dodson (New York: Cambridge University Press, 2015), 59.

[251] Ginsburg and Flagg, "Some Reflections," 17.

[252] Ibid.

[253] Goldberg, "Second Woman Justice."

[254] Ginsburg and Flagg, "Some Reflections," 18.

[255] Michael Martin, "Phyllis Schlafly Still Championing the Anti-Feminist Fight," National Public Radio, Mar. 30, 2011.

[256] Ibid.

23. HITTING DOWN
THE MIDDLE

[257] Todd C. Peppers, *In Chambers: Stories of Supreme Court Law Clerks and Their Justices* (Charlottesville: University of Virginia Press, 2013), 397.

[258] "Ginsburg Easily Wins Seat on High Court," in *CQ Almanac* (1994), 318–25.

[259] Ibid.

[260] Peppers, *In Chambers*, 399.

[261] Margolick, "Trial by Adversity," para. 28.

[262] Robert Barnes, "The Question Facing Ruth Bader Ginsburg: Stay or Go?" *Washington Post*, Oct. 4, 2013, www.washingtonpost.com/lifestyle/magazine/the-question-facing-ruth-bader-ginsburg-stay-or-go/2013/10/04/4d789e28-1574-11e3-a2ec-

b47e45e6f8ef_story.html.

263 "Originalism: A Primer on Scalia's Constitutional Philosophy," National Public Radio, *All Things Considered*, Feb. 14, 2016.

264 Robert Bork, "Civil Rights—A Challenge," *The New Republic*, Aug. 31, 1963, 21.

265 Scalia's dissent in *Webster v. Reproductive Health Services* 492 U.S. 490 (1989).

266 Scalia's concurrence in *Bond v. United States*, 529 U.S. (2014).

267 Barnes, "Question," para. 57.

268 Manuel Balce Ceneta, "Antonin Scalia: In His Own Unforgettable Words," *Los Angeles Times*, Apr. 22, 2016.

269 *Doe v. Commonwealth's Attorney*, 425 U.S. 901 (1976).

270 David G. Savage, "Gay Rights Case a Window to Ginsburg Centrist Views," *Los Angeles Times*, June 17, 1993.

271 Ibid.

272 Rosen, "New Look."

273 "Behind the Music," *Chicago Magazine*, Oct. 6, 2006.

274 Toobin, "Heavyweight," para. 27.

275 "NAACP to Fight Bork 'Till Hell Freezes Over," *Daily News Wire Service*, New York, July 6, 1987.

276 Jeffrey Toobin, *The Nine: Inside the Secret World of the Supreme Court* (New York: Anchor Books, 2008), 48.

277 David G Savage, "Supreme Court's Byron White Will Step Down after 31 Years," *Los Angeles Times*, Mar. 20, 1993.

24. I'M RUTH,
NOT SANDRA

278 Barnes, "Question," para. 18.

279 Toobin, *The Nine*, 81.

280 Ginsburg, "Changing Complexion," 306.

281 Catherine Yang, "Ruth Bader Ginsburg: So Principled, She's Unpredictable," *Businessweek*, June 27, 1993.

282 "Ruth Bader Ginsburg: Humble. Pursuits," Behrman House, www.behrmanhouse.com/RL/justice-ruth-bader-ginsburg-

humble-pursuits.

283 Ginsburg, "Interview," Academy of Achievement.

284 Ginsburg, "Ginsburg Supreme Court Nomination Speech."

285 Von Drehle, "Conventional Roles," para. 1.

286 Jessica Gresko, "Ruth Bader Ginsburg's Husband Became Court of Last Culinary Resort," *Portland Press Herald*, Jan. 4, 2012.

287 Philip Shenon, "After the Debate," *Washington Post*, Sept. 26, 1988.

288 Barnes, "Question," para. 21.

25. JUSTICE, SHALL
YOU PURSUE

289 Ginsburg, "Justice Ginsburg Addresses."

290 Ruth Bader Ginsburg, "Ruth Bader Ginsburg: From Brooklyn to the Bench," YouTube video, 43:44, Sept. 14, 2014, posted Feb. 24, 2015, by "Cornell University."

291 As quoted by Ruth Bader Ginsburg, "Remarks on Women's Progress in the Legal Profession in the United States," 33 *Tulsa L. Rev* 33 (1997): 13, 14.

292 Peppers, *In Chambers*, 393.

293 *United States v. Virginia*, 518 U.S. 515 (1996).

294 Ibid., 522.

295 Ibid., 523–524.

296 *United States v. Virginia*, 976 F.2d 890, 892–93 (4th Cir. 1992).

297 Mike Allen, "Defiant V.M.I. to Admit Women, But Will Not Ease Rules for Them," *New York Times*, Sept. 22, 1996.

298 "Women Enroll at VMI," *CNN*, Aug. 18, 1997.

299 "Remarks by Justice Ruth Bader Ginsburg, Associate Justice, Supreme Court of the United States," *Ann. Surv. Am. L.* 1 (1997): xii.

300 Ibid., xiii.

301 Phyllis Schlafly, "Open Letter to VMI Alumni," Eagle Forum, June 11, 1996.

302   *M.L.B. v. S.L.J.*, 519 U.S. 102, 124 (1996).

303   Kenneth Karst, "Those Appealing Indigents: Justice Ginsburg and the Claims of Equal Citizenship," *Ohio State L. Rev* 70 (2009): 942.

304   Ginsburg, "Legally Speaking."

305   Ariane de Vogue, "Ginsburg to Begin 'Precautionary' Chemo," *ABC News*, Mar. 19, 2009.

26. THE EYE OF
THE BEHOLDER

306   Linda Greenhouse, "My Florida Recount Memory," *New York Times*, Nov. 20, 2010.

307   *Bush v. Gore*, 531 U.S. 98, 109 (2000).

308   Ginsburg, "Conversation between Ruth Bader Ginsburg and Professor Robert A. Stein," 1, 5.

309   Lesley Stahl, "Justice Scalia on the Record," *60 Minutes*, Apr. 27, 2008.

310   "The Supreme Court's Heavyweight," *Fresh Air*, NPR, www.npr.org/2013/03/06/173466698/ruth-bader-ginsburg-the-supreme-courts-heavyweight.

311   Jeffrey Toobin, "Justice O'Connor Regrets," *New Yorker*, May 6, 2013.

312   Jessica Weisberg, "Supreme Court Justice Ruth Bader Ginsburg: Reigning Supreme," *Elle Magazine*, Sept. 23, 2014.

313   Ginsburg, "Justice Ginsburg Addresses."

27. THE POWER
OF DISSENT

314   *Nevada Dept. of Human Resources v. Hibbs*, 538 U.S. 721 (2003).

315   Ibid.

316   *Ledbetter v. Goodyear Tire & Rubber Co.*, 550 U.S. 618 (2007).

317   Ibid.

318   *Ledbetter v. Goodyear Tire & Rubber Co.*, opinion announcement,

www.oyez.org/cases/2006/05-1074.

28. THE CONTOURS
OF LIBERTY

[319] *Gonzales v. Carhart*, 550 U.S. 124 (2007).

[320] Jeffrey Rosen, "An Interview with Ruth Bader Ginsburg: Ruth Bader Ginsburg Is an American Hero," *The New Republic*, Sept. 28, 2004.

[321] *Gonzales v. Carhart*, 550 U.S. 124 (2007).

[322] *Citizens United v. FEC*, 588 U.S. 310 (2010).

[323] Richard Wolf, "Ginsburg's Dedication Undimmed after 20 Years on Court," *USA Today*, Aug. 1, 2013.

[324] Ruth Bader Ginsburg, "Inviting Judicial Activism: A 'Liberal' or 'Conservative' Technique?," *Georgia L. Rev.* 15 (1981): 539, 582.

[325] Ruth Bader Ginsburg, "Life at the Supreme Court: Ruth Joan Bader Ginsburg," YouTube video, 1:18:09, Mar. 26, 2016.

[326] Ruth Bader Ginsburg, "Ginsburg on Hobby Lobby," *Yahoo News*, July 31, 2014, www.yahoo.com/news/video/ginsburg-hobby-lobby-071640878.html?ref=gs.

[327] Ruth Bader Ginsburg, "Conversation with Justice Ruth Bader Ginsburg and Ted Olson," C-Span video, 46:36, Dec. 17, 2013.

[328] Jeffrey Rosen, "An Interview with Ruth Bader Ginsburg: Ruth Bader Ginsburg Is an American Hero," *The New Republic*, Sept. 28, 2004.

[329] Jeffrey Toobin, "Heavyweight: How Ruth Bader Ginsburg Has Moved the Supreme Court," *New Yorker*, Mar. 11, 2013, para. 58, www.newyorker.com/magazine/2013/03/11/heavyweight-ruth-bader-ginsburg.

[330] *Scalia/Ginsburg: (A Gentle) Parody of Operatic Proportions*, www.lawandarts.org/wp-content/uploads/sites/4/2015/02/5-38.2-Wangupdated3.4.pdf.

[331] Ibid.

[332] Ibid.

[333] Ann E. Marimow, "Personal Trainer Bryant Johnson's Clients Include Two Supreme Court Justices," *Washington Post*, Mar. 19, 2013.

[334] Ginsburg, "'Notorious RBG': Conversation," European University Institute.

[335] Ginsburg, "Conversation," Annual Stevens Lecture.

BIBLIOGRAPHY

HEARINGS

"Confirmation Hearing of Ruth Bader Ginsburg to the DC Circuit Court." 96th Cong. 15238 (June 16, 1980).

"Nomination of Ruth Bader Ginsburg to Be Associate Justice of the Supreme Court of the United States." 1994. www.loc.gov/law/find/nominations/ginsburg/hearing.pdf.

RUTH BADER GINSBURG'S
INTERVIEWS AND SPEECHES

"Advocating the Elimination of Gender-Based Discrimination: The 1970s New Look at the Equality Principle." Speech. U. of Cape Town, South Africa. Feb. 10, 2006. www.supremecourt.gov/publicinfo/speeches/sp_02-10-06.html.

"American University Commencement Address, May 10, 1981." *American University L. Rev* 30 (1981): 891.

"The Changing Complexion of Harvard Law School." Speech. Harvard Law School. *Harvard Women's Law Journal* 27: 303–308. Nov. 14, 2004. www.law.harvard.edu/students/orgs/jlg/vol27/bader-ginsburg.pdf.

"Conversation between Ruth Bader Ginsburg and Professor Robert A. Stein." *Minnesota Law Review* 99: 1–25. Sept. 16, 2014. www.minnesotalawreview.org/wp-content/uploads/2014/12/Ginsburg_MLR1.pdf.

"A Conversation with Associate Justice Ruth Bader Ginsburg." YouTube video, 1:17:45, from the Annual Stevens Lecture, University of Colorado Law School. Posted Sept. 25, 2012, by "Colorado Law." www.youtube.com/watch?v=xTKaTjFlfzs. Reprinted in *Colorado Law Review* 84 (2013): 909–932. Sept. 19, 2012. www.lawreview.colorado.edu/wp-content/uploads/2013/11/9.-Ginsburg_610_s.pdf.

"A Conversation with Justice Ruth Bader Ginsburg." *Kansas Law*

Review 53 (June 2005): 957.

"A Conversation with Justice Ruth Bader Ginsburg." By Abbe R. Gluck. *Faculty Scholarship Series*. Paper 4905. Mar. 1, 2013. www.digitalcommons.law.yale.edu/cgi/viewcontent.cgi?article=5910&context=fss_papers.

"A Conversation with Justice Ruth Bader Ginsburg: Her Life as a Woman, a Jew, and a Judge." PRX recording, 53:48, from an interview recorded by *Only in America*. Sept. 2, 2004. Posted Nov. 11, 2004. www.beta.prx.org/stories/2952.

"A Conversation with Justice Ruth Bader Ginsburg: Justice Ruth Bader Ginsburg in Conversation with Gillian Metzger, Stanley H. Fuld Professor of Law and Vice Dean, Columbia Law School, and Abbe Gluck, Associate Professor of Law, Columbia Law School." Columbia Law School video, 60:00. Feb. 10, 2012. web.law.columbia.edu/gender-sexuality/events/symposia/spring-2012.

"Conversation with Justice Ruth Bader Ginsburg and Ted Olson." C-Span video, 46:36. Dec. 17, 2013. www.c-span.org/video/?316839-1/conversation-supreme-court-assoc-justice-ruth-bader-ginsburg.

"Conversation with Ruth Bader Ginsburg and Her Former Law Clerk, California Supreme Court Justice Goodwin Liu." C-Span video, 1:03:27. June 13, 2015. www.c-span.org/video/?326578-1/conversation-supreme-court-justice-ruth-bader-ginsburg.

"Conversation with Ruth Bader Ginsburg at the Capitol City Constitution Day." By Maeva Marcus, New York Historical Society, Institute for Constitutional History. C-Span video, 50:59. Sept. 12, 2014. www.c-span.org/video/?93457-1/justice-ruth-bader-ginsburg-capital-city-constitution-day.

"Ginsburg on Hobby Lobby," Yahoo News, July 31, 2014. Ginsburg speaks with Katie Couric. www.yahoo.com/news/video/ginsburg-hobby-lobby-071640878.html?ref=gs.

"Ginsburg Speaks with Greg Stohr and Matthew Winkler in Washington D.C." YouTube video, 30:26. Posted Feb. 12, 2015, by "Bloomberg." www.youtube.com/watch?v=MPict1a-xQ8.

BIBLIOGRAPHY

"Ginsburg Supreme Court Nomination Speech in the White House Rose Garden." C-Span video, 23:42. June 14, 1993. www.c-span.org/video/?42908-1/ginsburg-supreme-court-nomination.

"Interview: Ruth Bader Ginsburg." Academy of Achievement. Aug. 17, 2010. www.achievement.org/autodoc/printmember/gin0int-1.

"Justice Ginsburg Addresses the Women's Law and Public Policy Fellowship Program." C-Span video, 1:01:01. Sept. 25, 2003. www.c-span.org/video/?178383-1/womens-law-public-policy.

"Justice Ginsburg Talks about Arias, the Law, and the Most Famous Plea Bargain in Opera." By Stephanie Francis Ward. *ABA Journal.* Aug. 5, 2012. www.abajournal.com/news/article/justice_ginsburg_talks_about_arias_and_the_law/

"Justice Ruth Bader Ginsburg Remarks." C-Span video, 1:02:30. Feb. 4, 2015.www.c-span.org/video/?324177-1/discussion-supreme-court-justice-ruth-bader-ginsburg.

"Justice Ruth Bader Ginsburg Speaks with Irin Carmon." MSNBC. Feb. 17, 2015. www.msnbc.com/msnbc/exclusive-justice-ruth-bader-ginsburg-interview-full-transcript.

"Legally Speaking: Ruth Bader Ginsburg." UCTV video, 1:25:47, from an interview by Joan Williams at Hastings College of the Law. Nov. 3, 2011. www.uctv.tv/shows/Legally-Speaking-Ruth-Bader-Ginsburg-22928.

"Life at the Supreme Court: Ruth Joan Bader Ginsburg." YouTube video, 1:18:09. Mar. 26, 2016. Posted by "oublidelinde." www.youtube.com/watch?v=wS3SkP9R9Ls.

"Lighter Side of Life at the United States Supreme Court." Speech. New England Law, Boston. Mar. 13, 2009. www.supremecourt.gov/publicinfo/speeches/viewspeech/sp_03-13-09.

"'Notorious RBG': Conversation with United States Supreme Court Justice Ginsburg." YouTube video, 1:55:05. Feb. 4, 2016. Posted by "European University Institute." www.youtube.com/watch?v=qRqe43iwhbw.

"Reflections of Justice Ginsburg." C-Span video, 1:28:36. Aug. 20, 1995.   www.c-span.org/video/?66855-1/reflections-justice-ginsburg.

"Ruth Bader Ginsburg: From Brooklyn to the Bench." YouTube video, 43:44. Posted Feb. 24, 2015, by "Cornell University." www. youtube.com/watch?v=htJXKesFpE8.

"Ruth Bader Ginsburg: Interview with Professor Deborah Jones Merritt and Professor Wendy Webster Williams." *Ohio State Law Journal* 70, no. 4: 806–825. Apr. 10, 2009. moritzlaw.osu.edu/ students/groups/oslj/files/2012/03/70.4.Interview.pdf.

"Ruth Bader Ginsburg Speaks with Dorit Beinisch and Nina Totenberg." YouTube video, 1:45:43. Oct. 22, 2014. Posted by "92Y Plus." www.youtube.com/watch?v=fkwXw8T_qso.

"Ruth Bader Ginsburg Speaks with Jessica Weisberg." *Elle Magazine*, 358–362. Sept. 23, 2014.

"Sex and Unequal Protection: Men and Women as Victims." Keynote speech at the Southern Regional Conference of the National Conference on Law, Duke University Law School. Oct. 1, 1971. Reprinted in *J. Fam. L.* 11 (1971): 347.

"Table for Three: Ruth Bader Ginsburg and Gloria Steinem Speak with Philip Galanes." *New York Times.* Nov. 14, 2015. www. nytimes.com/column/table-for-three.

"Transcript: Interview with Supreme Court Justice Ruth Bader Ginsburg." WNYC Public Radio, in collaboration with the *New York Times* and WGBH Boston. Sept. 16, 2013. www.wnyc.org/ story/transcript-interview-justice-ruth-bader-ginsburg.

"Transcript of Panel Discussion with Ruth Bader Ginsburg." *Journal of Gender, Social Policy & the Law* 20, no. 2, art. 1: 315–344. Nov. 17, 2001. digitalcommons.wcl.american.edu/jgspl/vol20/iss2/1.

ORAL ARGUMENTS BEFORE
THE SUPREME COURT

Califano v. Goldfarb, 430 U.S. 199 (1977), www.oyez.org/ cases/1976/75-699, Oct. 5, 1976.

Duren v. Missouri, 439 U.S. 357 (1979), www.oyez.org/ cases/1978/77-6067, Jan. 9, 1979.

Edwards v. Healy, 421 U.S. 772 (1975), www.oyez.org/

cases/1974/73-759, Oct. 16, 1974.

Frontiero v. Richardson, 411 U.S. 766 (1973), www.oyez.org/cases/1972/71-1694, Jan. 17, 1973

General Electric v. Gilbert, 429 U.S. 125 (1975), www.oyez.org/cases/1975/74-1589, Jan. 19 and Jan. 20, 1976.

Kahn v. Slevin, 416 U.S. 351 (1974), www.oyez.org/cases/1973/73-78, Feb. 25, 1974.

Lilly Ledbedder v. Goodyear Tire and Rubber Company, 550 U.S. 618 (2007), www.oyez.org/cases/2006/05-1074, May 29, 2007.

Reed v. Reed, 404 U.S. 71 (1971), www.oyez.org/cases/1971/70-4, Oct. 19, 1971.

Weinberger v. Wiesenfeld, 420 U.S. 636 (1975), www.oyez.org/cases/1974/73-1892, Jan. 20, 1975.

RUTH BADER GINSBURG'S
ESSAYS AND ARTICLES

"American Bar Association Delegation Visits People's Republic of China." *A.B.A. J.* 64 (1978): 1516.

"Comment: Frontiero v. Richardson." *Women's Rts. L. Rep.* 1 (1971–1974): 2.

"Equal Rights Amendment Is the Way." *Harv. Women's L. J.* 1 (1978): 19.

"A Feminist Lawyer Visits China." *Women's Agenda* 4 (1979): 5.

"From No Rights, to Half Rights, to Confusing Rights." *Human Rights* 7, no. 1 (1978): 12.

"Gender and the Constitution." *U. Cin. L. Rev.* 44 (1975): 1.

"Gender in the Supreme Court: The 1976 Term." In *Constitutional Government in America*, edited by R. Collins, 217. Carolina Academic Press, 1980.

"Honorable Ruth Bader Ginsburg." In *The Right Words at the Right Time*, edited by Marlo Thomas, 115–117. New York: Atria Books, 2004.

"In Memoriam: Benjamin Kaplan." *Harv. L. Rev.* 124 (2011): 1349.

"In Memory of Herbert Wechsler." *Colum. L. Rev.* 100 (2000): 1359.

"Introduction." *Colum. J. Gender and Law* 1 (1991): 1.

"Introduction to Women and the Law—A Symposium." *Rutgers L. Rev.* 25 (1970): 1.

"Inviting Judicial Activism: A 'Liberal' or 'Conservative' Technique?" *Georgia L. Rev.* 15 (1981): 539. (John A. Sibley Lecture)

"Is the ERA Constitutionally Necessary?" Update 16. A.B.A. Special Committee on Youth Education for Citizenship, Spring 1978.

"Judicial Authority to Repair Unconstitutional Legislation." *Cleveland-Marshall L. Rev.* 28 (1979): 301. (Cleveland-Marshall Fund Lecture)

"Let's Have ERA as a Signal." *A.B.A. J.* 63 (1977): 70.

"Memorial Tribute to Hans Smit." Columbia Law School, Feb. 9, 2012. www.law.columbia.edu/null/download?&exclusive=filemgr. download&file_id=62886

"My First Opera." *Opera America*, Spring, 2015.

"Need for the Equal Rights Amendment." *A.B.A. J.* 59 (1973): 1013.

"The Obligation to Reason Why." *U. of Fla. L. Rev.* 37 (1985): 205.

"Pregnancy and Discrimination." *New York Times.* Jan. 25, 1977. Written with Susan Deller Ross.

"Ratification of the Equal Rights Amendment: A Question of Time." *Tex. L. Rev.* 57 (1979): 919. (Will E. Orgain Lecture)

"Realizing the Equality Principle." In *Social Justice & Preferential Treatment*, edited by William T. Blackstone & Robert D. Heslep, 135. Athens: University of Georgia Press, 1977.

"Remarks by Justice Ruth Bader Ginsburg, Associate Justice, Supreme Court of the United States." *Ann. Surv. Am. L.* (1997): 1.

"Remarks on Women's Progress in the Legal Profession in the United States." *Tulsa L. Rev* 33 (1997): 13, 15.

"Ruth Bader Ginsburg." In *Particular Passions*, by Lynn Gilbert and Gaylen Moore, 153–160. New York: Clarkson Potter, 1981.

"Sex Equality and the Constitution." *Tulane L. Rev.* 52 (1978): 451. (George Abel Dreyfous Lecture)

"Sexual Equality under the Fourteenth and Equal Rights Amendments." *Wash. U. L.Q.* (1979): 161–178.

"Some Reflections on the Feminist Legal Thought of the 1970s." *U.*

Chi. Legal Forum 1 (1989): 9–11.

"Some Thoughts on Autonomy and Equality in Relation to *Roe v. Wade.*" *N.C. L. Rev* 63 (1985): 373.

"Some Thoughts on Benign Classification in the Context of Sex." *Conn. L. Rev.* 10 (Summer 1978): 813.

"Speaking in a Judicial Voice." *N.Y.U. L. Rev.* 67 (1992): 1185.

"A Study Tour of Taiwan's Legal System." *A.B.A. J.* 66 (1980): 165.

"Treatment of Women by the Law: Awakening Consciousness in the Law Schools, Remarks Made by Ruth Bader Ginsburg at the Annual Meeting of the Association of American Law Schools." *Val. U. L. Rev.* 5 (1971): 480.

"Women as Full Members of the Club: An Evolving American Ideal." *Human Rights* 6 (1977): 1.

"Women at the Bar—A Generation of Change." *U. Puget Sound L. Rev.* 2 (1978): 1.

"Women's Work: The Place of Women in Law Schools." *J. Legal Educ.* 32 (1982): 272.

SUPREME COURT BRIEFS
AUTHORED OR COAUTHORED
BY RUTH BADER GINSBURG

Craig v. Boren, 429 U.S. 190 (1976), Amicus Brief.

Duren v. Missouri, 439 U.S. 357 (1979), Petitioner's Brief.

Edwards v. Healy, 421 U.S. 772 (1975), Appellee's Brief.

Frontiero v. Richardson, 411 U.S. 766 (1973), Amicus Brief.

Frontiero v. Richardson, 411 U.S. 766 (1973), Jurisdictional Statement.

Kahn v. Shevin, 416 U.S. 351 (1974), Appellant's Brief.

Reed v. Reed, 404 U.S. 71(1971), Appellant's Brief.

Reed v. Reed, 404 U.S. 71(1971), Reply Brief.

Struck v. Secretary of Defense, 409 U.S. 409 U.S. 1071 (1972), Opposition to Motion to Dismiss for Mootness.

Struck v. Secretary of Defense, 409 U.S. 409 U.S. 1071 (1972), Petitioner's Brief.

Weinberger v. Wiesenfeld, 420 U.S. 636 (1975), Appellee's Brief.

BIBLIOGRAPHY

SUPREME COURT BRIEFS
OTHERS

Frontiero v. Richardson, 411 U.S. 766 (1973), Appellant's Brief.
Reed v. Reed, 404 U.S. 71(1971), Jurisdictional Statement.
Reed v. Reed, 404 U.S. 71 (1971), Petitioner's Reply Brief.

TABLE OF CASES

Moritz v. Commissioner of Internal Revenue, 469 F.2d. 466 (10th Cir. 1972).

Muller v. Oregon, 208 U.S. 412 (1908).

Nevada Dept. of Human Resources v. Hibbs, 538 U.S. 721 (2003).

Plessy v. Ferguson, 163 U.S. 537 (1986).

Reed v. Reed, 93 Idaho 511 (1970).

Reed v. Reed, 404 U.S. 71 (1971).

Roe v. Wade, 410 U.S. 113 (1973).

Sail'er Inn, Inc. v. Kirby, 5 Cal.3d 1 (1971).

Shelby County v. Holder, 570 U.S. 193 (2013).

State v. Munson (Circ. Ct. S.D. filed 1970).

Struck v. Secretary of Defense, 460 F.2d 1372 (1971).

United States v. Virginia, 976 F.2d 890 (4th Cir. 1992).

United States v. Virginia, 518 U.S. 515 (1996).

Webster v. Reproductive Health Services, 492 U.S. 490 (1989).

Weinberger v. Wiesenfeld, 420 U.S. 636 (1975).

White v. Crook, 251 F. Supp. 401 (M.D. Ala. 1966).

Wiesenfeld v. Secretary of Health, Education, and Welfare, 367 F. Supp. 981 (D.N.J. 1973).

BOOKS

Brownmiller, Susan. *Against Our Will: Men, Women, and Rape*. New York: Simon and Shuster, 1975.

Cahn, Susan K. *Sexual Reckonings: Southern Girls in a Troubling Age*. Cambridge: Harvard University Press, 2012.

Carmon, Irin, and Knizhnik, Shana. *Notorious RBG: The Life and Times of Ruth Bader Ginsburg*. New York: Dey Street Books, 2015.

Chemerinsky, Erwin. *Constitutional Law: Principles and Policies*. New York: Aspen Law and Business, 1997.

Collins, Gail. *When Everything Changed: The Amazing Journey of American Women from 1960 to the Present*. Boston: Little Brown, 2009.

Dworkin, Ronald. *The Supreme Phalanx: The Court's New Right Wing Bloc*. New York: New York Review Books, 2008.

Gilligan, Carol. *In a Different Voice: Psychological Theory and Women's Development*. Cambridge: Harvard University Press, 1982.

Greenhouse, Linda, and Reva Siegel, eds. *Before* Roe v. Wade*: Voices That Shaped the Abortion Debate before the Supreme Court's Ruling.* New York: Kaplan, 2010.

Gutmacher, Alan. *Margaret Sanger: An Autobiography.* New York: Pergamon Books, 1938.

Herbert, A. P. "The Myth of the Reasonable Man: The Case of Fardell v. Potts." In *Uncommon Law.* New York: Methuen, 1935.

Hirshman, R. *Sisters in Law: How Sandra Day O'Connor and Ruth Bader Ginsburg Went to the Supreme Court and Changed the World.* New York: HarperCollins, 2015.

Hymowitz, Carol, and Michaele Weissman. *A History of Women in America.* New York: Turtleback Books, 1984.

Kluger, Richard. *Simple Justice.* New York: Vintage Books, 1977.

Mathews, Donald G., and Jane S. DeHart. *Sex, Gender, and the Politics of ERA: A State and the Nation.* New York: Oxford University Press, 1990.

Mele, Christopher. *Selling the Lower East Side: Culture, Real Estate, and Resistance in New York City.* Minneapolis: University of Minnesota Press, 2000.

Peppers, Todd, C. *In Chambers: Stories of Supreme Court Law Clerks and Their Justices.* Charlottesville: University of Virginia Press, 2013.

Pogrebin, Abigail. *Stars of David: Prominent Jews Talk About Being Jewish.* New York: Broadway Books, 2007.

Roberts, Dorothy E. *Killing the Black Body: Race, Reproduction, and the Meaning of Liberty.* New York: Vintage, 1998.

Stephanopoulos, George. *All Too Human: A Political Education.* Boston: Little, Brown, 1999.

Strebeigh, Fred. *Equal: Women Who Reshape American Law.* New York: W.W. Norton, 2009.

Toobin, Jeffrey. *The Nine: Inside the Secret World of the Supreme Court.* New York: Anchor Books, 2008.

BIBLIOGRAPHY

PERIODICALS, JOURNAL ARTICLES, AND CHAPTERS IN COLLECTIONS

Alfiero, Gabrielle. "Queens of New York," Strausmedia. June 4, 2015. www.nypress.com/queens-of-new-york.

Allen, Mike. "Defiant V.M.I. to Admit Women, But Will Not Ease Rules for Them." *New York Times*. Sept. 22, 1996. www.nytimes.com/1996/09/22/us/defiant-vmi-to-admit-women-but-will-not-ease-rules-for-them.html.

Baer, Judith. "Advocate on the Court: Ruth Bader Ginsburg in the Limits of Formal Equality." In *Rehnquist Justice: Understanding the Court Dynamic*, ed. by Earl M. Maltz, 216–240. Lawrence: University Press of Kansas, 2003.

Barnes, Robert. "Ginsburg Performs Wedding." *Washington Post*. May 25, 2014.

Barnes, Robert. "The Question Facing Ruth Bader Ginsburg: Stay or Go?" *Washington Post*. Oct. 4, 2013. www.washingtonpost.com/lifestyle/magazine/the-question-facing-ruth-bader-ginsburg-stay-or-go/2013/10/04/4d789e28-1574-11e3-a2ec-b47e45e6f8ef_story.html?tid=a_inl.

Bartlett, Katharine. "Unconstitutionally Male?" *Duke Law Working Papers*. Paper 12 (2012). scholarship.law.duke.edu/cgi/viewcontent.cgi?article=2936&context=faculty_scholarship.

Bazelon, Emily. "The Place of Women on the Court." *New York Times Magazine*. July 7, 2009.

Becker, Mary. "Prince Charming: Abstract Equality." *Supreme Court Review* (1987): 201–247.

"Behind the Music." *Chicago Magazine*. Oct. 6, 2006. magazine.uchicago.edu/0610/peer/music.shtml.

Biskupic, Joan. "Female Justices Attest to Fraternity on Bench; O'Connor and Ginsburg, in Separate Speeches, Discuss Personal Aspects of Supreme Court Life." *Washington Post*. Aug. 21, 1994.

Bork, Robert. "Civil Rights—A Challenge." *The New Republic*. Aug. 31, 1963.

Bowman, Cynthia Grant. "Women in the Legal Profession from the

1920s to the 1970s: What Can We Learn from Their Experience about Law and Social Change?" *Cornell University Law School Faculty Publications*. Paper 12 (2009). scholarship.law.cornell.edu/cgi/viewcontent.cgi?article=1011&context=facpub.

Brennen, William J. "The Constitution of the United States: Contemporary Ratification." *S. Tex. L. Rev.* 27 (1985–1986): 433. (Originally delivered as a speech at Georgetown University on Oct. 12, 1985)

Campbell, Amy Leigh. "Raising the Bar: Ruth Bader Ginsburg and the ACLU Women's Rights Project." *Texas J. of Women and the Law* 11 (2002): 157. www.aclu.org/files/FilesPDFs/campbell.pdf.

Campbell, Linda, and Harrington, Linda. "Judge Ruth Bader Ginsburg: Portrait of a 'Steel Butterfly.'" *Chicago Tribune*. June 27, 1993.

Carlson, Margaret. "The Law According to Ruth." *Time*, June 28, 1993.

"Carter Selects Feminists for Two Important Posts." *United Press International*. Dec. 17, 1979.

Caruso, Michelle. "Benched! Shunned Woman Lawyer Hits Big Time." *Boston Herald*. June 15, 1993.

Ceneta, Manuel Balce. "Antonin Scalia: In His Own Unforgettable Words." *Los Angeles Times*. Apr. 22, 2016. www.latimes.com/nation/la-na-scalia-quotes-20160213-story.html.

"Chicago Tribune Names James Ginsburg A Chicagoan of the Year." *Chicago Tribune*. Dec. 28, 2009. AmericanTowns.com. www.americantowns.com/il/chicago/news/chicago-tribune-names-james-ginsburg-a-chicagoan-of-the-year-243115.

Clark, Mary L. "Changing the Face of the Law: How Women's Advocacy Groups Put Women on the Federal Judicial Appointments Agenda." *Yale J. of Law and Feminism* 14, no. 2, art. 6 (2002): 243–254. digitalcommons.law.yale.edu/cgi/viewcontent.cgi?article=1188&context=yjlf.

Cole, David. "The Liberal Legacy of Bush v. Gore." *Georgetown Law J.* 94 (2006): 1427–1474.

Cole, David. "Strategies of Difference: Litigating for Women's Rights in a Man's World." *J Law & Ineq* 2, no. 33 (1984): 55–56.

"Columbia Professor Studied for Federal Court Post." *New York Times*. Dec. 16, 1979.

Cooper, Gail. "Equal Rights May Be Painful." *Grand Rapids Gazette*. May 10, 1974.

Cowan, Ruth B. "Women's Rights through Litigation." *Colum. Human Rights L. Rev.* (1979): 373–412.

Crocker, Catherine. "Ginsburg Explains Origins of Sex, Gender." *Los Angeles Times*. Nov. 21, 1993.

"Election Day Suspense." *New York Times*. Nov. 8, 2000.

Epps, Garrett. "Justice Scalia's Outsized Legacy." *The Atlantic*. Feb. 13, 2016.

"Feminist Leaders Plan Coalition for Law Aiding Pregnant Women." *New York Times*. Dec. 15, 1976. ezproxy.sfpl.org/login?url=http:// search.proquest.com/docview/122946158?accountid=35117.

Francis, Roberta W. "The Equal Rights Amendment: Unfinished Business for the Constitution." National Council of Women's Organizations. www.equalrightsamendment.org/history.htm.

Franklin, Cary. "Justice Ginsburg's Advocacy and the Future of Equal Protection." *Yale Law J.* Feb. 21, 2013. www.yalelawjournal. org/forum/justice-ginsburgs-advocacy-and-the-future-of-equal-protection.

Freeman, Jo. "How 'Sex' Got into Title VII." *Law & Ineq.* 9 (1991): 163.

Gardener, Harris. "M.D. Ginsburg, 78, Dies, Lawyer and Tax Expert." *New York Times*. June 27, 2010.

"Ginsburg Easily Wins Seat on High Court." In *CQ Almanac 1993*, 49th ed., 318–25. Washington, DC: Congressional Quarterly, 1994. library.cqpress.com/cqalmanac/cqal93-1105802.

Goldberg, Stephanie. "The Second Woman Justice." *A.B.A. J.* Oct. 1993.

Goldstein, Tom. "Luce of Con Ed Recommended for U.S. Bench. 8 Others Also Considered for Appeals Assignment." *New York Times*. Mar. 2, 1979.

Greenhouse, Linda. "Burnita S. Matthews Dies at 93; First Woman on U.S. Trial Courts." *New York Times.* Apr. 28, 1988.

Greenhouse, Linda. "Learning to Listen to Ruth Bader Ginsburg." *N.Y. City L. Rev.* 7 (2004): 213.

Greenhouse, Linda. "My Florida Recount Memory." *New York Times.* Nov. 20, 2010.

Greenhouse, Linda. "On Privacy and Equality; Judge Ginsburg Still Voices Strong Doubts on Rationale Behind *Roe v. Wade* Ruling." *New York Times.* June 16, 1993.

Greenhouse, Linda. "Word for Word: A Talk with Ginsburg on Life and the Court." *New York Times.* Jan. 7, 1994.

Gresko, Jessica. "Ruth Bader Ginsburg's Husband Became Court of Last Culinary Resort." *Portland Press Herald.* Jan. 4, 2012.

Gunther, Gerald, "Ruth Bader Ginsburg: A Personal, Very Fond Tribute." *U. of Hawai'i L. Rev* 20 (1998): 583.

Gunther, Gerald. "The Supreme Court, 1971 Term-Foreword: In Search of Evolving Doctrine on a Changing Court: A Model for a Newer Equal Protection." *Harv. L. Rev* 86 (1972): 92.

Halberstam, Malvina. "Ruth Bader Ginsburg." *Jewish Women's Archives.* jwa.org/encyclopedia/article/ginsburg-ruth-bader.

Halberstam, Malvina. "Ruth Bader Ginsburg: The First Jewish Woman on the United States Supreme Court," *Cardozo L. Rev.* 19, no. 4 (1998): 1441.

Hand, Learned. "The Spirit of Liberty." Speech. 1944. www.providenceforum.org/spiritoflibertyspeech.

Herbert, A. P. "The Myth of the Reasonable Man: The Case of Fardell v. Potts." In *Uncommon Law.* New York: Methuen, 1935. alittlebitofjake.wordpress.com/2006/10/04/the-myth-of-the-reasonable-man-the-case-of-fardell-v-potts-a-p-herbert.

Hewitt, Bill. "Feeling Supreme." *People.* June 28, 1993.

Hodder, Sarah. "Like Mother, Like Daughter." *Legal Times.* Nov. 1, 1993.

Idelson, Holly. "Ginsburg's Abortion Anomaly: Support for Rights, Not Roe." *Congressional Quarterly.* July 17, 1993.

Idelson, Holly. "Quiet Confirmation Expected." *Congressional*

Quarterly. July 17, 1993.

"Immigration: The Lower East Side." Teaching materials. Library of Congress. www.loc.gov/teachers/classroommaterials/ presentationsandactivities/presentations/immigration/polish6. html.

"Justice for Women." *Vogue.* Oct., 1993.

Kagan, Elena. "Remarks Commemorating Celebration 55: The Women's Leadership Summit." *Harvard J. of Law and Gender* 32 (2009): 233. www.law.harvard.edu/students/orgs/jlg/ vol322/233-250.pdf.

Kaplan, David, and David A. Cohn. "A Frankfurter, Not a Hot Dog." *Newsweek.* June 29, 1993.

Karst, Kenneth. "Those Appealing Indigents: Justice Ginsburg and the Claims of Equal Citizenship." *Ohio State L. Rev* 70 (2009): 927.

Karst, Kenneth. "The Way Women Are: Some Notes in the Margins for Ruth Bader Ginsburg." *U. of Hawai'i Law School* 20 (1998): 619.

Kashina, Marisa M. "Stage Presence: Ruth Bader Ginsburg's Love of Arts." *Washingtonian.* Oct. 10, 2012.

Kay, Herma Hill. "Ruth Bader Extraordinaire." In *The Legacy of Ruth Bader Ginsburg,* edited by Scott Dodson. New York: Cambridge University Press, 1–11. 2015.

Kay, Herma Hill. "Ruth Bader Ginsburg, Professor of Law." *Columbia L. Rev* 104 (2004): 2.

Klarman, Michael. "Social Reform Litigation and Its Challenges: An Essay in Honor of Justice Ruth Bader Ginsburg." *Harv. L. Rev.* 32, no. 2 (Summer 2009): 251–302. www.law.harvard.edu/ students/orgs/jlg/vol322/251-302.pdf.

Kolbert, Elizabeth. "Firebrand: Phyllis Schlafly and the Conservative Revolution." *New Yorker.* Nov. 7, 2015.

Labaton, Stephen. "The Man behind the High Court Nominee." *New York Times.* June 17, 1993.

Labaton, Stephen. "Senators See Easy Approval for Nominee." *New York Times.* June 16, 1993. www.nytimes.com/1993/06/16/us/

senators-see-easy-approval-for-nominee.html.

Lewis, Neil. "Woman in the News; Rejected as a Clerk, Chosen as a Justice: Ruth Joan Bader Ginsburg." *New York Times*. June 15, 1993.

Liptak, Adam. "Justice Bids Farewells on Last Day." *New York Times*. June 28, 2010.

Liptak, Adam. "Kagan Says Her Path to Supreme Court Was Made Smoother by Ginsburg's." *New York Times*. Feb. 10, 2014.

Lyons, Richard D. "James Madison High School's Tradition of Success; From Cousin Brucie to Ruth Bader Ginsburg." *New York Times*. June 16, 1993.

MacKinnon, Katherine. "Reflections on Sexual Equality under Law." *Yal L.J.* 100 (1991): 1281.

MacLaughlin, Claudia. "Mr. Ginsburg's Campaign for Nominee." *National Law J.* June 27, 1993.

Margolick, David. "Day Cites Law Role of Women." *New York Times*. Apr. 14, 1984. www.nytimes.com/1984/04/14/nyregion/day-cites-law-role-of-women.html.

Margolick, David. "Trial by Adversity Shapes Jurist's Outlook." *New York Times*. June 25, 1993.

Marimow, Ann E. "Personal Trainer Bryant Johnson's Clients Include Two Supreme Court Justices." *Washington Post*. Mar. 19, 2013.

Markowitz, Deborah. "In Pursuit of Equality: One Woman's Work to Change the Law." *Women's Rights L. Rep.* 11 (1989): 73.

Martin, Michael, "Phyllis Schlafly Still Championing the Anti-Feminist Fight." National Public Radio. Mar. 30, 2011. www.npr.org/templates/story/story.php?storyId=134981902.

Mathews, Jay. "The Spouse of Ruth." *Washington Post*. June 19, 1993.

McMahon, Patrick. "The Barefoot and Pregnant Awards." *St. Petersburg Times*. Apr. 1, 1978.

Means, Marianne. "Clinton's Choice for the Court Third Time

Is a Charm." *Hearst Newspapers.* June 16, 1993.

Meyer, Carol. "On Feminism in Action: The First Activist Feminist I Ever Met." *AFFILIA* 9 (1994): 1984.

Murphy, Mary Jo. "Nancy Drew and the Secret of the 3 Black Robes." *New York Times.* May 30, 2009.

Murray, Pauli. "The Negro Woman's Stake in the Equal Rights Amendment." *Harv. Civ. Rights L.R.* 6 (1971): 253.

Murray, Pauli, and Mary Eastwood. "Jane Crow and the Law: Sex Discrimination and Title VII." *Geo. Wash. L. Rev* 34 (1965): 232.

"NAACP to Fight Bork 'Till Hell Freezes Over." *Daily News Wire Service.* New York. July 6, 1987.

Oelsner, Leslie. "Columbia Law Snares a Prize in the Quest for Women Professors." *New York Times.* Jan. 26, 1972.

Oelsner, Leslie. "Supreme Court Rules Employers May Refuse Pregnancy Sick Pay." *New York Times.* Dec. 8, 1976.

Olsen, Francis. "From False Paternalism to False Equality: Judicial Assaults on Feminist Community." *Michigan L. Rev* 84 (June 1986): 1581.

"On Becoming a Judge." *Judicature* 69 (1985–1986): 139.

"Operatic Tendencies." *A.B.A. J.* 80, no. 3 (Mar. 1994): 44.

"Originalism: A Primer on Scalia's Constitutional Philosophy." *All Things Considered.* National Public Radio. Feb. 14, 2016. www.npr.org/2016/02/14/466744465/originalism-a-primer-on-scalias-constitutional-philosophy.

"Oversexed." *A.B.A. J.* 80 (Mar. 1994): 45.

"Overview of Title IX of the Education Amendments of 1972." United States Department of Justice. www.justice.gov/crt/overview-title-ix-education-amendments-1972-20-usc-1681-et-seq.

Page, Clarence. "President Clinton's Stealth Justice." *Chicago Tribune.* June 20, 1993.

Pusey, Allen. "Ginsburg: Court Should Have Avoided Broad-Based Decision in *Roe v. Wade.*" *A.B.A. J.* May 13, 2013. www.abajournal.com/news/article/ginsburg_expands_on_her_disenchantment_with_roe_v._wade_legacy.

"The Real Story behind the Passage of Title IX 35 Years Ago." *Women in Higher Education.* Jossey Bass. wihe.com/the-real-story-behind-the-passage-of-title-ix-35-years-ago.

Reske, Henry. "Two Paths for Ginsburg." *A.B.A. J.* 79 (Aug. 1993): 16.

Roberts, John G. "What Makes the D.C. Circuit Different? A Historical View." *Virginia L. Rev* 92 (May 2006): 3. www.virginialawreview.org/sites/virginialawreview.org/files/375_0.pdf.

Rosen, Jeffrey. "The Book of Ruth." *New Republic* 209 (Aug. 2, 1993).

Rosen, Jeffrey. "An Interview with Ruth Bader Ginsburg: Ruth Bader Ginsburg Is an American Hero." *New Republic.* Sept. 28, 2004.

Rosen, Jeffrey. "The New Look of Liberalism on the Court." *New York Times Magazine.* Oct. 5, 1997.

"Ruth Bader Ginsburg: Humble. Pursuits." Behrman House. www.behrmanhouse.com/RL/justice-ruth-bader-ginsburg-humble-pursuits.

Saulnier, Beth. "Justice Prevails: A Conversation with Ruth Bader Ginsburg, '59." *Cornell Alumni Magazine.* Nov./Dec. 2013.

Savage, David G. "Gay Rights Case a Window to Ginsburg Centrist Views." *Los Angeles Times.* June 17, 1993.

Savage, David G. "Supreme Court's Byron White Will Step Down after 31 Years." *Los Angeles Times.* Mar. 20, 1993.

Savage, David G., and Karen Kaplan. "Ruth Bader Ginsburg Home after Cancer Surgery." *Los Angeles Times.* Feb. 14,

2009.

Schlafly, Phyllis. "Open Letter to VMI Alumni." Eagle Forum. June 11, 1996. www.eagleforum.org/column/1996/july96/7-11-96.html.

Schroth, Tracy. "At Rutgers, Ginsburg Changed." *New Jersey Law J.* June 21, 1993.

Shapiro, Ian. "Still Speaking in a Judicial Voice: Ruth Bader Ginsburg Two Decades Later." *Yale Law Journal* 122 (2013): 257–265.

Shenon, Philip. "After the Debate." *Washington Post*. Sept. 26, 1988. www.nytimes.com/1988/09/27/us/after-the-debate-aclu-reports-rise-in-membership-calls-in-wake-of-bush-s-attacks.html.

Sherman, Mark. "Ginsburg Anticipates Being 1 of 3 Female Justices." *Seattle Times*. Aug. 4, 2010.

Simon, Maria. "Reflections." *U. of Hawai'i L. Rev* 20 (1998): 559.

Slobogin, Christopher. "Justice Ginsburg's Gradualism in Criminal Procedure." *Ohio St. L.J.* 70 (2009): 867–887.

Stahl, Lesley. "Justice Scalia on the Record." *60 Minutes*. Apr. 27, 2008. www.cbsnews.com/news/justice-scalia-on-the-record.

"The Supreme Court's Heavyweight." *Fresh Air*, NPR. www.npr.org/2013/03/06/173466698/ruth-bader-ginsburg-the-supreme-courts-heavyweight.

Thomas, Jennifer S. "Ruth Ginsburg: Carving a Career Path through Male-Dominated Legal World." *Congressional Quarterly*. July 17, 1993.

Toobin, Jeffrey. "Heavyweight: How Ruth Bader Ginsburg Has Moved the Supreme Court." *New Yorker*. Mar. 11, 2013.

Toobin, Jeffrey. "Justice O'Connor Regrets." *New Yorker*. May 6, 2013. www.newyorker.com/news/daily-comment/justice-oconnor-regrets.

Totenberg, Nina. "Notes on a Life." In *The Legacy of Ruth Bader Ginsburg*, edited by Scott Dodson, 1–11. New York: Cambridge University Press, 2015.

Tracy, Carole E., and Terry L. Fromson. "Rape and Sexual Assault in the Legal System." June 5, 2012. www.womenslawproject. org/resources/Rape%20and%20Sexual%20Assault%20 in%20the%20Legal%20System%20FINAL.pdf.

"Tribute: The Legacy of Ruth Bader Ginsburg and the WRP Staff." ACLU website. 2016. www.aclu.org/tribute-legacy-ruth-bader-ginsburg-and-wrp-staff.

Vogue, Ariane de. "Ginsburg to Begin 'Precautionary' Chemo." *ABC News*. Mar. 19, 2009. abcnews.go.com/TheLaw/ SCOTUS/story?id=7101673.

Von Drehle, David. "Conventional Roles Hid a Revolutionary Intellect." *Washington Post*. July 18, 1993.

Von Drehle, David. "Redefining Fair with a Simple Careful Assault." *Washington Post*. July 19, 1993.

Ward, Stephanie. "Francis. Family Ties." *A.B.A. J.* Oct. 1, 2010. www.abajournal.com/magazine/article/family_ties1/.

"Weddings Lisa Brauston, James Ginsburg." *New York Times*. Nov. 19, 1995.

Weigand, Kate, and Horowitz, Daniel. "Dorothy Kenyon: Feminist Organizing 1919–1963." *J. of Women's History* 14, no. 2 (2002): 126.

Weisberg, Jessica. "Supreme Court Justice Ruth Bader Ginsburg: Reigning Supreme." *Elle Magazine*. Sept. 23, 2014.

Weisberg, Jessica. "Susan's Choice: Ruth Bader Ginsburg's Defining Case." *Elle Magazine*. Oct. 21, 2014.

Williams, Joan. "Beyond the Tough Guise: Justice Ginsburg's Reconstructive Feminism." In *The Legacy of Ruth Bader Ginsburg*, edited by Scott Dodson, 59–70. New York: Cambridge University Press, 2015.

Williams, Susan H., and Williams, David C. "Sense and Sensibility: Justice Ruth Bader Ginsburg's Mentoring Style a Blend of Rigor and Compassion." *University of Hawaii L. Rev* 20 (1998): 589.

Williams, Wendy Webster. "Ruth Bader Ginsburg's Equal Protection Clause: 1970–80." *Columbia J. of Gender and Law* (2013): 41–49. scholarship.law.georgetown.edu/cgi/viewcontent.cgi?article=2253&context=facpub.

Williams, Wendy. "Sex Discrimination: Closing the Law's Gender Gap." In *The Burger Years: Rights and Wrongs in the Supreme Court, 1969–1986*, edited by Herman Schwartz, 109–124. Viking Books, 1987.

"Without Precedent: Ruth Bader Ginsburg Honored at Law School." *Columbia Magazine*. Spring 2012. magazine.columbia.edu/news/spring-2012/without-precedent-ruth-bader-ginsburg-honored-law-school.

Wolf, Richard. "Ginsburg's Dedication Undimmed after 20 Years on Court." *USA Today*. Aug. 1, 2013.

"Women Enroll at VMI." *CNN*. Aug. 18, 1997. www.cnn.com/US/9708/18/vmi.women.

Yang, Catherine. "Ruth Bader Ginsburg: So Principled, She's Unpredictable." *Businessweek*. June 27, 1993.

OTHER SOURCES

"Free to Be . . . You and Me." YouTube video, from a TV special aired Mar. 11, 1974. Posted May 17, 2010, by "ftbfoundation." www.youtube.com/watch?v=_26FOHoaC78.

National Organization for Women. Philadelphia Chapter Records, 1968–1977. www2.hsp.org/collections/manuscripts/n/now2054.xml.

Scalia/Ginsburg: (A Gentle) Parody of Operatic Proportions.

lawandarts.org/wp-content/uploads/sites/4/2015/02/5-38.2-Wangupdated3.4.pdf

Supreme Court of the United States website. www.supremecourtpress.com/chance_of_success.html.

ABOUT THE

AUTHOR

Teri writes novels, short stories, essays, stories for children, nonfiction for both children and adults, and lots of legal briefs. Her books include *The Girl from the Tar Paper School*, winner of the 2015 Jane Addams Book Award and the 2015 Carter G. Woodson Middle-Level Book Award. Her next biography, *Alexander Hamilton*, will be published by Abrams in 2017. Her stories and essays have appeared in publications as diverse as *Education Week*, *Scope Magazine*, *The Iowa Review*, *The American Literary Review*, and *Cricket Magazine*.

Her law practice is limited to representing indigents on appeal from adverse rulings.

She lives with her family in California near the beach.

For more information about Teri and her books, please visit www.terikanefield.com.

Made in the USA
Monee, IL
21 September 2020